MW00686002

Sports Fan's
GUIDE TO
CHRISTIAN
ATHLETES
& SPORTS
TRIVIA

MOODY PRESS
CHICAGO

ISBN: 0-8024-3084-8

1 3 5 7 9 10 8 6 4 2

Printed in the United States of America

Contents

Foreword

In September 1998, I was fortunate enough to be offered a truly remarkable job. I was named the general manager of the Los Angeles Dodgers. That left me, a born-again Christian, with the difficult yet enjoyable task of restoring championship caliber baseball to one of the sport's most storied franchises.

In a way, this was symbolic of the increased visibility in recent years of Christians in sports as they have risen to prominence. Just think of the top sports events in the past few years, and you'll find believers in Jesus Christ at the center of many of them.

In baseball, players such as Travis Fryman, John Wetteland, Scott Brosius, Andy Pettitte, and Tim Salmon have taken home some of the diamond's most coveted awards.

In basketball, David Robinson has been the National Basketball Association MVP. A. C. Green played in more than 1,000 straight games, an NBA record. As a collegian, Bryce Drew hit one of the most memorable shots in NCAA tournament history.

In football, Reggie White was without peer. Randall Cunningham turned his career and his team around because of his faith. Top-notch Christians Mike Singletary, Anthony Muñoz, and Dwight Stephenson all joined the Hall of Fame.

It's truly been fun to watch as people who share my passion for the Lord and my love for living a godly life have stepped up and let people know it's okay to be a Christian and a great athlete.

Although I am now able to see all this from what some consider an important position with the Dodgers, I've watched it happen from another perspective too.

You see, even though God has, in His incredible way, allowed me to have this difficult but much-appreciated job, He made sure that I at first viewed sports from what some might say is not as lofty a perspective.

My sports career had its start at a small Christian college, Tennessee Temple University in Chattanooga, Tennessee. That's where I got my coaching start. That fact is important, because I know from firsthand evidence what it means to truly appreciate sports and competition without any thoughts of big money.

Like my life, this book speaks of sports from both the major league level and the small-scale level. Sure, there are the profiles of the players who compete at Dodger Stadium and L.A.'s Staples Arena, but there are also facts and figures about men and women who are playing their heart out at the NAIA level and the NCCAA level in colleges, just like my alma mater. Plus there is information about all kinds of other sports ministries, outlets, and organizations.

It's been my privilege to see sports from many angles. As a small-college coach, as an anonymous scout, as the general manager of a small-market team (the Montreal Expos), and now with this position. I love sports for what it can tell us about ourselves. And I love to watch the Christians in sports as they strive to make a difference both on the field and off.

If you like sports as I do, you'll be fascinated by the amount of information you'll find in this book. Perhaps it will give you an entirely new perspective of sports—from top to bottom.

Kevin Malone
Los Angeles Dodgers

Acknowledgments

All direct quotes from athletes, which are featured in chapter 4, were taken from three sources: *Sports Spectrum* magazine, *Sports Spectrum* radio programs, and books written by the compiler of the *Sports Fan's Guide*. In addition, the following resources were used to compile this book:

Sports Spectrum magazine
Sports Spectrum radio
Sharing the Victory magazine
Media guides, all professional sports teams
Safe at Home and *Safe at Home 2* (Moody)
First & Goal (Moody)
Slam Dunk, (Moody)
Competitor's Edge (Moody)
Baseball Register, NBA Register, Pro Football Register, and *Hockey Register* (The Sporting News Publishing Co.)
The LPGA Guide
Corel WTA Player Guide
PGA Tour Guide
Nike Tour Guide
1998 NASCAR Media Guide
Path To Victory New Testament (International Bible Society)
Pro Athletes Outreach testimony cards

Several books containing personal testimonies were very helpful in chapter 4. They are:

Breakaway, by Al Janssen (Here's Life)
More Than Winners, by Craig Massey (Cross Training Publishing)
Olympic Heroes, by Gerald Harris (Broadman & Holman)
Real Baseball Heroes, by Terry Hall (Full Court Press)
Shoot for the Star, by Bill Bates and Bill Butterworth (Word)
True Champions, by Mike Towle (Summit)
The Winning Spirit, by Bill Pennington (Barbour)

Other resources helpful in various sections of this guide were the Sports Outreach America web site, the tract "Winning Isn't Everything," by Steve Jones; *Linksletter,* published by the Linksletter foundation; *Christians In Sports* magazine, England; the National Christian College Athletic Association Membership Directory; and *The Baseball Encyclopedia* (MacMillan, 1993).

I also am grateful for E-mail communication from the following athletes and friends: Doug Bochtler, Rico Brogna, Paul Byrd, Tim Cash, Christin Ditchfield, Suzanne Hustead, Victor Lee, Bruce McDonald, Vince Nauss, and Danny Sheaffer.

Introduction

A HOME RUN OR A SERMON?

A monstrous Mark McGwire home run. A wondrous pass from Peyton Manning. Or a stupendous sermon from your pastor. Which of these events has imbedded itself the most deeply in your memory bank? Which has the most influence in your life?

As the twenty-first century unfolds, it has become increasingly clear that the world of sports is for many non-Christians a substitute for religion. Sundays mean baseball or football to millions of fans who would never think even briefly about spending time in church on that day. For them, devotion means spending hours of life talking about, reading about, shelling out money on, and watching favorite sports teams compete in majestic arenas. Steeples pointing to heaven are just landmarks on the horizon as they speed past them on the way to the stadium.

In its place, sports is both fun and positive. At the heart of it, sports is pure—encompassing exercise, healthy competition, sportsmanship, following rules, and a host of other positive concepts. However, along the way, sports has picked up a long list of unfortunate baggage. Among those are the greed that has tainted professional sports and the negative entanglements of alcohol, gambling, and tobacco. Equally significant, sports has developed an all-encompassing influence on many spectators and fans—drawing them away from family, faith, job, and other more important life realities.

When we combine the growing influence of sports in comparison to religion with the possible negative impact of an otherwise honorable avocation, we could come to the logical conclusion that sports are bad and that Christians must avoid contact lest they become contaminated.

Some Christians have drawn that conclusion, leading them to an abandonment of the games people play. Those well-meaning saints are probably not thumbing the pages through this book, though, so to address them would be futile.

Another group of believers in Jesus Christ exists, though—a group of Christians who have learned to keep their sports devotion in check and have avoided the negatives as much as is possible. More important, though, is the fact that this second group has taken an additional step. They've decided that sports can be used positively in our world. They are the kind of people who do the following:

- choose Christians for their fantasy sports team as a way of witnessing to non-Christians in their league
- send their kids to Christian sports camps
- point out strong Christian athletes to their children as possible role models
- have a prayer list that contains Christian athletes and pray for them regularly to carry the torch brightly and high
- travel overseas to participate in sports evangelism teams
- put up *Sports Spectrum* posters in their offices, lockers, dorm rooms
- help their church put together an evangelistic softball league
- hold a Super Bowl party at home to invite neighbors over and introduce the gospel to them through a halftime video
- support Christian college athletics

These are the people who have decided that while they value a great sermon by their pastor far more than they value a home run by Big Mac, they realize that their neighbor wouldn't step through a church door if Billy Graham himself were speaking. These are Christians who've decided that the best way to influence their friends for Christ is to use sports.

I discovered that concept as a young man just out of college while traveling overseas on a basketball evangelism trip. My college basketball coach modeled the concept of using sports as a tool. Later, through my time as a high school basketball coach and now in my position of managing editor of *Sports Spectrum,* I've been able to carry on that tradition.

I hope you can use this book as your ultimate Christian sports source and that it will spur you to find new ways to spread the gospel through sports. May it also help you to pray for these athletes to remain strong in God and ready to share their faith in this unique arena of professional and amateur sports.

Part 1

TRIUMPHS AND TRIVIA

Chapter 1

CHRISTIAN SPORTS HIGHLIGHTS

For any sports fan who professes to be a Christian, there is something heartwarming and special to see someone who shares the faith capture the top award in a sport. Whether it's watching Orel Hershiser drop to his knee in prayer after winning the 1988 World Series, hearing John Wetteland testify after winning the 1996 World Series, listening to Reggie White praise God after winning the 1997 Super Bowl, or hearing Jean Driscoll give her Savior the glory after winning one of her many Boston Marathons from a wheelchair—it's a great delight.

Watching fellow believers in Christ capture top awards is gratifying for a couple of reasons. First, it puts another nail in the coffin of the tired, old myth that Christians aren't winners. Second, it is encouraging to the Christian fan's faith to know that an athlete is willing to speak out about his or her salvation. Third, it introduces new people to the concept of salvation.

In the decade of the 1990s, more than ever before, Christian athletes represented the top echelon in sports. The lists on these pages can serve as a reminder of the great exploits of dozens of Christians over the past few years—and maybe even encourage fans and athletes that a life given to Jesus Christ should be the life of a winner.

Note: It is impossible to know who all the Christians in all the sports might be. Any omissions are inadvertent and not meant to slight any athlete who is a believer in Jesus Christ.

AWARDS

BART STARR AWARD

The Bart Starr Award is given annually during Super Bowl week at an NFL-sanctioned Super Bowl breakfast. The sponsoring body for the Bart Starr Awards is Athletes In Action. Following are the past recipients of this award, voted by peers and awarded to the person who exemplifies outstanding character and leadership in the home, on the field, and in the community.

1989	Steve Largent	1994	Warren Moon
1990	Anthony Muñoz	1995	Cris Carter
1991	Mike Singletary	1996	Jackie Slater
1992	Reggie White	1997	Darrell Green
1993	Gill Byrd	1998	Irving Fryar and Brent Jones

SPECTRUM AWARDS

In 1995, *Sports Spectrum* magazine awarded the Spectrum Awards to three sports figures who had made a great impact for Christ during the first ten years of the magazine's existence. The winners:

A.C. Green
Bill McCartney
Betsy King

Also, *Sports Spectrum* honored ten other athletes for a decade of dedication to serving Jesus Christ while making a difference in sports:

Dave Dravecky	Mike Gartner
Joe Gibbs	Darrell Green
Bobby Jones	David Robinson
Mike Singletary	Pat Williams
Kay Yow	Reggie White

TOP ACHIEVEMENTS IN PROFESSIONAL SPORTS

BASEBALL

1991

Brett Butler	NL runs leader (112)
Bryan Harvey	AL saves leader (46)
Howard Johnson	NL home run champ (38)
Howard Johnson	NL RBI champ (117)
Paul Molitor	AL hits (216) and runs (133) leader
Terry Pendleton	NL Most Valuable Player
Terry Pendleton	NL batting champ (.319)
Terry Pendleton	NL hits leader (187)

1992

Randy Johnson	AL strikeout leader (241)
Edgar Martinez	AL batting champ (.343)
Terry Pendleton	NL hits leader (199)
John Smoltz	NLCS Most Valuable Player
John Smoltz	NL strikeout leader (215)

1993

Cal Eldred	AL innings leader (258)
Randy Johnson	AL strikeout leader (308)
Paul Molitor	World Series Most Valuable Player
Paul Molitor	AL hits leader (211)
John Olerud	AL batting champ (.363)
Tim Salmon	AL Rookie of the Year
Todd Walker	Most Outstanding Player, NCAA

1994

Felipe Alou	NL Manager of the Year
Andy Benes	NL strikeout leader (189)
Randy Johnson	AL strikeout leader (204)
Randy Johnson	AL complete games leader (204)
Paul O'Neill	AL batting champ (.359)
Steve Ontiveros	AL ERA leader (2.65)

1995

Orel Hershiser	ALCS Most Valuable Player
Randy Johnson	AL winning percentage champ (18-2 .900)
Randy Johnson	AL ERA champ (2.48) and strikeout leader (294)
Randy Johnson	AL Cy Young Award
Edgar Martinez	AL batting champ (.356)
Mike Schmidt	Entered the Baseball Hall of Fame

1996

Jeff Brantley	NL saves leader (44)
Paul Molitor	AL hits leader (225)
Paul Molitor	Reaches 3,000 hits (21st player to do so)
Andy Pettitte	AL wins leader (21-8)
John Smoltz	NL wins leader (24-8)
John Smoltz	NL leader, strikeouts (276) and innings pitched (253.2)

John Smoltz	Winning pitcher, All-Star Game
John Wetteland	AL saves leader (43)
John Wetteland	World Series Most Valuable Player

1997

Charles Johnson	MLB record of catching 124 games without an error
John Smoltz	AL leader, innings pitched (256)

1998

Scott Brosius	World Series Most Valuable Player
Charles Johnson	Gold Glove, catcher

1999

Randy Johnson	NL strikeout leader (364)
Randy Johnson	NL ERA leader (2.48)
Randy Johnson	NL innings leader (271.2)
Edgar Martinez	AL DH batting leader (.337)
Edgar Martinez	AL on-base leader (.447)

BASKETBALL

1990–91

Kevin Johnson	All-NBA second team
Kevin Johnson	Walter J. Kennedy Citizenship Award
David Robinson	NBA Rookie of the Year
David Robinson	All-NBA first team
David Robinson	NBA All-Defensive first team
Buck Williams	Top field goal percentage (.620)
Buck Williams	NBA All-Defensive first team

1991–92

Kevin Johnson	All-NBA third team
Mark Price	Free throw percentage leader (.947)
Mark Price	All-NBA third team
David Robinson	NBA Defensive Player of the Year
David Robinson	NBA All-Defensive first team
David Robinson	All-NBA first team
Buck Williams	Field goal percentage leader (.604)
Buck Williams	NBA All-Defensive second team

1992–93

Jerry Colangelo	Executive of the Year (Phoenix Suns)
LaPhonso Ellis	NBA All-Rookie first team
Mark Price	All-NBA first team
Mark Price	AT&T Shootout three-point winner
Mark Price	Free throw percentage leader (.948)
David Robinson	NBA All-Star game starter
David Robinson	NBA All-Defensive second team

1993–94

Kevin Johnson	Most assists in one game (25)
Kevin Johnson	Most steals in one game (10)
Kevin Johnson	All-NBA second team
Mark Price	AT&T Shootout three-point winner
David Robinson	Leading scorer (29.8 ppg.)
David Robinson	Single-game high points (71)
David Robinson	Most triple doubles (5)
David Robinson	All-NBA second team
David Robinson	IBM Award (contribution to team)

1994–95

Vin Baker	Most minutes played (3,361)
David Robinson	NBA Most Valuable Player
David Robinson	All-NBA first team
David Robinson	NBA All-Defensive first team
David Robinson	IBM Award

1995–96

Avery Johnson	Assists to turnovers leader (4.05)
David Robinson	All-NBA first team
David Robinson	NBA All-Defensive first team
David Robinson	IBM Award

1996–97

Mark Jackson	Assists leader (11.4 apg.)
Mark Price	Free throw percentage leader (.906)

1997–98

Hersey Hawkins	Pacific Division Sportsmanship Award
Avery Johnson	NBA Sportsmanship Award
David Robinson	All-NBA second team

David Robinson	NBA All-Defensive second team
A. C. Green	Most consecutive games in a career (907)

1998–99

Hersey Hawkins	NBA Sportsmanship Award
Dikembe Mutombo	NBA All-Defensive second team
Dikembe Mutombo	IBM Award
David Robinson	NBA All-Defensive second team

FOOTBALL

1990

Bruce Matthews	All-NFL team
Anthony Muñoz	All-NFL team
John Offerdahl	All-NFL team
Reggie White	All-NFL team

1991

Joe Gibbs	NFL Coach of the Year
Darrell Green	Pro Bowl starter
Bruce Matthews	Pro Bowl starter
Guy McIntyre	Pro Bowl starter
Anthony Muñoz	Pro Bowl starter
Dan Reeves	AFC Coach of the Year
Reggie White	NFC Defensive Player of the Year
Reggie White	Pro Bowl starter

1992

Gill Byrd	Pro Bowl starter
Bruce Matthews	Pro Bowl starter
Guy McIntyre	Pro Bowl starter
Junior Seau	Pro Bowl starter
Junior Seau	AFC Defensive Player of the Year
Reggie White	Pro Bowl starter

1993

Gary Anderson	Pro Bowl starter
Robert Brooks	AFC top average kickoff returns (26.6)
Jason Hanson	NFC most points, kicker (130)
Jeff Hostetler	AFC top single game, passing (424 yards)
Raghib Ismail	AFC top average kickoff returns (24.2)

Norm Johnson	Pro Bowl starter
Bruce Matthews	Pro Bowl starter
Hardy Nickerson	Pro Bowl starter
Dan Reeves	NFC Coach of the Year
Eugene Robinson	AFC most interceptions (9)
Junior Seau	Pro Bowl starter
Steve Tasker	Pro Bowl starter
Reggie White	Pro Bowl starter

1994

John Carney	AFC top scorer, kickers (135)
John Carney	Pro Bowl starter
Cris Carter	NFC receptions leader (122)
Cris Carter	Pro Bowl starter
Irving Fryar	AFC most receptions yards, one game (211)
Brent Jones	Pro Bowl starter
Glyn Milburn	AFC all-purpose rushing leader (1,922)
Bryce Paup	Pro Bowl starter
Doug Pelfrey	NFL longest field goal (54 yards)
Fuad Reveiz	Pro Bowl starter
Fuad Reveiz	NFC top scorer, kicker (132)
Junior Seau	Pro Bowl starter
Steve Tasker	Pro Bowl starter
Herschel Walker	NFL longest run from scrimmage (91 yards)
Reggie White	Pro Bowl starter
Aeneas Williams	NFC most interceptions (9)
Aeneas Williams	Pro Bowl starter

1995

Jason Hanson	NFC top scorer, kickers (132)
Jim Harbaugh	AFC passing efficiency (100.7)
Jim Harbaugh	AFC Offensive Player of the Year
Norm Johnson	AFC top scorer, kickers (141)
Curtis Martin	AFC rushing leader (1,487 yards)
Curtis Martin	NFL Rookie of the Year
Bruce Matthews	Pro Bowl starter
Glyn Milburn	AFC all-purpose yards leader (2080)
Glyn Milburn	AFC kickoff returns leader (1,269 yards)
Glyn Milburn	Pro Bowl starter
Bryce Paup	AFC Most Valuable Player
Bryce Paup	NFL Defensive Player of the Year

Bryce Paup	AFC Defensive Player of the Year
Bryce Paup	AFC sacks leader (17.5)
Bryce Paup	Pro Bowl starter
Steve Tasker	Pro Bowl starter
Reggie White	Pro Bowl starter
Reggie White	NFC Defensive Player of the Year
Aeneas Williams	Pro Bowl starter

1996

Isaac Bruce	AFC reception yards (229)
Mark Brunell	AFC, single-game high, passing (432 yards)
John Kasay	Pro Bowl starter
John Kasay	NFC leading scorer, kickers (145)
Curtis Martin	AFC leader, touchdowns (17)
Bruce Matthews	Pro Bowl starter
Junior Seau	Pro Bowl starter
Reggie White	Pro Bowl starter
Aeneas Williams	Pro Bowl starter

1997

Tony Boselli	Pro Bowl starter
Isaac Bruce	NFC most yards, game, receiving (233)
Mark Brunell	AFC most yards per attempt (7.54)
Cris Carter	NFC most receiving TDs (13)
Bruce Matthews	Pro Bowl starter
Hardy Nickerson	Pro Bowl starter
Bryce Paup	Pro Bowl starter
Deion Sanders	Pro Bowl starter
Heath Shuler	NFC longest gain, pass, (89 yards)
Reggie White	Pro Bowl starter
Aeneas Williams	NFC most interceptions in game (2)
Aeneas Williams	Pro Bowl starter

1998

Gary Anderson	Single-season record, highest percentage, field Goals (100 percent); most PATs without a miss (59); most points scored without a touchdown (164)
Tony Boselli	Pro Bowl starter
Peter Boulware	Pro Bowl
Randall Cunningham	Pro Bowl starter

Randall Cunningham	Outstanding Player, Pro Bowl
Bruce Matthews	Pro Bowl starter
Hardy Nickerson	Pro Bowl starter
Dan Reeves	NFL Coach of the Year
Mark Schlereth	Pro Bowl
Junior Seau	Pro Bowl starter
Michael Sinclair	Pro Bowl starter
Reggie White	Pro Bowl starter

GOLF

Men

1990

Paul Azinger	Infiniti Tournament of Champions
Jim Gallagher Jr.	Greater Milwaukee Open

1991

Paul Azinger	AT&T Pebble Beach National Pro-Am
Corey Pavin	Bob Hope Chrysler Classic
Corey Pavin	BellSouth Atlanta Golf Classic
Payne Stewart	U.S. Open

1992

Paul Azinger	The Tour Championship
Corey Pavin	Honda Classic

1993

Paul Azinger	Memorial Tournament
Paul Azinger	PGA Championship
Jim Gallagher Jr.	The Tour Championship
Bernhard Langer	Masters Tournament
Larry Mize	Northern Telecom Open
Larry Mize	Buick Open
Scott Simpson	GTE Byron Nelson Golf Classic

1994

Bob Estes	Texas Open
Tom Lehman	Memorial Tournament
Corey Pavin	Nissan Los Angeles Open
Loren Roberts	The Nestle Invitational

1995

Jim Gallagher Jr.	KMart Greater Greensboro Open
Jim Gallagher Jr.	FedEx St. Jude Classic
Tom Lehman	Colonial National Invitation
Corey Pavin	Nissan Open
Corey Pavin	U.S. Open
Loren Roberts	The Nestle Invitational

1996

Steve Jones	U.S. Open
Tom Lehman	British Open
Tom Lehman	The Tour Championship
David Ogrin	Lacantera Texas Open
Corey Pavin	Mastercard Colonial
Loren Roberts	Greater Milwaukee Open
Paul Stankowski	BellSouth Classic
Paul Stankowski	Lincoln-Mercury Kapalua International

1997

Tom Lehman	Skins Game
Steve Jones	Phoenix Open
Steve Jones	Bell Canada Open
Loren Roberts	MCI Classic
Loren Roberts	CVS Classic
Paul Stankowski	United Airlines Hawaiian Open

1998

Steve Jones	Quad City Classic
Scott Simpson	Buick Open

Women

1990

Betsy King	Nabisco Dinah Shore Classic
Betsy King	U.S. Open
Betsy King	JAL Big Apple Classic
Betsy King	Itoman LPGA World Match Play Championship
Barb Mucha	Boston Five Classic

1991

Betsy King	LPGA Corning Classic
Betsy King	JAL Big Apple Classic

1992

Betsy King	Mazda LPGA Championship
Betsy King	The Phar-Mor Classic
Betsy King	Mazda Japan Classic
Barb Mucha	Oldsmobile Classic

1993

Betsy King	JCPenney/LPGA Skins Game
Betsy King	Toray Japan Queens Cup

1994

Barb Mucha	State Farm Rail Classic

1995

Betsy King	ShopRite LPGA Classic
Alison Nicholas	PING-AT&T Wireless Services Championship
Barb Thomas	Cup-o'-Noodles Hawaiian Open

1996

Barb Mucha	Chick-fil-A Charity Championship

1997

Betsy King	Nabisco Dinah Shore Classic
Alison Nicholas	U.S. Open
Wendy Ward	Fieldcrest Cannon Open

1998

Barb Mucha	Sara Lee Classic
Wendy Ward	Hawaiian Open

TOP ACHIEVEMENTS IN AMATEUR SPORTS

COLLEGE FOOTBALL

1990

Walter Camp Player of the Year	Raghib Ismail, Notre Dame
Outland Trophy	Russell Maryland, Miami (Fla.)
All-purpose yardage	Glyn Milburn, Stanford (2,222)
Division I-AA interception leader	Aeneas Williams, Southern (La.)

1991

Johnny Unitas Award	(Top senior QB) Casey Weldon, Florida State
Heisman runner-up	Casey Weldon, Florida State

1992

Scoring (kickers)	Joe Allison, Memphis State
Field goals	Joe Allison, Memphis State
Lou Groza Award (top kicker)	Joe Allison, Memphis State
Coach of the Year	Gene Stallings, Alabama

1993

Butkus Award	Trev Alberts, Nebraska
Coach of the Year	Terry Bowden, Auburn
Passing efficiency	Trent Dilver, Fresno State
Heisman Trophy	Charlie Ward, Florida State
Player of the Year	Charlie Ward, Florida State
Davey O'Brien Award	Charlie Ward, Florida State
Johnny Unitas Award	Charlie Ward, Florida State

1994

Johnny Unitas Award	Jay Barker, Alabama
Coach of the Year (Dodd)	Fred Goldsmith, Duke
Coach of the Year (AFCA)	Tom Osborne, Nebraska

1995

Scoring	Eddie George, Ohio State
Rushing (one game)	Eddie George, Ohio State
Heisman Trophy	Eddie George, Ohio State
MVP, Copper Bowl	Byron Hanspard, Texas Tech
Passing efficiency	Danny Wuerffel, Florida
O'Brien Award	Danny Wuerffel, Florida

1996

Walker Award	Byron Hanspard, Texas Tech
Heisman Trophy	Danny Wuerffel, Florida
Maxwell Trophy	Danny Wuerffel, Florida
O'Brien Award	Danny Wuerffel, Florida
Unitas Award	Danny Wuerffel, Florida
MVP, Sugar Bowl	Danny Wuerffel, Florida

1997

NCAA passing efficiency leader (168.6 points)	Cade McNown, UCLA
Consensus All-American, defense	Andre Wadsworth, Florida State

1998

Lombardi Award; Bednarik Award	Dat Nguyen, Texas A & M
Consensus All-American	Cade McNown, UCLA
Coach of the Year	Phillip Fulmer, Tennessee

SUMMER OLYMPICS

GOLD MEDALS

1992

Evelyn Ashford	4 x 100m
Gail Devers	100m
Mary Joe Fernandez	Tennis doubles
Jackie Joyner-Kersee	Heptathlon
Mike Marsh	200m
Mike Marsh	Leroy Burrell, 4 x 100m
David Robinson	Basketball
Mel Steward	200m fly (swimming)

1996

Michelle Akers	Soccer
Jennifer Azzi	Basketball
Ruthie Bolton	Basketball
Amanda Borden	Gymnastics team
Josh Davis	Swimming (3 gold)
Gail Devers	100m
Gail Devers	4 x 100m
Mary Joe Fernandez	Tennis doubles
Penny Heyns	100m and 200m breaststroke
Jaycie Phelps	Gymnastics team
David Robinson	Basketball
Katy Steding	Basketball
Sheila Taormina	4 x 200m free (swimming)

Chapter 2

SPORTS AND THE ISSUES

There are so many issues that can be raised through the avenue of sports. Through sports, we learn about competition, about fair play, and about how we get along. Also, by observing people in sports, we sometimes learn from bad examples. We've all watched coaches fling themselves about the court or field like mad dogs, and we've made mental notes to ourselves never to act that way. We've seen greed and disloyalty and unkindness and a hundred other characteristics displayed.

The thoughtful sports person, whether a fan or a participant, can gain an education through experience and observance. In these essays by this author, taken from the pages of *Sports Spectrum,* some of those lessons are discussed.

THE DAD FACTOR

COULD IT BE THAT DADS ARE MAKING A COMEBACK IN OUR SOCIETY?

You're sitting at home watching the NBA Finals. It's a time out, and the benchcam focuses on one of the pine-riders. As the player notices the camera, he grins, raises his index finger to the sky, looks into the lens, and says, "Hi, Dad!"

Sure. And Dick Vitale is a monk.

As any sports fan knows, the on-camera anthem of all athletes is not sung to Dad. It goes like this: "Hi, Mom!"

And it's not just the players. Fans who happen to be near the camera also pay homage to mother when they get a chance. It's become a part of Americana.

Yet a growing number of athletes seem to be discovering that Mom had some help. I noticed this in the past few months as I gathered interviews for a book I am writing. Almost to a man, the NBA players I talked to singled out Dad as their most important influence as a kid.

Of course, there are exceptions to this pattern in all sports, for not everyone has the advantage of a two-parent situation. Notably, Kevin Johnson, All-Star guard of the Phoenix Suns, and Harold Reynolds, former major league pitcher and baseball analyst for ESPN, came from dad-less families.

Interestingly, both KJ and Reynolds were, in a sense, raised by two parents. In their cases, each had a mom and a grandma who teamed up to help. Both became highly educated, well-read athletes. Both started foundations to help young people. Both received a Point of Light award from the George Bush administration. And both have a strong faith in Jesus Christ.

Indeed, good people come from one-parent backgrounds. Yet I would venture to guess that both Johnson and Reynolds would have liked to have had a dad to play catch with, to talk to, to model their lives after.

Think with me for a moment about the dad-advantage that some other successful athletes have. Athletes who are respectable role models and who love God. Athletes who are not afraid to give credit to Dad.

One is Charlie Ward, point guard for the New York Knicks and the 1993 Heisman Trophy winning quarterback of the Florida State Seminoles. Charlie Ward Sr. was not only a vital force in the Ward home, but he also got involved in Junior's life as a coach. When young Charlie was in high school, his dad was his assistant football coach and his head basketball coach. Charlie credits his parents—both of them—with being "the main leaders in my life."

In the NBA, besides Ward, several other key players are not ashamed to mention that Dad played a vital role in their lives. The Dallas Mavericks' A.C. Green, another athlete who is named after his dad, credits A.C. Sr. with setting the tone for his life. "My father was a great example. He taught me to work hard, to have a strong work ethic." According to the junior Green, his dad would work two or three jobs if necessary to provide for his family.

Avery Johnson, the quick little point guard of the San Antonio Spurs, also minces no words in talking about his father, who, AJ proudly says, "taught me how to be a man—a godly man. He taught me how to be a father and how to provide for my family. My father and I had a great relationship."

One of the most noteworthy facts about the stories of Ward, Green, and Johnson is that they help to explode the stereotype that black dads desert their kids. Clearly, Charlie Ward Sr., A.C. Green Sr., and Jim Johnson went against the grain of the stereotypical African-American male. Each stood by his wife and children, supporting them spiritually, financially, physically, and psychologically. Each worked hard to keep the family cared for, educated, and instructed in the things of God.

And now their sons are continuing that legacy.

The list could go on. David Robinson is grateful to his dad Ambrose, a Navy man about whom David says, "More than anybody was the biggest influence on my life."

New York Knicks' forward Terry Cummings' father taught him how to handle life on the streets of Chicago and how to be loyal to his family.

Former Indiana Pacer Clark Kellogg and current network TV analyst credits his dad, a police officer and a great athlete himself, with guiding Clark toward excellence.

The stories of these stars show how important the combination of both parents' influence can be. These dads stuck to the task, worked hard, dispensed wisdom, provided for the family, and led by example. They are like the father who is described in Psalm 128 in the Bible. Because of his hard work and dedication to God, his life had divine blessing.

When the roving camera at sporting events is turned on those briefly famous people, maybe they respond "Hi, Mom" because they know for sure that Mom is watching. That Mom is always there.

Perhaps dads Johnson, Green, *et. al.* are on the cutting edge of a new trend—one in which dads from all socioeconomic strata—from suburbs to the inner city—recognize what kind of positive impact they have. And then put out the effort to be the influence-makers they are supposed to be. The more dads who do, the easier life will be for everybody. Mom included.

—June 1994

PAY THEM TO PLAY? NO WAY

Some people say college athletes should draw a salary. Is that such a good idea?

I had a rare free evening recently, so I grabbed the newspaper and a Coke. With the TV to myself, I did what I normally do with such a unique opportunity. I looked for sports.

Eureka! Two NBA games were on the tube.

As I sat back to monitor both games through the magic of remote control, though, I suddenly found myself intensely disinterested in the action. The quality of play was mediocre, yet I knew the payrolls were anything but average.

I was upset with myself. Why wasn't I enjoying this? Trying to figure out why I didn't seem to care who threw down the next dunk or who trash-talked whom, I hit upon a theory: The players' love of money had made it all seem so pointless. They were making too much money for me to care about them.

Perhaps that doesn't make sense, but stay with me.

Those players were representatives of a league that had given us the following off-putting scenarios during signing season. One player called an offer of $19 million over 7 years "a slap in the face." Another player was able to negotiate a contract for $35 million for 7 years after averaging just 2 points a game. And then there's the $80 million man who averages 12 points a game, the coach who felt insulted by an offer of $4.3 million, and the multitude of players who simply don't understand how selfish they look when they whine about the millions they are making.

I reached for the remote control and began to search for something else. It wasn't long until I found something that displayed enthusiasm, skill, excitement, drama, and passion. It was college basketball.

The contrast startled me.

Even though I had the opportunity to watch what were supposed to be the best players in the world, I discovered that the amateur athletes played a more enjoyable brand of basketball. And they played it hard from tip-off to buzzer, endline to endline.

This encounter with basketball reminded me why I am against the increasingly popular idea of paying college athletes.

Behind such thinking is the notion that college players are unhappy with the measly $60,000 college scholarship they've been allotted. After all, they don't have any spending money. If they are low on cash, the thinking goes, they are not happy and they might be tempted to take money under the table. It's not fair, theorists conclude, to make these athletes work so hard for so little.

So, the thinking continues, let's pay them so they can be happy. If you need proof that paying athletes doesn't make them happy, flick the remote back to the NBA—the league in which a large percentage of the athletes do drugs to try to get happy; the league with the high divorce rate and the aforementioned unhappy millionaires. And I don't suppose joy was on the heart of P. J. Carlisemo's $35 million attacker in December of 1997.

Think of it this way. If I'm a happy athlete—one with no concerns but to win championships for my team, and if I'm made exceptionally happy because I do not have, nor will my descendants for the next 10 generations have, a financial care in the world—I think I would be flying around the basketball court like a freed puppy. To earn that kind of money, I ought to be playing so hard my tongue is too busy dragging to talk trash.

If that money made me happy, I wouldn't be slouching my way through the first quarter as if it were a bad day running a punch-press in a metal-stamping plant. I wouldn't allow myself to go on national TV and shoot free-throws like a junior-higher. My goodness, my daughter had a better free-throw shooting percentage as a senior in high school than every member of the 1996–97 Portland Trail Blazers last season (.800; the Blazers' highest was .796 by Isaiah Rider). And nobody paid her a dime to practice.

Money runs the NBA, and it is one major reason the competition level of the NBA has diminished in recent years. Seeking more of the green stuff, the NBA has expanded to 230 teams (okay, it's just 29). Watch a game for a few minutes. You'll see that there just aren't enough high-quality basketball players to go around.

Also, the immense lure of money is making pros out of guys who should still be in college, learning to play. Consider that the league's $126 million man signed that contract when he would normally have been a college junior, polishing his skills. Think of the difference it makes in a pro league to add players who have not matured athletically.

Let's turn back to the college game. If we think guys are going to stay in college if we pay them, what dream world are we living in? Remember, pro players switch teams to follow the dollars as often as we change shoes. If you give an athlete a scholarship and then pay him $30,000 a year to play for good, old Hometown University, how's he going to respond when the NBA waves a few million in his face? He'll be gone before the shot clock runs out.

And another thing. The greed, selfishness, lack of loyalty, and arrogance we see in so many big money pro athletes would soon trickle down to the colleges. Gargantuan salaries haven't made players any happier than NBA players were in the 60s and 70s when they were making peanuts. The same highfalutin posturing we see in pro ball will pollute the colleges if we start paying the athletes.

Flip the channel back to the college game, where the fans are rabid, the players are dripping sweat, and the game is fundamentally sound. Is paying these guys going to change anything for the better? Of course not.

Those guys wouldn't play any harder if you paid them.

What a mistake it would be to try.

—March 1998

RESERVATIONS

CAN WE CONTINUE TO TOLERATE THE BAD TO GET THE GOOD FROM THE WORLD OF SPORTS?

Sometimes I get very tired of the sports scene. There is so much of it that I wish would go away. When I stop and think about what is happening with sports, I begin to have reservations about even being involved.

- I have reservations because of the salary demands and contract squabbles of today's players. To demand more money than anyone could ever possibly spend in a lifetime is absurd, and the owners who give in to those demands need some free time to contemplate what would cause them to spend money so foolishly. Isn't there any athlete who is embarrassed enough about all this to say enough is enough, as Detroit Tiger great Al Kaline once did when management offered him more money than he thought he was worth?
- I have reservations because of the growing violence on the field and on the courts. To be sure, personal wars have always been in the game. Ty Cobb was no angel, and battles have erupted on playing fields since teams started playing each other. Yet the growing mean-spiritedness of trash talk and belligerence is more than just competitiveness. Some of this is an overflow of deep-seated anger that is ready to explode even before the contest begins. This is not the proverbial 110-percent effort that we all applaud. This is chip-on-the-shoulder pugilism, just itching for an excuse to erupt.
- That's why I have reservations about pro basketball, which threatens to degenerate into an exchange of body slams and irritatingly horrific offense. This semi-controlled violence has soured many who were turning to the city game to watch in-

credibly skilled athletes do remarkable things. What they have begun to see is a combination of roller derby and big-time wrestling. Why have we replaced the graceful moves and creative play of men like Pete Maravich, Julius Erving, David Thompson, Earvin Johnson, and Michael Jordan with bumping, banging, and battering?

- I have reservations because American football, at all levels, is almost a religion in this land (of course, that is one of the problems with soccer in other parts of the world). More than any other sport, it seems, people spend an inordinate amount of time, energy, and effort in following their favorite football team. Families are neglected, responsibilities go unfinished, and spiritual activities are ignored in favor of the games.
- I have reservations because the continued expansion in all sports is leading to a thinning of talent. It seems that the sports moguls will not be happy until every city in America has a major league team. Yet as we see in baseball with the dearth of quality pitchers, many teams are major league in name only. As the quantity rises, the quality diminishes.
- I have reservations because the alcohol industry continues to be a major player in sports—both pro and college. Sports are intrinsically youthful, and the young people who love sports are easily influenced to associate sports and its related elements. Growing up with a constant reminder of alcohol at every sporting event—whether through video commercials, print ads, or signs at the games—makes it easy for them to connect the good times in sports with drinking. It's unfair to tie sports in with a drug that has so many debilitating side effects, yet never speak of those dangers.

Life is a balancing act. We cannot control all of its elements, so we sometimes have to balance the bad with the good and see where it leads. For instance, I have reservations about the way people drive their cars. I don't like tailgating, going through red lights, and discourteous behavior. Yet I still drive. I wish those people would change, but they aren't going to. I still derive benefit from driving, so I tolerate the miscreants and feel good when I see others driving as they should.

Following sports is a balancing act as well. In a world that is imperfect, its recreations will follow suit. Yet my connections to the games—and the connections of a [book] like this one—don't have to be influenced by the downside. We can still find athletes who have values higher than their bank account. We can help readers see that no sport and no person is worthy of worship—except Jesus Christ. We can expose the dangers of substance abuse. And we can be a light that exposes those things we do not think are right.

I have reservations about sports. But as an athlete and as an observer I have also seen the great value they can bring. That's enough incentive to influence me to stay in the game.

—October 1994

THE RETURN OF A KING

When superstar Michael Jordan (sometimes known simply as MJ) returned to basketball in 1995, you would have thought something of biblical proportions happened. This allegory looks into that overreaction.

Once there was a kingdom called Hoopalia. In this dominion dwelt King EmJay, a benevolent ruler who reigned without equal over the entire land. Except for a few disloyal subjects who were simply jealous of his incredible powers, everybody liked this potentate, for he brought smiles to their faces with his incredible feats of skill at the game of Baskets.

One day, though, in the dry time between two seasons of Baskets, King EmJay abdicated his throne, leaving it in the shakey hands of the venerable Sir Chuck and the young pretender Duke Shack. In an emotional speech before the people, King Emjay told the Hoopalians that he simply didn't want to be King anymore. He just wanted to be average citizen EmJay, free to spend a lot more time with his own little serfdom.

Soon, however, a spell of sorts seemed to overtake him, causing the former King EmJay to make a strange decision. He wanted to immigrate to another land—the Land of the Diamonds. It seems that as a young prince he had been quite talented at their leisure time activity called Bases, and he felt that he might entertain the subjects of his new homeland by attempting their game.

People of both kingdoms knew immediately that the ex-king would not find it easy to transcend the throne in this land. There was no fear from the young reigning potentates who ruled the land from a rare double throne: King Frank of Hurt and King Junior of Griff. All over the countryside, the subjects of the Land of the Diamonds made derisive remarks about EmJay, this king in exile. He may have been good at Baskets, they said, but not all of his skills had transferred to Bases—leaving him often looking no better for his efforts than those who played in the lowest levels of the leagues called minor.

Yet EmJay persevered. Former king or no former king, he was not about to quit. He was, as many people were fond of saying about him, a Competitor. It was something all the people of the dominion appreciated.

Then something very sad happened in the Land of the Diamonds. An uprising among the best players of Bases—the ones in the League of Majors—took place. It seems that they had been paid handsomely to play at Bases, . . . [but they became afraid] when the men and women who hired them to play—and paid many of them millions of Facets to do so—had decided that they might not pay them quite so much in the future.

Besides causing consternation among fans of Bases everywhere, this also bummed out Sir EmJay immensely. He had been trying to get to the League of Majors, but now he didn't know if that would be possible. He was growing impatient. And besides, he was making very small amount of Facets playing at Bases.

As he pondered his situation, nostalgia swept over him.

He missed his old country, Hoopalia. He missed the game of Baskets. He missed being King.

So, in an amazing and very popular move, he packed away his Bases gear and returned to Hoopalia. As the townsmen and townswomen of his original town of Sheekaga cheered and cheered, he swept into town on his favorite horse, Range Rover.

Immediately he was reinstalled as King and asked to restore the game of Baskets to its former immense popularity. Indeed he was so well-received on his return that the people who wrote articles about Baskets began to use terms that had never before been used to describe people who played sporting games.

They wrote about a "resurrection." And a "second coming." And some even used the term "Messiah."

As impressed as King Emjay must have been, he knew better.

"I'm only human," he protested to the masses of Hoopalia amid the hoopla.

And indeed he was. For even in the the land of Baskets—where he was surely King—there were people who knew that there was a bigger world out there outside of Hoopalia and the Land of the Diamonds.

It was called the Real World. The world where one day a Man who was a Real King had lived a perfect life. He had been killed by people who didn't understand who He really was.

Yet He had come back to life three days later in the only true Resurrection ever. Then, in a most astonishing road trip, He returned to His original home: heaven.

He is the One who will make a Second Coming of importance. He is the ultimate King.

And His name is Jesus.

He alone is King. Indeed He is The King of kings.

—June 1995

SIMPLE CHOICES; COMPLEX RESULTS

IN SPORTS—AS WELL AS IN REAL LIFE—OUR CHOICES HAVE FAR-REACHING IMPLICATIONS THAT WE OFTEN DON'T SEE UNTIL MUCH LATER.

When you have an elementary-aged boy, you spend a lot of time explaining simple things. In my case, Steven and I discuss many of these profound yet basic ideas.

Simple things like why it doesn't make sense to drink a whole can of Coke right before trying to go to sleep for the night. Like why it's vital to learn to dribble a basketball with either hand. Like why an 11-year-old isn't ready to drive a car.

Making right choices is a simple concept that occupies many of our conversations.

"It's pretty simple," I tell Steven. "You make right choices; you avoid trouble. You make lousy choices; you pay the consequences."

As simple as this concept is, though, we continue to see people in the sports world—men and women who are old enough to know better—making some incredibly poor choices. As I always tell Steven—and as sports figures prove almost daily—every bad choice you make has bad consequences. Notice how it works.

NBA Player

CHOICE: Drink alcohol while under the league's drug treatment program OR Avoid the drinks and earn millions and millions of dollars.

DECISION: Drink the booze.

CONSEQUENCE: Lose the money.

Former Major League Baseball Players

CHOICE: Hide assets from autographs sessions OR Pay the rightful amount of taxes on autograph session money—making money and staying on the law's good side.
DECISION: Lie about income to the IRS.
CONSEQUENCE: Suffer embarrassment and loss of stature among fans (and lose that extra dough too).

College Coaches

CHOICE: Violate NCAA rules OR Run a clean program and enjoy a clear conscience and post-season games.
DECISION: Cheat.
CONSEQUENCE: Coach the team while looking over your shoulder in fear, followed by an investigation, followed by stiff sanctions from the NCAA, followed by fleeing the school to find another job.

Too Many Athletes

CHOICE: Beat up wife/girlfriend OR Act like a real man and demonstrate self-control.
DECISION: Loose control and hit her—or worse.
CONSEQUENCE: Jeopardize your career, damage a woman for life, and destroy your reputation.

Athletes Under Contract

CHOICE: Renegotiate/hold out for even more money OR Gratefully play out the length of the contract with intensity, demonstrating enough value to make the next contract better.
DECISION: Hold out and whine about not having enough security or not getting enough respect.
CONSEQUENCE: Coerce more bucks but lose the respect of a nation of sports fans.

Those are simple choices, really. To be fair, there may be extenuating circumstances that make a person more predisposed to a negative action; but that only makes the decision understandably difficult. It doesn't make the wrongdoing acceptable.

Yet not all sports figures make the wrong choices. They don't all practice violence or cheat on taxes or act greedy. Many athletes make choices that can be admired and applauded.

Cal Ripken made a conscious choice each day between 1982 and 1998 to quietly and effectively go about his job—and he ended up as baseball's ironman.

Ernie Irvan chose to battle back from a near-fatal crash by overcoming physical and psychological obstacles—and he drove again on the NASCAR circuit.

Junior Seau decided to avoid the drugs and gang involvement that surrounded him as he grew up—and became one of the best football players in the land.

Choices have consequences, and these athletes have enjoyed the good fruit of their wise decisions.

When I first heard about Calvin Duncan's choice, I was reminded that not everyone will agree what a good choice might be. Duncan, a basketball coach who had an opportunity to move to the NBA as a coach but chose to stay in the CBA because he thought that's where God wanted him, found peace in that decision.

While I would applaud Duncan's choice to turn down an NBA career so he could be a basketball missionary (and I would have given anything to have had a shot at the NBA), some would call Duncan's move questionable.

Sometimes it depends on your perspective.

And your perspective ultimately depends on another choice you may or may not have made.

Every Person on Earth

CHOICE: Accept Jesus Christ as your personal Savior OR Reject what Jesus did for you and choose an eternity separated from God in a place the Bible describes as "a lake of fire."
DECISION: It's up to you.

Sounds like a simple decision. But it has consequences that will affect how you perceive things now and where you will spend eternity.

No choice was ever more important.

—February 1996

DON'T BRING THAT UP!

ONE OF THE NEWEST ADDITIONS TO THE SPORTS MEDIA WORLD IS THE ALL-SPORTS RADIO STATIONS AND NETWORKS. THE HOSTS PRIDE THEMSELVES IN BEING OPEN-MINDED AND WILLING TO DISCUSS ANYTHING. WELL, MAYBE NOT ANYTHING.

"Our next caller's from Paducah, Kentucky. Hello, Bob. You're next on sports talk radio with Buck Blather. Our topic today is things that bug you about the world of sports! Any subject you want to talk about is fair game."

"Yeah. Hi. Uh. Am I on?"

"Yes, you're on the air coast-to-coast."

"Uh, okay. Hey, Buck, how ya' doin'?"

"Great, go ahead."

"Yeah, I'm Bob, and I'm calling from Paducah, Kentucky, and I'd like to say I think the Kentucky Wildcats had the best team in college basketball in 1998."

"Bob! Bob! I think that's pretty well established. Let that one rest, okay? What's your gripe? We're looking for your biggest sports gripes today on the program."

"Well, I do have a complaint, Buck. I'm a big Reds fan, and I'm tired of people picking on Marge Schott. She was all right, you know. I even own a car from her car dealership."

"That was Bob from Kentucky. Well, hey! I don't agree, but the man's entitled to his opinion. You've got to admit, at least Marge had the folks in Cincinnati talking about baseball. Who am I to deny Bob his fun?

"Let's go out to Modesto, California, where Kevin's on a car phone waiting to talk to us. Kevin, go ahead."

"Buck, you know what I'm sick of? I'm sick of Michael Jordan. All I ever hear is Michael Jordan this, Michael Jordan that. Has everybody forgotten Elgin Baylor? Jordan couldn't carry Baylor's gym bag! The next time I hear some guy in a suit with a microphone in his hand bragging about Jordan, I'm going to throw a shoe at my TV."

"Hey, Kevin, that's okay. Let it out, man. If you think Baylor's better, who am I to question you? Everybody's entitled to an opinion. That's why we have sports talk radio.

"Buck Blather here. And we're doing 'What's bugging me' day on the radio from sea to shining sea. You bring up the topic, and we'll discuss it. No holds barred. My producer Chet says all of our lines are lit up, so let's go back to the phones. Tiffany from Topeka is on next. Hi, Tiffany!"

"Hi there, Buck. Love your program. I listen to it every day on my earphones while I walk the dog. I'm so excited to get through to you. Buck, you know, I've been reading a lot about Zen, and I think it is so neat that Phil Jackson is so big into it. He was such a Zen-master with that basketball team of his. But I have a gripe. They make him look a little kooky when they mention it."

"You mean the broadcasters?"

"Yeah, Buck. Why don't they just leave him alone?"

"You know, Tiffany, you've hit the nail on the head here. This is a free country last time I checked, and everyone should be able to do his or her own thing. And hey, if Phil Jackson has a yen for Zen, that's okay by me. Who am I to argue?

"It's gripe day here on the old radio, and we've got to keep moving. From Topeka we go out to Portland, where Thomas is on the line. Thomas, take it away."

"First-time caller here, Buck."

"Super. What's your beef?"

"Women's basketball. I been watching the WNBA, and I don't think it'll work. Sure some of those women are pretty good, but there's not a one of them who could play in the NBA. I mean, how long are people gonna to watch these games anyway? I don't think it'll stay."

"Hey, Thomas, you're stepping on some toes out there, big guy. But I'm sure a lot of people agree with you too. It's one of those deals where we'll just have to wait and see. You know, the women are very talented, so it may work out. But I'm not here to tell you how to think, Thomas. You may be right.

"My good friend Roadrunner is calling in from Rhode Island. You haven't called in a while, Roadrunner. What's up, my man?"

"You know what's getting me down, Buck? It's this whole Dennis Rodman thing. The man is outrageous, and I think that's great. He brings a whole new dimension to sports. It bothers me that some people think he's a problem."

"Nicely said, Roadrunner. Variety is the spice of sports, to coin a phrase, and DR certainly gives us that. Hey, so what if he's looking at the world differently! What harm's he doing! I'm an anything-goes kind of guy myself. Thanks for the call, Roadrunner!

"Hey, I think we have time for one more call before we call it quits for today. Let's head back to the Midwest, where Mike from Carol

Stream, Illinois, is on the phone. Mike, go ahead."

"Hello, Buck. I have a minor complaint about the way some athletes are treated."

"Okay, Mike. We're open to any subject, so go ahead. That's what we're here for."

"Well, a lot of times Christian athletes are looked down on, and people say they are wimps, but I disagree."

"Hey, now wait a minute, there, Mike. I'm not sure I want to talk about this."

"You said anything in sports was open to discussion."

"But religion? I'm not so sure. Be careful."

"Okay. I just want to say that there are lots of Christian athletes who have proved that they are tough and can compete. I mean, think of Orel Hershiser in 1988. And Joe Carter in 1993. And Jeff Gordon in 1995. And Scott Brosius in 1998. And people like Reggie White, Betsy King, and A.C. Green throughout their whole careers. I just think people need to know that just because a person loves Jesus Christ, he or she is not a pushover."

"Well, Mike, thanks for the sermon. What's with him? You know, I just don't understand why some people don't get it. This is a sports program, and I don't know why they have to bring their religion into it.

"Hey, that's our program for today. I've got to run. Call me tomorrow, and we'll talk about anything you care to discuss. Well, almost anything."

—July 1996

THE ONLY WAY TO WIN

NOTHING ELSE MATTERS FOR ANY OF US UNLESS WE GET ONE THING STRAIGHT. FOOTBALL, BASEBALL, OR ANY OTHER SPORT HAS NOTHING TO DO WITH OUR ULTIMATE DESTINY.

In football, there are as many ways to win as there are creative coaches. No one has a corner on the only way to rise to the top.

But what if you were interested in winning at something even more important than football? What if you want to win at life?

- Perhaps you're struggling through life, wondering why you aren't happy no matter how hard you work at it.

- Perhaps you can't seem to find purpose in life.
- Maybe you've wondered about your eternal destiny.

You need to find a way to win. You need a strategy.

Can we suggest the one we have found that works every time? It's endorsed by NFL stars Irving Fryar, Chad Hennings, Darrell Green, Reggie White, Cris Carter, Jim Harbaugh, Curtis Martin, Hardy Nickerson, Mark Brunell, Brent Jones, and dozens of others.

Here's how this winning plan works.

1. Recognize The Problem: *You can't get to God on your own.*

   Your way to God is blocked by sin. The Bible says, "All have sinned and fall short of the glory of God" (Romans 3:23).

   Need proof? Look at the Ten Commandments in Exodus 20. If you've failed to keep any of those commands, you've sinned.

   God is perfect and holy, and He cannot allow sin in His presence.

   Unless something changes, you are doomed to godless, hopeless living and an eternity separated from the One who created you and wants the best for you.
2. Understand The Plan: *The cross covers your sin.*

   God has a plan that will allow you to develop a relationship with Him despite your sin. He sent Jesus Christ, His only Son, to earth. Jesus lived without sinning yet was killed by being hung on a cross. When He died, Jesus took your sins on Himself, becoming your substitute. Three days after He died, Jesus rose from the dead to prove that He had power over death and sin. "He was delivered over to death for our sins and was raised to life for our justification" (Romans 4:25).
3. Accept God's Salvation: *You cross over through faith in Jesus Christ.*

   Despite what Jesus did, you are still on the other side—until you receive God's gift of salvation. The Bible says, "If you confess with your mouth, 'Jesus is Lord,' and believe in your heart that God raised him from the dead, you will be saved" (Romans 10:9).

Just put your faith in Jesus, believing that through His death He will forgive your sin. When you do, you use the cross to come over to God's side. You then have a relationship with God. He is your guide on earth, and He promises you an eternal home in heaven.

Do you want to cross over to God's side?

Pray a prayer like this:

Dear God,

Thank You for sending Jesus to earth as my substitute. Thank You for His death on my behalf. I realize that I have sinned, and I ask You to forgive my sins. I put my faith in Jesus Christ as my Savior. Help me to understand my new relationship with You. Thank You for taking away my sin and letting me be one of Your children.

If you prayed this prayer, you've just won the game of life! You are on God's side now, joining millions of others who love Him and have found His ways to be best.

—January 1997

Chapter 3

SPORTS PEOPLE

Ever since the recent surge in interest in Christians in sports began, fans everywhere have been thirsting to know who the Christian athletes are and what they stand for. Over the years, a number of resources have come on the scene attempting to provide profiles of well-known athletes who have in one way or another been noted for their faith.

One of the difficulties in putting together or depending on resources such as those is that people have a wide range of definitions for the term *Christian athlete*. For some fans, just hearing a sports figure mention the name of God in a positive way causes them to conclude that the person is a Christian. Others hear of their good works, and others just observe that the athlete "just acts like a Christian."

All of this makes compiling lists of Christian athletes problematic. Added to that, the difficulty of getting definitive word about every professed or assumed Christian's testimony makes the task even more difficult.

For the compilation of the listing of athletes that follows, two major considerations were made: First, has the person gone on record as saying that he or she is a Christian by virtue of putting genuine faith in the death, burial, and resurrection of Jesus Christ for the forgiveness of sins? Some evidence of that happening in the person's life is essential for consideration. Second, does the athlete strive to live a morally clean life as revealed in the Bible? This is something that is usually manifested in what others say about him or her—and even in what is reported in the media.

This list cannot be considered exhaustive. Every attempt was made through reasonable means to secure the testimony of as many athletes as possible. Some athletes were not included simply because there was no way to secure a clear salvation testimony. Although there are hundreds of athletes in this chapter, you can rest assured that there are many, many others who deserve to be in such a grouping.

Be encouraged by what you read in this chapter, and if you think you know of others who should be included in a later version of this book, please refer to the information at the end of the chapter.

BASEBALL (MLB)

RICK AGUILERA

New York Mets, Minnesota Twins, Boston Red Sox, Twins, Chicago Cubs
Right-handed pitcher

High school: Edgewood High (West Covina, Calif.)
College: Brigham Young University
Draft: Selected in the third round by the New York Mets in the 1983 draft

Highlights

Minnesota Twins all-time save leader
1991, 1996: Played in the World Series
1993: Selected Twins Pitcher of the Year

Salvation

"It didn't happen until I was called up to the majors. In May 1985, I was with the Mets, and Clint Hurdle was there with us. He was a tremendous witness. I wondered what this relationship with Jesus was all about. Through Baseball Chapel, I began to learn and understand about having a relationship with Jesus Christ. I kind of went through a period where I felt I had a relationship with Jesus Christ, but I really didn't. I was kind of using Jesus—hoping to have a good game and hoping to have some success. It wasn't until 1988 when I truly recommitted myself and surrendered my life fully to Him. I finally realized, 'Lord, I can't do it by myself. I need Your help.'"

Family: Wife, Sherry; and two children, Rachel and Austin
Ministries: Baseball Chapel, working with Native Americans in Minneapolis, and fishing ministry to athletes

---

FELIPE ALOU

Player: San Francisco Giants, Milwaukee/Atlanta Braves, Oakland A's, New York Yankees, Montreal Expos, Milwaukee Brewers
Outfielder (R/R)
Manager: Montreal Expos

Hometown: Haina, Dominican Republic
College: University of Santo Domingo (Dominican Republic)
Draft: Signed as free agent by the New York Giants in 1955

Highlights

1966: Led NL with 355 total bases
1994: Named NL Manager of the Year

Salvation

When Felipe was a minor league baseball player, a friend from the Dominican Republic handed him a Bible one day when he returned home from his minor league season. Felipe read the Bible, but it was not until several months later—after he had made his major league debut in 1958—that he trusted Christ as Savior. He finally understood after a teammate, Al Worthington, explained the gospel to him.

Family and personal: Wife, Lucie; and five children, Moises, José, Felipe José, Felipe Jr, and Valerie. Son Moises plays for the Houston Astros.

CHRIS BANDO

Retired after the 1989 season
Player: Cleveland Indians, Detroit Tigers, Oakland A's
Catcher, S/R (switch hitter, throws right)
Coach: Milwaukee Brewers

High school: Solon (Ohio) High
Draft: Selected by Milwaukee Brewers in twenty-second round of 1987 draft

Highlights

1984: Had most productive year as a hitter with 12 home runs

Salvation

Sal Bando had been led to faith in Christ by his manager, Al Dark. When Sal got saved, he encouraged his brother Chris to trust in Jesus too. However, Chris was not ready. It wasn't until he faced some disappointments, including some injuries during his minor league days, that he began to take Sal's words seriously. "The Lord had to get my attention," Chris says. Finally, though, in 1980, Chris became a Christian.

Family: Wife, Beth; and six children, Ben, Philip, Michael, Nico, Luke, and Angela
Ministries: Unlimited Potential, Inc. and his church in Scottsdale, Arizona, where he has served on staff

SAL BANDO

Retired after the 1981 season
Player: Kansas City A's/Oakland A's, Milwaukee Brewers
Third baseman, R/R (hits right, throws right)
General manager: Milwaukee Brewers

Hometown: Cleveland, Ohio
College: Arizona State University
Draft: Selected by the Athletics in the 1965 draft

Highlights

1973: Led the AL in doubles (32)
1975: Batted .500 in play-offs against Boston
Selected to play in four All-Star Games

Salvation

A Christian family had its benefits for Sal Bando, but one of them was not that he became a Christian. It was not until Bando came under the teaching of one of his managers while he was playing that he trusted Jesus Christ. The manager, Al Dark, was an outspoken Christian, and he was able to lead Sal to Christ. In 1975, Bando finally entrusted his life to Jesus Christ.

Family and personal: Wife, Sandy; and three children, Sal Jr., Sonny, and Stefano. Chuck Colson's book *Born Again* was influential in Sal's life.
Ministries: Fellowship of Christian Athletes, Boys' and Girls' Clubs

JESSE BARFIELD

Retired after the 1993 season
Player: Toronto Blue Jays, New York Yankees, Yomiuri (Japan)
Outfielder (R/R)
Coach: Houston Astros, Texas Rangers, Seattle Mariners

High school: Joliet (Ill.) Central
Draft: Selected in the ninth round by the Toronto Blue Jays in the 1977 draft

Highlights

1985, 1986: Led AL outfielders in double plays
1986: Selected to AL All-Star team; led AL in home runs (40)

Salvation

When Jesse Barfield joined the Toronto Blue Jays, he met relief pitcher Roy Jackson. Jesse had heard that Jackson was a Christian, so he kept an eye on him. He watched him when he won, and he watched him when he lost. He was impressed with Jackson's balance. Later, Jackson shared a gospel tape with Barfield—a tape that led both Jesse and his girlfriend, Marla, to accept Christ as Savior.

Family: Wife, Marla; and three children, Joshua, Jessica, and Jeremy
Ministries: Has led several major leaguers to faith in Christ.

JAY BELL

Cleveland Indians, Pittsburgh Pirates, Kansas City Royals, Arizona Diamondbacks
Shortstop (R/R)

High school: Tate High (Gonzalez, Fla.)
Draft: First-round pick in 1984 by the Minnesota Twins

Highlights

1996: Led all major league shortstops in fielding (.986)
1997: Kansas City Royals Player of the Year
1997: Tied for second in AL fielding (.985)

Salvation

Bell grew up in a Christian home and became aware of Jesus Christ at an early age. "I understood what the relationship with Jesus Christ was all about. I've been a Christian since 1976, when I made a decision to trust Jesus Christ."

Family and personal: Wife, Laura; and two children, Brianna and Brantley. "One of my favorite verses is Proverbs 3:5 and 6. It says that if you allow God to direct your paths, He's going to lead your way. That's one of the things I try to do—allow Him to lead my path and to make sure I trust Him in all my judgments."

ANDY BENES

San Diego Padres, Seattle Mariners, St. Louis Cardinals, Arizona Diamondbacks
Right-handed pitcher

High school: Central High (Evansville, In.)
College: University of Evansville
Draft: First-round draft pick in 1988 by the San Diego Padres

Highlights

1989: Named *The Sporting News* NL Rookie Pitcher of the Year
1993: Pitched in the All-Star Game
1994: Led NL in strikeouts (189)

Salvation

Benes came to faith in Christ in 1989, an event that he says, "changed my life. It is a great privilege to be called one of His children."

Family and personal: Wife, Jennifer; and two children, Andrew and Shane. Andy has two brothers in professional baseball. In 1997, they all were members of the St. Louis Cardinals organization.
Ministries: Children Ministries International

DOUG BOCHTLER

Retired after the 1998 season
Montreal Expos, San Diego Padres, Detroit Tigers, Los Angeles Dodgers
Right-handed pitcher

High school: John I. Leonard High (Lake Worth, Fla.)
College: Indian River Junior College (Fla.)
Draft: Selected in the ninth round of the 1989 draft by the Montreal Expos

Highlights

1996: Limited opponents to .195 batting average, third lowest in NL among relief pitchers
1997: Tied for third on San Diego Padres staff in appearances (54)

Salvation

While playing in the Midwest League in 1990, Doug trusted Jesus as Savior. "I came to the point in my life where the Holy Spirit convicted me of my sin, and while in an apartment in Rockford, Illinois, [home of his minor league team] I fell to my knees and repented."

Family and personal: Wife, Darcy. When Doug was in high school, his friend Greg Kennard died. The friend's dad, Curley Kennard, gave Doug his friend's baseball glove and told him, "Take this to the majors." When Bochtler made it to the big leagues in San Diego, he wore Greg's glove.

SHAWN BOSKIE

Retired after the 1998 season
Chicago Cubs, Philadelphia Phillies, Seattle Mariners, California Angels, Baltimore Orioles, Montreal Expos
Right-handed pitcher

High school: Reno (Nev.) High
College: Modesto (Calif.) Junior College
Draft: Selected in the first round of the 1986 draft by the Chicago Cubs

Highlights

1990: Recorded a complete game in his major league debut on the mound
1994: After going from Chicago to Philadelphia, he beat the Cubs in back-to-back games
1995: Won his first five starts (fourth starter in Angels history to do so)

Salvation

While a minor leaguer, Shawn began to grow tired of the women, drugs, and alcohol scene. He knew he needed a change. He went to a Baseball Chapel service and heard for the first time about the need for a personal relationship with Jesus Christ. He began to read his Bible, and he discovered in its introduction a plan of salvation. "A few nights later, while I was lying on my bed, I prayed the sinner's prayer. I said, 'Jesus, forgive me of my sins.' "

Family and personal: Wife, Pam; and one child, Brad. While in college, Boskie was an infielder.
Ministry: Unlimited Potential, Inc.

KENT BOTTENFIELD

Montreal Expos, Colorado Rockies, San Francisco Giants, Chicago Cubs, St. Louis Cardinals
Right-handed pitcher

High school: James Madison (Portland, Ore.)
Draft: Selected in the fourth round by the Montreal Expos in the 1986 draft

Highlights

1993: While pitching for Colorado, started the first-ever major league at Denver's Mile High Stadium
1999: Won 18 games for the St. Louis Cardinals
1999: Led Cardinals in wins, strikeouts (124), and starts (31)

Salvation

While playing in the Florida Instructional League in October, 1987, Kent began attending a church in West Palm Beach. Time after time, the church would have an altar call, but on one particular night, he says, "It just kind of struck me that I wanted to get right with God." Having grown up in a Christian home, this idea was not new to Kent, but now he understood he had to make the decision for himself. "I didn't go forward that night, but when I got back to my apartment, I prayed to receive Christ."

Family and personal: Wife, Pamela; and two children, Eli and Emma. Kent writes songs in his spare time.

SID BREAM

Retired after the 1994 season
Los Angeles Dodgers, Pittsburgh Pirates, Atlanta Braves
First baseman (L/L)

High school: Carlisle (Penn.) High
College: Liberty University, Lynchburg, Va.
Draft: Selected in the second round by the LA Dodgers in the 1981 draft

Highlights

1986: Set NL record for assists by a first baseman (166)
1990: Winner of the Hutch Award
1991: Hit two doubles in the World Series
1992: Scored winning run in league championship series

Salvation

"My mom and dad are tremendous Christians," Bream says. Those parents taught Sid early on about faith in Jesus Christ. In 1973, Bream became a Christian just before becoming a teenager when he trusted Christ as Savior during a church revival meeting.

Family: Wife, Michelle; and sons, Michael and Tyler
Ministries: Unlimited Potential, Inc.

RICO BROGNA

Detroit Tigers, New York Mets, Philadelphia Phillies
First baseman (L/L)

High school: Watertown (Conn.) High
College: Recruited by Clemson University to play football; did not attend
Draft: Selected in the first round in the 1988 draft by the Detroit Tigers

Highlights

1992: Hit a double in first major league at bat (August 8)
1995: Led NL first basemen with .998 fielding percentage
1997: Tied for second on Phillies with 20 home runs

Salvation

In 1991, Rico was diagnosed with an arthritic disease. It made him ask a lot of questions about baseball and about life. "I was really searching," he says. "God was steering me to the right people. I was sent down to Double A ball, where a good friend of mine opened the Bible and led me to Jesus. That's meant everything in my life to me."

Family and personal: Wife, Melissa; and daughter, Alexa. Rico suffers from an arthritic disease known as ankylosing spondylitis, yet has been able to battle it to be a top-notch first baseman. Rico has coached high school basketball in past winters at his alma mater.

SCOTT BROSIUS

Oakland A's, New York Yankees
Third baseman (R/R)

High school: Rex Putnam High (Milwaukie, Ore.)
College: Linfield College (McMinnville, Ore.)
Draft: Selected in the twentieth round by the Oakland A's in the 1987 draft

Highlights

1996: Hit .306 with 22 home runs for the A's
1998: Named World Series Most Valuable Player

Salvation

When Scott Brosius was playing in the minor leagues in 1989, he met a former player named Rocky Coyle. "Rocky started talking to me about a relationship with Christ," Brosius says. Later, after a family death made him think about his own future, Brosius prayed to receive Jesus as his Savior.

Family and personal: Wife, Jennifer; and three children, Allison, Megan, and David. Scott pitched two innings of a minor league game and posted a perfect 0.00 ERA.

TIM BURKE

Retired during spring training in 1993
Montreal Expos, New York Mets, New York Yankees
Right-handed pitcher

High school: Roncalli High (Omaha, Nebr.)
College: University of Nebraska
Draft: Selected in the second round by the Pittsburgh Pirates in the 1980 draft

Highlights

1985: Set NL record for most appearances by a rookie (78)
1989: Selected to the NL All-Star team

Salvation

When Tim played for Buffalo in the minor leagues, he and his young wife Christine were struggling with their new marriage. They were searching for answers when they were invited to Bible studies with team members. Before the season was over, their lives and marriage were rescued when they trusted Jesus Christ as Savior. According to Tim, that decision helped him to "see Christine in a different light. With Christ in me, all of a sudden I could see her with truly loving eyes."

Family: Wife, Christine; and four children, Stephanie, Ryan, Nicole, and Wayne
Ministries: Unlimited Potential, Inc.

BRETT BUTLER

Retired after the 1997 season
Cleveland Indians, San Francisco Giants, New York Mets, Los Angeles Dodgers, Outfielder (L/L)
High school: Libertyville (Ill.) High
Draft: Selected in the twenty-third round in the 1979 draft by the Cleveland Indians

Highlights

1987: Led AL in runs scored (109)
1990: Tied for AL lead in hits (192); led AL in runs scored (112)
1991: Had a 23-game hitting streak
1995: Tied for NL lead in triples (9)

Salvation

While in high school, Brett attended a Fellowship of Christian Athletes conference in Fort Collins, Colorado. Although he had grown up in a Christian home, it wasn't until someone at the FCA conference confronted him with the question, "If you were to die tonight, would you go to heaven?" that he knew he needed to take care of matters. "I wanted assurance. I got down on my knees by myself and asked Christ to come into my life."

Family and personal: Wife, Eveline; and four children, Abbi, Stefanie, Katie, and Blake. At the beginning of the 1996 season, Butler was diagnosed with throat cancer. He had the cancer removed, and he returned to play for the Dodgers before the season was over.

PAUL BYRD

New York Mets, Atlanta Braves, Philadelphia Phillies
Right-handed pitcher

High school: St. Xavier High (Louisville, Ky.)
College: Louisiana State
Draft: Selected in the 13th round by the Cincinnati Reds in the 1988 draft

Highlights

1998: Hurled a shutout against Randy Johnson in his first game with the Phillies

Salvation

While a sophomore at Louisiana State, Paul was introduced to the gospel by a Campus Crusade for Christ staff member. Growing up, Paul had gone to church and was a self-described "good person," but until attending Bible studies at Wayne Waddell's home, Paul didn't understand salvation. It was at his friend's home "that I then understood that Jesus is a living person who loved me." And it was then that Paul Byrd trusted Jesus as Savior. "That was the most important decision I ever made," Paul says.

Family: Wife, Kym; and two children, Grayson and Colby

BERNIE CARBO

Retired after the 1980 season
Cincinnati Reds, Boston Red Sox, St. Louis Cardinals
Outfielder (L/L)

Hometown : Detroit
Draft: Drafted by the Cincinnati Reds

Highlights

1970: Named *The Sporting News* NL Rookie of the Year
1975: Hit a dramatic three-run home run in one of the most exciting World Series games in baseball history as the Red Sox came back to beat the Reds. Carbo's blast tied the game, and Carlton Fisk's body-English home run won it to push the Series to seven games.

Salvation

One of the most incredible stories among Christians in sports, Bernie Carbo was nearly gone when the Lord rescued him. His life was in a shambles, messed up by drugs and alcohol. So sick of it he had almost nowhere to turn, he had himself admitted to a hospital. There, he met a man who told him about the saving power of Jesus Christ. After some resistance, Bernie turned his life over to Christ. He still contends that if God had not intervened, he would be a dead man now.

Family: Wife, Tammy
Ministries: Diamond Club, a baseball ministry to young people

---

GARY CARTER

Retired after the 1992 season
Montreal Expos, New York Mets, San Francisco Giants, Los Angeles Dodgers
Catcher (R/R)

High school: Sunny Hills High (Fullerton, Calif.)
College: Recruited by UCLA to play football, but never attended
Draft: Selected in the third round by the Montreal Expos in the 1972 draft

Highlights

1977, 1985: Hit 3 home runs in a single game
1978: Set major league mark for fewest passed balls (1)
1981, 1984: Named the MVP of the All-Star Game
1988: Won the Danny Thompson Award and the Roberto Clemente Award

Salvation

As a teenager just starting out in pro baseball, Gary Carter had all the tools and all the ambition he needed. He was also brokenhearted over the death of his mother when he was just twelve. When Carter told his teammate, John Boccabella, about his aching heart, his fellow catcher told Gary about the peace he could find in Jesus Christ. "On March 22, 1973, I asked Christ into my life," Carter recalls.

Family and personal: Wife, Sandy; and three children, Christy, Kimmy, and D. J. Now works as a broadcaster with the Montreal Expos.
Ministries: Carter serves as president of Baseball Chapel.

JOE CARTER

Retired after the 1998 season
Chicago Cubs, Cleveland Indians, San Diego Padres, Toronto Blue Jays, Baltimore Orioles, San Francisco Giants
Outfielder (R/R)

High school: Millwood High (Oklahoma City, Okla.)
College: Wichita State University
Draft: Selected in the first round by the Chicago Cubs in the 1981 draft

Highlights

1986: Led majors in RBI (121) and runs produced (200)
1990: Only NL player to appear in all 162 games
1991: Selected as an All-Star
1993: Won World Series with his last-at-bat home run
1994: Won the Danny Thompson Award for Christian character

Salvation

When Joe Carter was a student at Wichita State University, his roommate Kevin became a Christian—a very outgoing Christian. Carter, who had grown up in the church, knew what Kevin was talking about. But he wasn't ready to take the leap of faith. "I was straddling the fence on the subject," he says. Soon, everywhere he looked, Carter saw another mention of Jesus. Finally, the message got through. "It was the first time in my life I made the decision to trust Jesus Christ," he recalls.

Family: Wife, Diana; and three children, Kia, Ebony, and Jordan

---

CHAD CURTIS

California Angels, Detroit Tigers, Los Angeles Dodgers, Cleveland Indians, New York Yankees, Texas Rangers
Outfielder (R/R)

High school: Benson (Ariz.) Union High
College: Grand Canyon College
Draft: Picked in the forty-fifth round of the 1989 draft by the California Angels

Highlights

1994: Led Angels in at bats (453), doubles (23), triples (4), and steals (25)
1995: Led Tigers with 27 steals
1997: Batted .291 for the Yankees

Salvation

"I accepted Jesus Christ as Savior in my hometown church when I was nine years old. I had a good youth program with Awana and things like that. But there were times when I wasn't living for the Lord. While at Grand Canyon College, God . . . showed me that I was putting baseball and other things before Him. God showed me that I needed to put Him as my top priority."

Family and personal: Wife, Candace; and two children, Corazon and Cassidy. Chad and his wife Candace were married in 1990 while Chad wore his baseball uniform. He had a minor league game later that day, and he didn't want to be late.
Ministries: Frequent speaker to youth groups during the off-season

---

DARREN DAULTON

Retired after the 1997 season
Philadelphia Phillies, Florida Marlins
Catcher (R/R)

High school: Arkansas City High (Ark.)
College: Crowley County Community College (Ark.)
Draft: Selected in the twenty-fifth round by the Philadelphia Phillies in the 1980 draft

Highlights

1992: Led the NL in RBIs with 109
1993: Played in the World Series; hit a home run
1992, 1993, 1995: Selected to the All-Star Game
1997: Played in the World Series for the Marlins

Salvation

While going through a tough time in his life, Darren Daulton met Nicole, who is now his wife. Nicole introduced him to Jesus Christ. One night a few years ago in Clearwater Beach, Florida, Daulton prayed to accept Jesus Christ as Savior.

Family: Wife, Nicole

ALVIN DAVIS

Retired after the 1992 season
Seattle Mariners, California Angels, Osaka Kintutsu Buffaloes (Japan)
First baseman (L/R)

High school: John North High (Riverside, Calif.)
College: Arizona State University
Draft: Selected in the sixth round by the Seattle Mariners in the 1982 draft

Highlights

1984: Hit home runs in first two big league games
1984: National League Rookie of the Year
1988: Set major league record for most putouts by a first baseman in one game (22)

Salvation

Alvin Davis had the advantage of growing up in a Christian home in a family that attended a strong church. "The combination of being taught the Word and seeing it lived out in front of me by my parents—that showed me the proper relationship you should have with the Lord." He came to faith in Christ as a youngster.

Family: Wife, Kim; and three children, Jordan, Justin, and Kayla
Ministries: Pro Athletes Outreach

MARK DEWEY

Retired before the 1997 season
San Francisco Giants, New York Mets, Pittsburgh Pirates, Giants, Milwaukee Brewers
Right-handed pitcher

High school: Jenison (Mich.) High
College: Grand Valley State University (Allendale, Mich.)
Draft: Selected in the twenty-third round by the San Francisco Giants in the 1987 draft

Highlights

1996: Compiled a 6–3 record out of the bullpen for the Giants
1996: Pitched in 78 games

Salvation

Six months after being challenged with the gospel at a Professional Athletes Outreach conference, Mark was presented a New Testament. After reading it, he decided that the Bible was pretty relevant. About a year and a half later, he finally came to the place where he wanted to trust Christ. "The Lord showed me who I was, and that I had absolutely no righteousness on my own. Then I truly understood what it means to trust Jesus as your Lord and Savior."

Family and personal: Wife, Monique; and two children, Caleb and Seth. Mark's reading tastes tend toward the classics in Christian literature—authors like Calvin and Spurgeon.

JERRY DIPOTO

Cleveland Indians, New York Mets, Colorado Rockies
Right-handed pitcher

High school: Toms River (N. J.) High
College: Virginia Commonwealth
Draft: Selected in the third round by the Cleveland Indians in the 1989 draft

Highlights

1993: Collected 11 saves for the Cleveland Indians
1996: Compiled a 7–2 mark for the New York Mets

Salvation

In February 1994, Jerry DiPoto was feeling sluggish and was putting on weight. After doctors ran a series of tests, they discovered that he had thyroid cancer. He was twenty-five years old. "It was a wake-up call. That's when I received Christ as my Savior." The cancer was arrested in time through surgery, and DiPoto was considered healed. Now he says, "There's nothing that goes on in my life that Christ doesn't have some hand in."

Family: Wife, Tamie; and three children, Taylor, Jordan, and Jonah

---

DAVE DRAVECKY

Retired during the 1989 season
San Diego Padres, San Francisco Giants
Left-Handed pitcher

High school: Boardman (Ohio) High
College: Youngstown State University
Draft: Selected in the twenty-first round by the Pittsburg Pirates in 1978

Highlights

1983: Named to the National League All-Star team
1984, 1987: Played in the postseason for San Diego and San Francisco
1989: Made a stirring comeback after having cancer surgery

Salvation

Dave trusted Christ in Amarillo, Texas, in 1981. His roommate challenged him to read the Bible and understand the claims of Christ. As he read God's Word, he began to see how "precious this gift is that God has given us through Jesus Christ." And he put his faith in Jesus.

Family and personal: Wife, Jan; and two children, Jonathan and Tiffany. Dave's career was ended by cancer. His pitching arm was amputated when the cancer worsened.
Ministries: Outreach of Hope, Inc., working with people who have had cancer or amputation

---

J. D. DREW

St. Louis Cardinals
Outfielder (L/R)

High school: Lowndes County High (Hahira, Ga.)
College: Florida State University
Draft: Selected in the twentieth round by the San Francisco Giants in the 1994 draft, did not sign; selected in the first round by the Philadelphia Phillies in the 1997 draft, did not sign; selected in the first round by the St. Louis Cardinals in the 1998 draft.

Highlights

1998: Hit .417 in his first partial year with the Cardinals
1999: Finished eighth in *Baseball America*'s college Player of the Century poll

Salvation

J. D. trusted Jesus as his Savior while a young boy. As a collegian, J. D. was known for his outspoken beliefs and his strong faith in God.

Family and personal: Single. "My faith is very important. God blessed me with the talent to play this game, so . . . I can glorify Him."

CAL ELDRED

Milwaukee Brewers
Right-handed pitcher

High school: Urbana Community (Iowa)
College: University of Iowa
Draft: Selected in the first round of the 1989 draft by the Milwaukee Brewers

Highlights

1992: Selected *The Sporting News* AL Rookie Pitcher of the Year
1993: Named Milwaukee's Most Valuable Pitcher
1997: Led the Brewers in innings pitched (202) and strikeouts (122)

Salvation

As a minor leaguer in the Milwaukee Brewers system, Cal played for Chris Bando, the brother of Brewer GM Sal Bando. As happened so often when prospects played for Chris, this young pitcher was exposed to the gospel through Bando. When Cal's manager told him that he needed a personal relationship with Jesus, the pitcher, "didn't know what that was." Bando and his wife, MaryBeth, explained it to Eldred, and he trusted Christ as Lord and Savior.

Family: Wife, Christi; and two children, CJ and Luke
Ministries: Unlimited Potential, Inc.

SAL FASANO

Kansas City Royals
Catcher (R/R)

High school: Hoffman Estates (Ill.) High
College: University of Evansville (Ind.)
Draft: Selected in the thirty-seventh round by the Kansas City Royals in the 1993 draft

Highlights

1996: Hit his first major league home run on April 12 against the Brewers
1998: Tied for second in AL for being hit by the pitch (16)

Salvation

Sal was visiting with Kevin Seitzer at a batting practice facility Seitzer and Mike McFarland own in Kansas City. As Kevin, Sal, and Keith Lockhart talked, Sal began to sense the excitement Kevin and Keith had for Jesus Christ. To Sal, the Bible was just a dry history book. But as his teammates talked about Jesus, they were excited. "They spoke with passion," he says. "That really influenced me." Right there at the batting cages, Fasano prayed to trust Jesus as Savior.

Family: Wife, Kerri

TONY FERNANDEZ

Toronto Blue Jays, San Diego Padres, New York Mets, Blue Jays, Cincinnati Reds, New York Yankees, Cleveland Indians, Blue Jays
Shortstop (S/R)

High school: Gaston Fernando de Ligne High (San Pedro de Macoris, Dominican Republic)
Draft: Signed as a free agent by Toronto Blue Jays in 1979

Highlights

1986: Led AL in singles (161)
1989: Led AL shortstops in fielding percentage (.992)
1993: Had 9 RBIs in the World Series
1994: Hit for the cycle on September 3

Salvation

While a kid in the Dominican Republic, Tony attended the local Baptist church regularly. Although Tony would have preferred to be playing baseball, he did as his parents told him, but the gospel didn't sink in. It wasn't until 1984, as Fernandez was playing in his rookie year for the Toronto Blue Jays that he came to Christ. Two of his teammates, Jesse Barfield and Roy Lee Jackson, confronted him about his need for salvation. Barfield told Tony, "Jesus loves you and He wants to bless you." Later, after attending a Baseball Chapel service, Tony cornered Barfield and told him he wanted to be saved. Surrounded by other Christians on the team, Tony trusted Jesus Christ.

Family and personal: Wife, Clara; and three children, Joel, Jonathan, and Abraham. One of Tony's goals after baseball is to finish his education and study theology.

DARRIN FLETCHER

Los Angeles Dodgers, Philadelphia Phillies, Montreal Expos
Catcher (L/R)

High school: Oakwood (Ill.) High
College: University of Illinois
Draft: Selected in the sixth round by the Los Angeles Dodgers in the 1987 draft

Highlights

1994: Played for the NL in the All-Star Game
1999: Collected 120 hits and batted .291

Salvation

As the product of a Christian home, Darrin Fletcher trusted Jesus Christ as his Savior as a youngster. Once he got a little older and had played a couple of years of professional baseball, he realized he need to recommit himself to "living the way Christ wanted me to live." He did that in 1989 through the influence of Baseball Chapel.

Family and personal: Wife, Sheila; and one child, Casey. Darrin's wife, Sheila, trusted Christ while attending a Pro Athletes Outreach conference.
Ministries: Fellowship of Christian Athletes

TRAVIS FRYMAN

Detroit Tigers, Arizona Diamondbacks, Cleveland Indians
Third baseman (R/R)

High school: Tate High (Gonzalez, Fla.)
Draft: Selected in the supplemental round in the 1987 draft by the Detroit Tigers

Highlights

1992–94, 1996: Selected to the AL All-Star team
1998: Hit 28 home runs in first year with Cleveland

Salvation

Travis Fryman accepted Christ as his Savior as a youngster. Both parents were Christians and he grew up going to church, so he knew about matters of faith. "I understood what I did when I accepted Christ as a boy, but I didn't know how to make Him Lord of my life." During the baseball strike of 1994, after he had observed the faith of strong Christian teammates such as Frank Tanana, Travis vowed that he would make his relationship with God a top priority.

Family: Wife, Kathy; and one child, Mason

GARY GAETTI

Minnesota Twins, California Angels, Kansas City Royals, St. Louis Cardinals, Chicago Cubs
Third baseman (R/R)

High school: Centralia High (Ill.)
College: Lake Land Junior College (Mattoon, Ill.)
Draft: Selected in the fourth round by the St. Louis Cardinals in the 1978 draft

Highlights

1986–89: Won four straight Gold Glove awards
1987: Named ALCS Most Valuable Player; Twins won World Series
1988, 1989: Played in the All-Star Game
1998: Hit a home run in the first game of the NL play-off series

Salvation

In 1988, Gary Gaetti was one year removed from the glory and excitement of the 1987 World Series. He hurt his knee during 1988, and while he was injured he began to seriously consider the way he was living. He knew that his rough lifestyle was not good for him. When he heard someone talking about the rapture of the church (when Christians go immediately to heaven), he began to wonder about his own destiny. After talking to some Christian players and reading more about Christ, he decided to trust Jesus as his Savior.

Family: Wife, Donna; and two children, Joseph and Jacob

GREG GAGNE

Retired after the 1997 season
Minnesota Twins, Kansas City Royals, Los Angeles Dodgers
Shortstop (R/R)

High school: Somerset (Mass.) High
Draft: Selected in the fifth round by the New York Yankees in the 1979 draft

Highlights

1986: Tied major league mark with 2 inside-the-park home runs in the same game
1987: Drove in the winning run in the World Series
Set Twins record for consecutive errorless games by a shortstop (76)

Salvation

While a minor leaguer, Greg Gagne was enduring one of those notorious bus rides when he spotted some teammates in the front of the bus having a discussion. Bored, he decided to join them. They were reading from a Bible, and they were talking about the fact that everyone is a sinner who needs Jesus Christ. Gagne listened, and he decided that what they said made sense. That night, Greg went into his room and cried—and prayed. "I confessed all my sins and asked Christ to come into my life. That's when I was born again."

Family and personal: Wife, Michelle; and two children, Zachary and Lucas. Once Greg returned home to Somerset, Massachusetts, he was on familiar ground. During his career, he had donated the money to build a baseball field for the Christian school his children attended. After he retired, Gagne returned to coach the school's high school baseball team.

JOE GIRARDI

Chicago Cubs, Colorado Rockies, New York Yankees, Cubs
Catcher (R/R)

High school: Spalding Institute (Peoria, Ill.)
College: Northwestern University (Evanston, Ill.)
Draft: Selected in the fifth round by the Chicago Cubs in the 1986 draft

Highlights

1989: Became first Cubs rookie catcher to start Opening Day in 23 years
1991: Hit a 2-run home run in first-ever pinch-hitting role
1996: Batted 294 and led Yankees with 11 sacrifice bunts

Salvation

When Joe was nineteen, his mother died. Left with a huge void, he struggled for a long time to find meaning in life. A few years later, Kim was able to help Joe see the difference Jesus Christ could make in his life. While he was playing for Winston-Salem in the minor leagues, he listened as "Kim explained to me about a relationship with Jesus Christ." During the summer of his second year in the minors, he put his faith in Jesus.

Family: Wife, Kim

BRIAN HARPER

Retired from baseball after the 1995 season
California Angels, Pittsburgh Pirates, St. Louis Cardinals, Detroit Tigers, Oakland A's, Minnesota Twins, A's
Catcher (R/R)

High school: San Pedro (Calif.) High
Draft: Selected in the fourth round by the California Angels in the 1977 draft

Highlights

1991: Named second team All-Star (AP)
1991: Hit .381 in the World Series
1992: Hit .307, ninth best average in the AL

Salvation

As a teenager, one of the most profound events in Brian Harper's life was the day a friend was killed in a car accident. From then until his first year of professional baseball in the 1977 draft, he wondered what happened to a person when he died. During that first year of pro ball, Brian's roommate shared a Bible verse with him: John 3:16. After some discussion, Brian prayed to trust Jesus. Still, he didn't understand about turning his life over completely to Christ as Lord. That would come a few years later when he decided that he had to give everything—including baseball—to Jesus.

Family and personal: Wife, Chris; and three children, Brett, Derek, and Lance. Brian and Chris work with women who have had abortions to help them cope with their situation.
Ministries: Works with Pro Athletes Outreach, Athletes in Action, Fellowship of Christian Athletes

---

DOUG HENRY

Milwaukee Brewers, New York Mets, San Francisco Giants, Houston Astros
Right-handed pitcher

High school: Tennyson High (Hayward, Calif.)
College: Arizona State University
Draft: Selected in the sixteenth round by the New York Mets in the 1982 draft

Highlights

1992: Set a record by converting 16 straight save opportunities
1993: Led Brewers in saves for third straight year (17)
1997: Was unscored upon in 54 of 75 outings

Salvation

As a teenager, Doug attended a youth retreat where he trusted Jesus Christ as Savior. In 1995, while with the Mets, he dedicated himself to grow stronger spiritually, and that included praying daily and reading the Bible regularly.

Family: Wife, Monique; and four children, Danielle, Mikayla, Jason, and Zachary

OREL HERSHISER

Los Angeles Dodgers, Cleveland Indians, San Francisco Giants, New York Mets, Dodgers
Right-handed pitcher

High school: Cherry Hills East (N.J.)
Draft: Selected in the seventeenth round of the 1979 draft by the Los Angeles Dodgers

Highlights

1988: Broke MLB consecutive scoreless innings record (set by Don Drysdale)
1988: Won Cy Young Award, and named World Series MVP
1991: Named NL Comeback Player of the Year
1995: Won ALCS MVP Award

Salvation

While playing minor league ball in Clinton, Iowa, a teammate asked Orel if he was a Christian. Hershiser thought it was a strange question because he thought everyone in America was a Christian. The friend explained the gospel to Orel. Several months later, while in Arizona playing winter league baseball, Orel asked Jesus Christ to be his Savior on the basis of the finished work on the cross.

Family and personal: Wife, Jamie; and two children, Quinton and Jordan. Nicknamed Bulldog by Tommy Lasorda. After his 1988 season, published his life story with Jerry Jenkins in the book *Out of the Blue.*

STERLING HITCHCOCK

New York Yankees, Seattle Mariners, San Diego Padres
Left-handed pitcher

High school: Armwood High (Seffner, Fla.)
Draft: Selected in the ninth round by the New York Yankees in the 1989 draft

Highlights

1992: Was the youngest pitcher in the AL
1995: Made two appearances in the Division Series against Seattle
1998: MVP of the American League Championship Series

Salvation

In spring training 1994, Yankee teammate Kevin Maas invited Sterling and his wife to attend a Bible study. While there, Sterling heard the gospel of Jesus Christ explained by a potter who was there. "The message was just what Carrey and I needed. We had been searching." At the study, they both turned their lives over to Jesus Christ for salvation.

Family: Wife, Carrey; and one child, Calyn

TODD HOLLANDSWORTH

Los Angeles Dodgers
Outfielder (L/L)

High school: Newport High (Bellevue, Wash.)
Draft: Selected in the third round by the Los Angeles Dodgers in the 1991 draft

Highlights

1996: Named Rookie of the Year

Salvation

Todd Hollandsworth trusted Christ when he was a youngster, but it wasn't until his high school years that he understood what it means to trust Him completely. He began to read his Bible more faithfully and discovered that "God was a factor in my life in everything I did. I discovered that I needed to honor the Lord in all my deeds."

Family and personal: Wife, Clare. Todd was introduced to his future wife while they were both attending a party hosted by Brett Butler.

REX HUDLER

Retired midway through the 1998 season
New York Yankees, Baltimore Orioles, Montreal Expos, St. Louis Cardinals, Yakult Swallows (Japan), California Angels, Philadelphia Phillies
Outfielder (R/R)

High school: Bullard High (Fresno, Calif.)
College: Made recruiting visits to Michigan State and Notre Dame as a football prospect; didn't attend either
Draft: Selected in the first round by the New York Yankees in the 1978 draft

Highlights

1988: Was successful in first 19 steal attempts
1995: Was 12 for 12 in stolen base chances for the Angels
1996: Batted .313 with 16 home runs—career bests

Salvation

Rex Hudler walked down the aisle of a Baptist church when he was eight years old to accept Jesus Christ as Savior. And he grew up trying to be the best kid he could be to honor his parents. Yet he drifted away from his relationship with Christ. After ten years of trying to make it to the majors and struggling with sin in his life, he and his young wife Jennifer rededicated their lives to Christ. "We wanted to do things God's way."

Family and personal: Wife, Jennifer; and two children, Alyssa and Cade. Jennifer is a Christian recording artist; Rex has worked with Fox Sports as a baseball analyst.

JEFF HUSON

Montreal Expos, Texas Rangers, Baltimore Orioles, Milwaukee Brewers, Seattle Mariners
Infielder (L/R)

High school: Mingus Union High (Cottonwood, Ariz.)
College: Glendale (Ariz.) Community College, University of Wyoming
Draft: Not drafted. Signed as a free agent by the Montreal Expos in 1985

Highlights

1990: Named to *Baseball Digest* All-Rookie team
1995: Was starting third baseman for Orioles the night Cal Ripken broke Lou Gehrig's consecutive games streak
1998: Played 5 positions for Seattle: all 4 infield spots and the outfield

Salvation

While playing with the Montreal Expos, Jeff got to know believers such as Tim Burke, Andy McGaffigan, and Tom Foley. They invited him to a Professional Athletes Outreach conference. While he was there, he was impressed by the testimony of the Christian baseball players, and he decided to do what they had done and put his trust in Jesus Christ.

Family: Wife, Wendy; and three children, Lindsay, Kyle, and Cody

MIKE JACKSON

Philadelphia Phillies, Seattle Mariners, San Francisco Giants, Cincinnati Reds, Mariners, Cleveland Indians, Phillies
Right-handed pitcher

High school: Forest Brook High (Houston, Tex.)
College: Hill Junior College (Tex.)
Draft: Selected in the twenty-ninth round by the Philadelphia Phillies in the 1983 draft

Highlights

1989: Led Seattle with 65 appearances, sixth best in AL
1993: Made 81 appearances for San Francisco, a club record
1997: Pitched in the World Series against Florida

Salvation

Jesse Barfield had given Mike Jackson his phone number and asked the relief pitcher to give him a call. Barfield is always on the lookout for someone new to share his faith with. Jackson threw the number away. Later, when Jackson and his wife went out to eat, Barfield and his wife were also there. They talked, and Barfield invited the Jacksons to go on a cruise with them. While on the cruise, through the influence of Jesse and Marla, both Tammy and Mike Jackson turned their lives over to Jesus Christ.

Family: Wife, Tammy; and two children, Lindsey and Ryan

CHARLES JOHNSON

Florida Marlins, Los Angeles Dodgers, Baltimore Orioles
Catcher (R/R)

High school: Ft. Pierce (Fla.) Westwood High
College: University of Miami
Draft: Selected in the first round by the Montreal Expos in the 1989 draft; did not sign. Selected in the first round by the Florida Marlins in the 1992 draft

Highlights

1995: Selected Marlins Rookie of the Year; won a Gold Glove
1996: Won second Gold Glove; led NL catchers with .995 fielding percentage
1997: Set MLB record by catching in 123 games without making an error (across two seasons): 172 straight games with no errors

Salvation

It was the death of Charles's grandmother that got him thinking seriously about spiritual things. "I had always had a knowledge of Christ, but my faith didn't come alive until then," he says. That day he prayed to ask Jesus to come into his life. As a relatively young Christian, Charles took on the role of chapel leader for the Marlins. He says, "My hope is that my faith and my beliefs will continue to draw me closer to God."

Family and personal: Wife, Rhonda. Favorite verse: Philippians 4:13

HOWARD JOHNSON

Retired after the 1995 season
Detroit Tigers, New York Mets, Colorado Rockies, Mets
Third baseman (S/R)

High school: Clearwater (Fla.) High
Draft: Selected in the secondary phase of the 1979 free-agent draft

Highlights

1991: Led NL in home runs (38) and RBIs (117)
1989, 1991: Selected to NL All-Star team

Salvation

In about 1990, Howard Johnson's wife Kim grew concerned that they were not raising their children properly. She felt they needed some spiritual assistance. Earlier, she had accepted Christ as her Savior, and she began to pray for Howard. Through her persistent prayers, Johnson says, he came to faith in Christ. "I realized that if you love Christ you need to obey Him."

Family: Wife, Kim; and three children, Shannon, Kayla, and Glen

---

RANDY JOHNSON

Montreal Expos, Seattle Mariners, Houston Astros, Arizona Diamondbacks
Left-handed pitcher

High school: Livermore (Calif.) High
College: University of Southern California
Draft: Selected in the third round by the Atlanta Braves in the 1982 draft, did not sign. Selected in the second round by the Montreal Expos in the 1985 draft

Highlights

1992: Struck out 18 batters in one game on September 27
1993: Led majors in strikeouts (241)
1995: Cy Young Award winner; led league in strikeouts for fourth straight year
1997: Became Mariners first-ever 20-game winner; joined 2,000 strikeout club

Salvation

"I was on the brink of becoming a Christian, but when my dad passed away [in the early '90s] I finally made the vow to the Lord that He could have my life, and that I would glorify Him on and off the field. I didn't dedicate my life to Him until I had a tragic experience in my life."

Family: Wife, Lisa; and two children, Samantha and Tanner

DOUG JONES

Milwaukee Brewers, Cleveland Indians, Houston Astros, Philadelphia Phillies, Baltimore Orioles, Chicago Cubs, Indians, Oakland A's
Right-handed pitcher

High school: Lebanon (Ind.) High
College: Central Arizona Junior College, Butler University (Ind.)
Draft: Selected in the third round by the Milwaukee Brewers in the 1978 draft

Highlights

1988–90, 1992, 1994: Named to the All-Star team
1997: Brewers Most Valuable Player and Most Valuable Pitcher

Salvation

Doug grew up going to church and was saved as a young teenager while attending a church camp in California. It wasn't until much later, though, through the influence of his wife, that he realized that he needed to commit all of his life to the Lord.

Family: Wife, Debbie; and three sons, Dustin, Dylan, and Dawson
Ministries: Has worked in the past with Teen Challenge, an Arizona-based ministry that helps kids struggling with drug abuse

---

SCOTT KARL

Milwaukee Brewers, Colorado Rockies
Left-handed pitcher

High school: Carlsbad (Calif.) High
College: University of Hawaii
Draft: Selected in the sixth round of the 1992 draft by the Milwaukee Brewers

Highlights

1996: Led Brewers in wins, complete games, and shutouts
1997: Won eight straight games
1998: Hit single in first major league at bat

Salvation

While pitching for the New Orleans Zephyrs, a Brewers farm team, Scott heard his manager Chris Bando and his teammate Steve Sparks talk about Jesus Christ. Sparks especially answered a lot of questions Scott had. Struggling as he was with anger, he wanted someone to help him. Sparks helped him see that he needed Jesus. "I got down on my knees and asked the Lord to come into my heart," Karl recalls.

Family and personal: Single. One of Scott's hobbies is scuba diving.

PAT KELLY

Retired after the 1981 season
Minnesota Twins, Kansas City Royals, Chicago White Sox, Baltimore Orioles, Cleveland Indians
Outfielder (L/L)

Hometown: Philadelphia, Pa.

Highlights

1969: Stole 40 bases for the Kansas City Royals
1973: Selected to AL All-Star team
1979: Hit .364 in play-offs for Baltimore

Salvation

Pat turned his back on his Christian upbringing and as a major leaguer began to spiral down into an existence of loose living. After struggling with a failed relationship with his girlfriend, Pat was invited to a Bible study by an executive. At the study, Pat gave his life to Jesus Christ and experienced His peace.

Family and personal: Wife, Phyllis; and one child, April. His brother, Leroy, played for the Cleveland Browns in the NFL.
Ministries: Pat has a ministry called Life Line. He is an outstanding preacher.

JEFF KING

Retired during the 1999 season
Pittsburgh Pirates, Kansas City Royals
Infielder (R/R)

High school: Rampart High (Colorado Springs, Colo.)
College: University of Arkansas
Draft: Selected in the first round by the Pittsburgh Pirates in the 1986 draft

Highlights

1989: Hit a double off Rick Aguilera in his first at bat in the majors; also hit his first home run off Aggie
1992: Played each infield position for the Pirates
1996: Became ninth Pirate to hit at least 30 home runs
1997: Led AL first basemen with .996 fielding percentage

Salvation

When he was thirteen, Jeff accompanied his father, who was coaching an Athletes In Action baseball team, on a trip to Alaska. While on the journey, Jeff was impressed by the testimonies of the players. He knew about Jesus Christ, but it wasn't until he was on that trip that he put his faith in Him.

Family and personal: Wife, Laura; and five children, Audrey, Jeffrey, Cody, Hannah, and Wyatt. His father, Jack, played with the Phillies organization in the '50s.

MIKE KINGERY

Retired after the 1996 season
Kansas City Royals, Seattle Mariners, San Francisco Giants, Oakland A's, Colorado Rockies, Pittsburgh Pirates
Outfielder (R/R)

High school: Atwater High (St. James, Minn.)
College: Willmar (Minn.) Community College
Draft: Not drafted; signed as a free agent with the Kansas City Royals in 1979

Highlights

1987: Hit .280 in his first full major league season with Seattle
1994: Batted .349 with Colorado Rockies
1995: Played in the Division Series for Colorado

Salvation

It wasn't until Mike's first year at spring training that he heard about the importance of putting his faith in Jesus Christ. Soon after hearing the gospel, he says, "I trusted in Him and asked Him to come in and forgive me for my sins and be my Lord and Savior. When I trusted in Christ, it put my priorities in order: God first, then family, then athletics."

Family: Wife, Christy; and four daughters, Rachel, Anna, Michelle, and Rebekah

---

CHUCK KNOBLAUCH

Minnesota Twins, New York Yankees
Infielder (R/R)

High school: Bellaire High (Houston, Tex.)
College: Texas A & M
Draft: Selected in the first round by the Minnesota Twins in the 1989 draft

Highlights

1991: Named AL Rookie of the Year
1992, 1994: Selected to All-Star team
1997: Was 67 of 72 in stolen base attempts
1998: Most home runs by a Yankees second baseman since 1943 (17)

Salvation

Chuck was led to faith in Jesus Christ during spring training of 1998 by teammates.

Family and personal: Wife, Lisa. As a teenager, was member of Mickey Mantle League national champions.

CHAD KREUTER

Texas Rangers, Detroit Tigers, Seattle Mariners, Chicago White Sox, Anaheim Angels, White Sox
Catcher (S/R)

High school: Redwood High (Calif.)
College: Pepperdine University (Malibu, Calif.)
Draft: Selected in the fifth round by the Texas Rangers in the 1985 draft

Highlights

1988: Collected 2 hits in 1 inning during his first major league game
1989: Ranked fourth among AL catchers in fielding (.992)
1994 Cleared the rightfield roof at Tiger Stadium, just 15th player to do so in 82 years

Salvation

Although Chad grew up in a family that attended church, he says he wasn't saved until he attended Pepperdine University. "I started getting involved with our chapels there, both with the baseball team and at the school. I felt it was the right thing to do to become a Christian. It was back in 1982 at Pepperdine University."

Family and personal: Wife, Kelly; and two children, Caden and Coleton. Chad was severely injured in a home-plate collision in 1996, an accident that nearly took his life and cost him much of the season. Chad's father-in-law is Mike Gillespie, the coach of the 1998 national champion University of Southern California baseball team.

KEITH LOCKHART

San Diego Padres, Kansas City Royals, Atlanta Braves
Infielder (L/R)

High school: Northview High (Covina, Calif.)
College: Mount San Antonio (Calif.) Junior College, Oral Roberts University
Draft: Selected in the eleventh round by the Cincinnati Reds in the 1986 draft

Highlights

1995: Led Royals in batting (.321)
1996: Banged out 33 doubles to tie for team lead
1998: Played in the NLCS

Salvation

Keith Lockhart became a Christian while a student at Oral Roberts University. A friend one day asked him if he wanted to receive Christ, and Lockhart surprised him by saying yes. The friend then led him in the sinner's prayer as Lockhart asked for forgiveness and put his trust in Jesus.

Family: Wife, Lisa; and two children, Danny and Sydney

SCOTT McGREGOR

Retired after the 1988 season
Baltimore Orioles
Left-handed pitcher

High school: El Segundo (Calif.) High
Hometown: Inglewood, Calif.
Draft: Selected in the first round by the New York Yankees in the 1972 draft.

Highlights

1980: Won 20 games for Baltimore
1979, 1983: Pitched for Baltimore in the World Series

Salvation

In 1979, promising young pitcher Scott McGregor developed tendinitis in his pitching arm. It appeared that his much-anticipated career could be over much earlier than anyone expected. McGregor began to wonder if perhaps there wasn't more to life than baseball. He attended Baseball Chapel services and noticed the peace of some of the others who attended. Soon McGregor realized that Jesus Christ gave that peace, and he accepted Christ as his Savior.

Family: Wife, Cara; and three children, Eric, Katherine, and Michael

---

MARK McLEMORE

California Angels, Cleveland Indians, Houston Astros, Baltimore Orioles, Texas Rangers, Seattle Mariners
Second baseman (S/R)

High school: Mores High (San Diego, Calif.)
Draft: Selected in the ninth round by the California Angels in the 1982 draft

Highlights

1993: Batted .284 with 165 hits for Baltimore
1996: Led AL second basemen in assists (473) and total chances (798)

Salvation

During 1991, Mark and his wife were challenged about matters of faith by his cousin. "She talked to us about Jesus Christ and what He could do. We were ready to listen." After listening, both Mark and Capri prayed to trust Jesus Christ as Savior.

Family and personal: Wife, Capri; and three children, DeMarca, Darien, and Derek. Mark's favorite basketball team is the Phoenix Suns.

GREG McMICHAEL

Atlanta Braves, New York Mets, Los Angeles Dodgers, Mets, Oakland A's
Right-handed pitcher

High school: Webb High (Knoxville, Tenn.)
College: University of Tennessee
Draft: Selected in the seventh round by the Cleveland Indians in the 1988 draft

Highlights

1993: Converted his first 15 save opportunities
1994: Tied for fifth in the National League with 21 saves
1995: Pitched 18 straight scoreless innings (July 22–August 27)

Salvation

When Greg was eleven, his parents divorced. This threw his life into a mess as he tried to find his identity in things that were counterproductive. But as Greg struggled his way through junior high, something remarkable happened. His parents, Allen and Sylvia, both trusted Christ as Savior. Within a couple of years, they were remarried, this time as Christians. Greg did not come around immediately. "It took me about two years. I'd lie awake at night for hours with a spiritual warfare going on." During his junior year of high school, he sat down with his parents, who led him to Christ.

Family and personal: Wife, Jennifer; and two children, Erin and Slade. One of Greg's hobbies is collecting knives.
Ministries: Unlimited Potential, Inc.

MICKEY MANTLE

Retired after the 1968 season
Died: August 13, 1995
New York Yankees
Outfielder (S/R)

High school: Commerce (Okla.) High

Highlights

1955: Led the AL in slugging percentage (.611)
1956: Led the AL in hitting (.353), home runs (52), runs (132), RBIs (130)
1956, 1957, 1962: AL Most Valuable Player
Hit 514 career home runs; 18 career home runs in the World Series

Salvation

Bobby Richardson visited Mickey Mantle just a few days before the Yankee slugger died on August 13, 1995. Mickey told Bobby, "I've been meaning to tell you. I've received Christ as my Savior." Bobby leaned over the bed of the dying legend of baseball and went through the plan of salvation with him. When Richardson was done, Mickey said, "That's what I've done."

Family: Wife, Marilyn; and three children, Mickey Jr., David, and Donny

---

EDGAR MARTINEZ

Seattle Mariners
Designated Hitter

High school: Dorado High (Puerto Rico)
College: American College (Puerto Rico)
Draft: Signed as a nondrafted free agent by the Seattle Mariners in 1982

Highlights

1992: Named third baseman on *The Sporting News* All-Star team
1992, 1995: Led AL in hitting (.343 and .356, respectively)
1992, 1995, 1996: Played in All-Star Game

Salvation

In 1991, during the early part of his career with Seattle, Martinez made a decision to trust Christ while on a Pro Athletes Outreach retreat. The speaker who influenced Edgar to trust Christ was Mickey Weston, then a minor league pitcher. Edgar says that since he turned his life over to Jesus, "I'm able to enjoy myself a lot more."

Family: Wife, Holli; and son, Alexander

MATT MIESKE

Milwaukee Brewers, Chicago Cubs, Seattle Mariners, Houston Astros
Outfielder (R/R)

High school: Bay City Western (Auburn, Mich.)
College: Western Michigan University
Draft: Selected in the twentieth round by the Oakland A's in the 1989 draft

Highlights

1996: Batted .278 for the Milwaukee Brewers
1998: Hit .421 for May; .299 for the year.

Salvation

Five days before spring training ended in 1992, Matt was traded from San Diego to Milwaukee. He wanted so much to impress his new team, plus during this season he was moving up from Single A to Triple A baseball. The pressure was great. "I had never failed in my life," he says, but the pressure of the new situation caused trouble. "I was miserable for the first two months." But teammates and chapel speakers gave him a message of hope. They were teaching about "the peace that transcends all understanding. I wanted that." So, in June 1992, Matt prayed and asked Jesus to be his Savior.

Family: Wife, Lynn; and two children, Zachary and Jessica

PAUL MOLITOR

Retired after the 1998 season
Milwaukee Brewers, Toronto Blue Jays, Minnesota Twins
Infielder (R/R)

High school: Cretin High (St. Paul, Minn.)
College: University of Minnesota
Draft: Selected in the first round by the Milwaukee Brewers in the 1977 draft

Highlights

1978: Named AL Rookie of the Year by *The Sporting News*
1982: Set World Series record with five hits in one game
1991: Played in fourth All-Star Game
1993: Became oldest player in majors (37) to have 100 RBI season
1996: Collected the 3,000th hit of his career

Salvation

Growing up for Paul Molitor meant being a part of a churchgoing family, but he didn't make faith in Christ a part of his life until much later. He began to grow interested in spiritual things when he attended Fellowship of Christian Athletes functions while at the University of Minnesota. Later, though, after he became a pro baseball player, is when he really committed his life to Christ. "With the help of my wife and other Christians in baseball, I was able to walk right with the Lord," he says.

Family: Wife, Linda; and one child, Blaire
Ministries: Fellowship of Christian Athletes

MIKE MUÑOZ

Los Angeles Dodgers, Detroit Tigers, Colorado Rockies, Texas Rangers
Relief pitcher

High school: Bishop Amat (La Puente, Calif.)
College: California Polytechnic
Draft: Selected in the third round by the L. A. Dodgers in the 1986 draft

Highlights

1992: Made a career-high 65 relief appearances
1995: Appeared in the division series for the Rockies

Salvation

In the early '90s, Mike spent a couple of years with the Detroit Tigers. While there, he was influenced by Frank Tanana and team chaplain Jeff Totten. While Frank and Jeff were ministering to Mike, Ed and Gwen Diaz, who work with the Tigers at spring training in a spiritual capacity, were witnessing to Mike's wife, Lee Ann. Soon both of them saw their need of a Savior and were saved. Prior to this, Mike says, "I knew Jesus died on the cross for me, but as far as accepting Him personally, it was hard for me to grasp that." Now, thanks to some dedicated Christians, he knows.

Family and personal: Wife, Lee Ann; and one daughter, Kailey Ann. When Mike began his college studies, he intended to become a firefighter.

DAVE NILSSON

Milwaukee Brewers
Infielder (L/R)

High school: Kedron High (Brisbane, Australia)
Draft: Signed as a nondrafted free agent in 1987

Highlights

1994: Named the Brewers Most Valuable Player
1996: Led AL in batting average against right-handers (.359)
1997: Appeared in 156 games (most on team)

Salvation

Impressed by the lives of teammates such as Kevin Seitzer, Nilsson began to ask them questions about their faith. After they explained to him what it meant to have a personal relationship with Christ, he wanted what they had. "On July 23, 1995, I decided to accept Christ." His girlfriend, Amanda, trusted Christ about a month earlier. During the off-season, they were married.

Family and personal: Wife, Amanda. David grew up in Australia and was discovered when a scout for the Brewers, Kevin Greatrex, saw him play.

JOHN OLERUD

Toronto Blue Jays, New York Mets, Seattle Mariners
First baseman (L/L)

High school: Interlake High (Wash.)
College: Washington State University
Draft: Selected in the third round by the Toronto Blue Jays in the 1989 draft

Highlights

1992: Hit .308 in the World Series against Atlanta
1993: Won the AL batting title by hitting .363; collected 200 hits
1996: Led AL first basemen in fielding (.998; just 2 errors)
1997: Hit for the cycle on September 11

Salvation

"My wife Kelly had become a Christian at a very early stage in her life. Personally, I didn't know a lot about Christianity before I met Kelly. I always thought I was a Christian and that I was born into Christianity. After thinking things through between 1989 and 1990, I finally realized that I could not get to heaven on my own. Kelly was really patient with me. She took the time to spell it out for me, clearly pointing out that I was a sinner and that I needed to be forgiven by God. I put my faith in Jesus Christ in the summer of 1990, my first full year with the Blue Jays."

Family and personal: Wife, Kelly; and one child, Garrett. While playing for Washington State, Olerud collapsed and was diagnosed with a subarachnoid hemorrhage. Surgery was performed to remove a brain aneurysm at the base of the brain.
Ministries: Unlimited Potential, Inc.

STEVE ONTIVEROS

Retired after the 1998 season
Oakland A's, Philadelphia Phillies, Seattle Mariners, A's, St. Louis Cardinals
Right-handed pitcher

High school: St. Joseph High (South Bend, Ind.)
College: University of Michigan
Draft: Selected in the second round by the Oakland A's in the 1982 draft

Highlights

1987: Won 10 games for the Oakland A's
1995: Pitched for AL in the All-Star Game

Salvation

After a stellar career at Michigan, Ontiveros embarked on his minor league days with a clear shot at the majors. However, he felt a void in his life. He had grown up in a churchgoing family, but he knew he was missing something important in his life. "There was a yearning or a void that was becoming more evident," he says. "I knew the void was Jesus Christ." So, Steve put his trust in the Savior while in the minor leagues.

Family: Wife, Cindy; and one daughter, Eve-Ana

FRANK PASTORE

Retired after the 1986 season
Cincinnati Reds, Minnesota Twins
Right-handed pitcher

High school: Damien High (La Verne, Calif.)
College: Stanford University
Draft: Selected in the first round by the Cincinnati Reds in the 1975 draft

Highlights

1979: As a rookie, pitched in the NLCS
1980: Won 13 games in his second season with the Reds

Salvation

When Frank Pastore was a pitcher for the Reds, he began his time with them as a man who was very skeptical about Christianity. Also, he was very self-assured. All that changed when an injury sidelined him and threatened his career. When he was hurt, the Christians on the team prayed earnestly for him. He was touched by their prayers. Later, he attended a players' Bible study just to argue how wrong Christianity is. While he studied the Bible to try to refute it, he was touched by its truth. Soon, he accepted Christ as his Savior.

Family: Wife, Gina
Ministries: Frank is an apologetics expert and the director of Talbot Institute for Biblical Studies.

TERRY PENDLETON

Retired after the 1998 season
St. Louis Cardinals, Atlanta Braves, Florida Marlins, Cincinnati Reds, Kansas City Royals
Third baseman (S/R)

High school: Channel Island High (Calif.)
College: Oxnard (Calif.) Junior College, Fresno State University
Draft: Selected in the seventh round by the St. Louis Cardinals in the 1982 draft

Highlights

1986: Led NL third basemen in games (156), putouts (133), assists (371)
1987: Won Gold Glove
1991: Selected NL Most Valuable Player and captured league batting title (.319)

Salvation

Although Terry trusted Christ at an early age, he didn't get serious about his faith until late in his career. During the baseball strike of 1994, he visited with his spiritual mentor Tim Cash, who helped Terry see that he had his priorities out of order. "I decided that I had to rededicate my life to Christ," he says. "Baseball had pushed me away from Him."

Family: Wife, Catherine; and two children, Stephanie and Terry
Ministries: Unlimited Potential, Inc.

RICO PETROCELLI

Retired after the 1976 season
Player: Boston Red Sox
Infielder (R/R)
Coach: Boston Red Sox minor league organization

Hometown: Brooklyn, N.Y.

Highlights

1967, 1975: Played in the World Series for the Red Sox
1975: Batted .308 against the Reds in the World Series

Salvation

When Petrocelli played for the Boston Red Sox, he was struggling because his wife had cancer. He knew he needed some kind of foundation in his life, and discovered what it was when team chaplain Pat Jantomaso explained to him the importance of trusting Christ. Rico did so, and turned to prayer to help his wife. She was healed of the disease.

Family: Wife, Elsie; and four children, Michael, Billy, Jimmy, and Danny

---

ANDY PETTITTE

New York Yankees
Left-handed pitcher

High school: Deer Park (Tex.) High
College: San Jacinto Junior College (Tex.)
Draft: Signed by the Yankees as a free agent in 1991

Highlights

1996: Led all major league pitchers with 11 pickoffs
1996: Won 21 games and finished second in Cy Young voting
1997: Led AL pitchers with 35 starts and 14 pickoffs

Salvation

At the age of twelve, Andy's sister encouraged the family to begin attending a church she was going to. They went, and one day soon afterward, Andy responded to the pastor's invitation to accept Christ as Savior. One by one, the whole Pettitte family was saved at that church.

Family: Wife, Laura; and one child, Joshua

LOU PINIELLA

Retired after the 1984 season
Player: Baltimore Orioles, Cleveland Indians, Kansas City Royals, New York Yankees
Outfielder (R/R)
Manager: New York Yankees, Cincinnati Reds, Seattle Mariners
High school: Jesuit High (Tampa, Fla.)
College: University of Tampa
Draft: Signed as a free agent by the Cleveland Indians in 1962

Highlights

1969: AL Rookie of the Year
1995: AL Manager of the Year

Salvation

When some business deals went bad, Lou became nervous and anxious. While he fumed, his wife, Anita, stayed calm. She had become a Christian, and Lou noticed her even demeanor. She suggested to Lou that they attend church together. When they did, the light began to come on in Lou's heart. Soon, he too had trusted Jesus as Savior. He characterized that decision as "the best thing that's happened in my life."

Family: Wife, Anita; and three children, Lou Jr., Derek, and Kristi

---

JODY REED

Retired after the 1998 season
Boston Red Sox, Los Angeles Dodgers, Milwaukee Brewers, San Diego Padres, Detroit Tigers
Second baseman (R/R)
High school: Brandon (Fla.) High
College: Manatee Junior College (Fla.)
Draft: Selected in the eighth round by the Boston Red Sox in the 1984 draft

Highlights

1990: Tied for lead in AL in doubles (45)
1993: Led NL in fielding among second basemen (.993)
1994: Led AL in fielding among second basemen (.995)

Salvation

When Jody was in the minors in the Red Sox organization, he ran across Chris Cannazaro. Chris was a Christian who was not afraid to share his faith. He invited Jody to Baseball Chapel, and then he began to tell Jody the advantages of being a Christian. One that caught Reed's fancy was the fact that Jesus said His followers could cast their cares on Him. At a later Baseball Chapel meeting that summer, the speaker gave an invitation, and Jody answered. He prayed to trust Jesus that day.

Family: Wife, Michelle

HAROLD REYNOLDS

Retired after the 1994 season
Seattle Mariners, Baltimore Orioles, California Angels
Second baseman (S/R)

High school: Corvallis (Ore.) High
College: San Diego State
Draft: Selected by the Seattle Mariners in the 1980 draft

Highlights

1986: Tied the record for assists in one game (12)
1987: Led the American League in stolen bases (60)
1987, 1988: Named to the American League All-Star team

Salvation

Although his mother had taken Harold to church his whole life as he was growing up in Eugene, Oregon, the message of the gospel didn't sink in at first. It wasn't until Harold was in his junior year of high school that he finally realized that he needed to establish a personal relationship with Jesus Christ. While attending a Fellowship of Christian Athletes huddle group, Harold realized that he didn't have the faith his friends were talking about. "I got on my face before the Lord and asked Him to come into my heart," he says.

Family and personal: Single. Harold currently serves as a baseball analyst for ESPN. Harold won a Presidential Point of Light Award in 1990.
Ministries: Role Models Unlimited; Harold Reynolds Children's Foundation

BOBBY RICHARDSON

Retired after the 1966 season
New York Yankees
Second baseman (R/R)

High school: Sumter (S.C.) High

Highlights

1960: Named Most Valuable Player of the World Series
1960: Set new Series record with 12 RBIs
1965: Won his fifth Gold Glove
1966: Named to AL All-Star team for seventh time

Salvation

Bobby was just a kid when his mother opened her Bible and explained the plan of salvation to him. She used John 1:12 as her reference point. "It came alive," Bobby recalls, and he trusted Christ as Savior right then. He has been one of baseball's pioneer Christian statesmen.

Family and personal: Wife, Betsy; and five grown children. Former coach at both South Carolina and Liberty University
Ministries: Past president, Baseball Chapel

TIM SALMON

Anaheim Angels
Outfielder (R/R)

High school: Greenway High (Phoenix, Ariz.)
College: Grand Canyon College (Ariz.)
Draft: Selected in the third round by the Angels in the 1989 draft

Highlights

1993: Named AL Rookie of the Year
1995: Selected Angels Most Valuable Player
1995: Became first Angel to hit .300, 30 home runs, score 100 runs, and knock in 100 runs

Salvation

While he was at Grand Canyon College, a teammate, catcher Acey Martin, witnessed to Tim about Jesus Christ. Because Acey was a senior, Tim, as a freshman, listened to him. While at Grand Canyon, Salmon trusted Christ as his Savior. He and Marci, a strong Christian, began to date a month after he was saved.

Family and personal: Wife, Marci; one child, Callie. Tim's wife battled thyroid cancer in 1997. In early 1998 she received a clean bill of health.

KEVIN SEITZER

Retired after the 1997 season
Kansas City Royals, Milwaukee Brewers, Oakland A's, Brewers, Cleveland Indians
Infielder (R/R)

High school: Lincoln (Ill.) High
College: Eastern Illinois
Draft: Selected in the eleventh round by the Kansas City Royals in the 1983 draft

Highlights

1987: Tied for AL lead in hits with 207
1987, 1995: Played for the AL in the All-Star Game
1994–1996: Batted .311 or better each year

Salvation

Kevin Seitzer thought teammate Mike Kingery was his friend. Until he walked into a Pro Athletes Outreach conference that Kingery invited him to and found out it was a Christian get-together. Instead of getting mad, Seitzer listened to the speaker, who hit him right between the eyes with his message of salvation. At the time, Kevin and his wife were not getting along, and it looked as if their marriage was headed for the scrap heap. Instead, Kevin turned his life over to Jesus that day. He's been a bold witness for Christ since, his marriage is strong, and he's still friends with Kingery.

Family and personal: Wife, Lisa; and two children, Brandon and Cameron. In 1993, Seitzer made his only appearance as a pitcher in the majors and struck out the only batter he faced. Career ERA: .000

JOHN SMOLTZ

Atlanta Braves
Right-handed pitcher

High school: Lansing (Mich.) Waverly High
Draft: Signed as a free agent by the Detroit Tigers on September 22, 1985

Highlights

1989: Became youngest Braves All-Star pitcher in team history (22)
1992: Led NL with 215 strikeouts; selected to All-Star team
1996: Won NL Cy Young Award
1997: Struck out 241 batters

Salvation

While in Atlanta, Smoltz realized that it wasn't his good works or his being nice that would get him to heaven. With the help of friends Tim Cash and Mike McCoy, he began to understand what it means to have a relationship with Jesus Christ. "Some people think, I'll wait until all the problems are behind me and then I'll turn my life around," Smoltz says. "But someone told me, 'You may never see that day.' " Thinking all this through, Smoltz decided to put his faith in Christ.

Family and personal: Wife, Dyan; and three children, John, Rachel, and Carly. John was a champion accordion player as a kid.
Ministries: Unlimited Potential, Inc.

STEVE SPARKS

Milwaukee Brewers, Anaheim Angels
Right-handed pitcher

High school: Holland Hall High (Tulsa, Okla.)
College: Sam Houston State
Draft: Selected in the fifth round by the Milwaukee Brewers in the 1987 draft

Highlights

1998: Returned from the minors to become a starter for the Angels

Salvation

While playing Class A ball in 1990, Steve Sparks and his wife were invited by Chris Bando to attend a Bible study. It was quite a revelation for the young couple. "We thought we were Christians because we believed in God." Three months after being introduced to the saving power of Jesus Christ, both Steve and his wife trusted Him as Savior.

Family and personal: Wife, Michelle. Sparks learned how to hold a knuckleball by studying pictures on baseball cards. He learned to throw it with the help of Tom Candiotti.
Ministries: Speaking engagements through the Fellowship of Christian Athletes. Also has traveled with Unlimited Potential, Inc. (UPI), a baseball-based ministry

ANDY STANKIEWICZ

New York Yankees, Houston Astros, Montreal Expos, Arizona Diamondbacks
Infielder (R/R)

High school: St. Paul High (Santa Fe, Calif.)
College: Pepperdine University (Calif.)
Draft: Selected in the 12th round by the New York Yankees in the 1986 draft

Highlights

1992: First Yankee rookie in 16 years to have 100 hits
1996: Batted .310 as a pinch hitter for Montreal

Salvation

Andy knew all the information as a kid growing up in Southern California. "I knew the story, the story of Christ," he says. "And if someone had asked me if I was a Christian, I would say, 'Yeah.' " But it wasn't until he was a college student on an Athletes in Action baseball trip that he finally understood what it means to become a believer in Christ. "It was while we were in Alaska that I made a commitment to Christ and asked Him to come into my heart."

Family: Wife, Mari Anna; and three children, Drew, Marisa, and Dane
Ministries: Athletes in Action

MIKE STANLEY

Texas Rangers, New York Yankees, Boston Red Sox, Toronto Blue Jays, Red Sox
Catcher (R/R)

High school: St. Thomas Aquinas (Fort Lauderdale, Fla.)
College: University of Florida
Draft: Selected in the sixteenth round by the Texas Rangers in the 1985 draft

Highlights

1993: Named catcher on *The Sporting News* AL All-Star team
1995: Hit 3 home runs in 1 game on August 10
1999: Collected his 1,000th hit during the season

Salvation

During his time with the New York Yankees, Mike came to trust Jesus Christ through the influence of teammates such as Matt Nokes, Kevin Maas, and John Wetteland. "I have Jesus Christ in my life and the Holy Spirit working in me," he says.

Family and personal: Wife, Erin; and three children, Ryan, Tanner, and Jenna. Mike enjoys using the daily devotional guide *Our Daily Bread* as a tool for spiritual growth.

FRANK TANANA

Retired after the 1993 season
California Angels, Boston Red Sox, Texas Rangers, Detroit Tigers, New York Mets, New York Yankees
Left-handed pitcher

High school: Catholic Central (Detroit, Mich.)
Draft: Selected by the California Angels in the 1973 draft

Highlights

1974: Led the AL in strikeouts (269)
1977: Led the AL in shutouts (7) and ERA (2.54)
1982: Led the AL in wins (18)
1987: Pitched the game that clinched the Eastern conference title for Detroit

Salvation

While a member of the California Angels, Frank Tanana was a fireballing lefty who led the league in strikeouts and partying. As so often happens, he had reached the professional peak of baseball, but he was miserable. When Frank told Angels chaplain John Werhas that he admired him, John explained to Frank that his relationship with Jesus Christ was what made the difference. After quite a few months of thinking this over, and after his Angels teammate Lyman Bostock was killed in a shooting, Tanana realized he needed to be saved. After the season, both he and his wife Cathy trusted Jesus Christ as Savior.

Family: Wife, Cathy; and four daughters, Lauren, Jill, Kari, and Erin

EDDIE TAUBENSEE

Cleveland Indians, Houston Astros, Cincinnati Reds
Catcher (R/L)

High school: Lake Howell High (Maitland, Fla.)
Draft: Selected in the sixth round by the Cincinnati Reds in the 1986 draft. Selected by Oakland in Rule 5 draft in 1990

Highlights

1996: Stole two bases in one game; first Reds catcher to do so since Johnny Bench in 1976
1997: Led Reds with 10 pinch hits

Salvation

In 1995, while attending a Pro Athletes Outreach conference for baseball players, Eddie saw clearly that he needed to turn his life over to Jesus Christ. Before that, he says, "I believed in God, but I did things my own way." At the conference, he asked Jesus to "take control, clean up my life, and redeem" his life.

Family: Wife, Rene; and two children, Justin and Benjamin

DAVE VALLE

Retired after the 1996 season
Seattle Mariners, Texas Rangers, Oakland A's
Catcher (R/R)

High school: Holy Cross High (Flushing, N.Y.)
Draft: Selected in the second round by the Seattle Mariners in the 1978 draft

Highlights

1990: Led AL catchers in fielding percentage (.997)
1993: Led AL batters in being hit by the pitch (17)

Salvation

Dave Valle and a minor league teammate, Dave Edler, were sent to different teams, meaning they couldn't continue their partying for a while. Later, they were reassigned to the same team again. When they were, Valle discovered that Edler had become a Christian. Edler's life was so different, so refreshing, so inviting, that instead of rejecting what he saw in his transformed teammate, Valle investigated this salvation stuff. He began attending Baseball Chapel services and soon accepted Christ as his Savior.

Family: Wife, Vicki; and three children, Philip, Natalia, and Alina
Ministry: Esperanza. This word means "hope" in Spanish, and it is also the name of a ministry Dave Valle founded. The purpose of it is to provide low-interest loans to women in the Dominican Republic to help them get on their feet financially and to care for their families.

ANDY VAN SLYKE

Retired after the 1995 season
St. Louis Cardinals, Pittsburgh Pirates, Baltimore Orioles, Philadelphia Phillies
Outfielder (R/R)

High school: New Hartford (N.Y.) High
Draft: Selected in the first round by the St. Louis Cardinals in the 1979 draft

Highlights

1988: Named *The Sporting News* NL Player of the Year
1988, 1992, 1993: Selected to All-Star team
1992: Led NL in doubles (45) and second in batting (.324)

Salvation

Van Slyke became a believer in Jesus Christ during his second year of pro baseball in 1981. "I was challenged by a chapel speaker who was more excited over Jesus than anyone I had ever seen. After the game, I knelt on the field and asked the Lord into my life."

Family: Wife, Lauri; and three children, A.J., Scott, and Jared

TURNER WARD

Cleveland Indians, Toronto Blue Jays, Milwaukee Brewers, Pittsburgh Pirates, Arizona Diamondbacks
Outfielder (S/R)

High school: Satsuma (Ala.) High
College: Faulkner State Junior College, University of South Alabama
Draft: Selected in the eighteenth round by the New York Yankees in the 1986 draft

Highlights

1995: Led Milwaukee Brewers with 8 outfield assists
1997: Hit 2 home runs in 1 game vs. St. Louis

Salvation

"I put baseball so high on the pedestal for so many years," says Turner. That all changed in 1994 when, as he puts it, "I turned my life over to Christ." Since his salvation, he says he puts "the Lord first, then my family, then my job. . . . The Lord has given us peace," he says.

Family and personal: Wife, Lisa; and two children, Samantha and Tanner. Turner and Lisa have known each other since they were fifteen years old.

WALT WEISS

Oakland Athletics, Florida Marlins, Colorado Rockies, Atlanta Braves
Shortstop (S/R)

High school: Suffern (N.Y.) High
College: University of North Carolina
Draft: Selected in the first round by the Oakland A's in the 1985 draft

Highlights

1988: Selected AL Rookie of the Year
1989: Hit a home run in the World Series against San Francisco
1997: Rated best defensive shortstop in majors
1998: Selected to be starting shortstop in the All-Star Game

Salvation

In 1994, Terri Weiss talked Walt into attending a Professional Athletes Outreach conference. While he was there, Weiss asked a lot of questions about faith in Jesus Christ, and had them answered. Also, he had observed the faith of his friend Joe Girardi, and had been impressed. After pursuing the claims of the gospel, Weiss decided, "To me, it is either all true or it isn't, and it's all true." At the conference, Weiss prayed to accept Jesus as his Savior.

Family and personal: Wife, Terri; and three sons, Blake, Brody, and Bo. Son Brody suffered from near-fatal case of e-coli bacteria in 1998 after being infected while at a water park near Atlanta.
Ministries: Unlimited Potential, Inc.

JOHN WETTELAND

Los Angeles Dodgers, Montreal Expos, New York Mets, New York Yankees, Texas Rangers
Right-handed pitcher

High school: Cardinal Newman High (Santa Rosa, Calif.)
College: College of San Mateo (Calif.)
Draft: Selected by the Detroit Tigers in 1987

Highlights

1996: Named to the AL All-Star team; led AL in saves (43)
1996: Selected the World Series Most Valuable Player

Salvation

John Wetteland's first interest in the things of God came after he discovered Michelle McCracken, a beautiful usher for the Shreveport Captains in Class AA baseball. Michelle, a Christian, didn't want anything to do with John and his somewhat outlandish behavior. John began reading the Bible in an effort to impress Michelle. Instead, he was impressed with its power. On his own, after being touched by what he read, Wetteland trusted Jesus as Savior. Although his initial call to Michelle to tell her about it was met with skepticism, she later believed him—and married him.

Family: Wife, Michelle; and two daughters, Addie and Katie

DAN WILSON

Cincinnati Reds, Seattle Mariners
Catcher (R/R)

High school: Barrington (Ill.) High
College: University of Minnesota
Draft: Selected in the twenty-sixth round by the New York Mets in the 1987 draft; did not sign. Selected in the first round by the Cincinnati Reds in the 1990 draft

Highlights

1995: Led AL catchers in putouts (895) and total chances (952)
1997: Led majors in games caught (144); second in AL in throwing out opposing runners trying to steal (41 percent)

Salvation

Dan Wilson grew up going to church in Barrington, Illinois. When he was in the eighth grade, he trusted Christ as Savior with the help of his pastor.

Family and personal: Wife, Anne; and two children, Sofia and Josephine. Dan played on a Little League team (Barrington, Ill.) that finished third in the Little League World Series. His team lost to Gary Sheffield's team (Tampa, Fla.).

BASKETBALL
NATIONAL BASKETBALL ASSOCIATION

STEVE ALFORD

Retired after the 1991 season
Dallas Mavericks; now head coach of University of Iowa

High school: Chrysler High (New Castle, Ind.)
College: Indiana University
Draft: Selected in the second round by the Dallas Mavericks in the 1987 draft

Highlights

1984: Selected to play for the U.S. Olympic team
1987: Voted the Big Ten Most Valuable Player
1989: Career-high 3-pointers, 20 for 55 (36.4%)

Salvation

During his junior year in high school, Steve made a decision to trust Jesus Christ. "It's the biggest decision I've ever made," he says. And he credits his parents for bringing him up in a Christian home and showing him the way to the Cross.

Family: Wife, Tanya; and two sons, Kory and Bryce

NICK ANDERSON

Orlando Magic, Sacramento Kings
Guard/Forward

High school: Prosser Vocational (Chicago, Ill.)
College: University of Illinois
Draft: Selected in the first round by the Orlando Magic in the 1989 draft

Highlights

1995: Set NBA Finals single-game record for most three-point field goal attempts
1999: Became all-time leading scorer for Orlando (10,650 points)

Salvation

Nearly thirty years old, Nick Anderson had lost the fun of playing ball. So, he searched for answers—which he found by putting his faith in Jesus Christ. "I've accepted Christ into my life," he was quoted as saying in *Magic Magazine,* the official publication of the Orlando Magic. Teammates and fans alike noticed the difference during the 1997–98 season.

Family and personal: Single. Won Rich and Helen De Vos Community Enrichment Award in 1996

TONY BENNETT

Retired from the NBA after the 1995 season
Charlotte Hornets
Guard

High school: Preble High (Green Bay, Wisc.)
College: University of Wisconsin, Green Bay
Draft: Selected in the second round by the Charlotte Hornets in the 1992 draft

Highlights

1992: Named Mid-Continent Player of the Year
1993: Scored 20 points in his third career start in NBA
Set NCAA record for highest 3-point field-goal percentage (49.7%)

Salvation

Going to summer basketball camps was a natural event for Tony Bennett, who grew up around basketball as the son of a college coach. One summer as a young high-schooler, he attended a Christian basketball camp. There he heard the gospel. "The gospel was presented in such a way that I understood God gave His Son Jesus Christ." Before, Tony had known that he wanted to go to heaven when he died, and the gospel presentation told him that he could. He accepted Christ at that basketball camp.

Family and personal: Wife, Laurel. Tony's dad is head basketball coach at the University of Wisconsin.
Ministries: Tony and Laurel moved to New Zealand after his playing career in the NBA ended. They went to be missionaries, using his basketball talents to attract the attention of people who need the gospel.

KENT BENSON

Retired after the 1987 season
Indiana Pacers, Detroit Pistons
Center

High school: New Castle (Ind.) High
College: Indiana University
Draft: Selected in the first round by the Milwaukee Bucks in the 1977 draft

Highlights

1977: Named first-team All-American
1977–87: Played in 680 NBA games and pulled down 3,881 rebounds

Salvation

In 1971, Kent Benson was nominated as one of five athletes to attend the Fellowship of Christian Athletes national conference. Ironically, he was not a Christian athlete at the time. "I didn't go there for the Christian fellowship," he says, "I went there for the athletic part." But the Christian fellowship is what ended up impressing him the most. Being around all those Christian athletes, he was impressed. "Jesus was the center of their lives," he recalls. That week, after an evening assembly, Benson asked Jesus to be his Savior.

Family and personal: Wife, Monica; and four daughters, Andrea, Elizabeth, Genevieve, and Ashley. Works with various charities in his hometown
Ministries: Chaired Youth Fest—a weekend event that promoted sexual purity

CALBERT CHEANEY

Washington Bullets/Wizards, Boston Celtics
Guard/Forward

High school: Harrison High (Evansville, In.)
College: Indiana University
Draft: Selected in the first round by the Washington Bullets in the 1993 draft

Highlights

1993: College basketball Player of the Year
1997: Average 15 ppg. for Washington in the play-offs
1998: Went over the 5,000-point plateau in his career

Salvation

When Calbert was twelve years old, attending St. James Missionary Baptist Church in Evansville, Indiana, he trusted Jesus Christ as his Savior.

Family: Single
Ministries: Assisted his home church in Evansville by helping them purchase land and construct a recreational center. Participated in Jammin' Against the Darkness

---

HUBERT DAVIS

New York Knicks, Toronto Rapters, Dallas Mavericks
Guard

High school: Lake Braddock Secondary (Burke, Va.)
College: University of North Carolina
Draft: Selected in the first round by the New York Knicks

Highlights

1996: Shot .476 from behind the 3-point line (127-267)
1998: Averaged a career-high 11.1 points a game

Salvation

Bobbie Webb Davis had just died of cancer, and her sixteen-year-old son Hubert was mad at God for taking her away. At first, Hubert simmered. Gradually, though, the love of family members softened him. His dad and his friends comforted him by sharing strategic Bible verses. Little by little, they led him on a pathway that included going to church, attending Bible studies, and finally trusting Jesus Christ as his Savior.

Family: Single

ANDREW DECLERCQ

Golden State Warriors, Boston Celtics, Cleveland Cavaliers
Forward/Center

High school: Countryside High (Clearwater, Fla.)
College: University of Florida
Draft: Selected in the second round by the Golden State Warriors in the 1995 draft

Highlights

1998: Accumulated career-highs in rebounds (392) and points (439)
1999: Scored career-high 17-point game (against Milwaukee)

Salvation

As a kid, Andrew attended church with his mom and sisters, but never got serious about what was going on. While in college, though, things changed. "I began to understand how you have a personal relationship with God and how you have to give something back to that relationship to keep it going. Later, a weekly Bible study get-together at the University of Florida helped him keep his relationship with Christ strong.

Family: Single

MICHAEL DICKERSON

Houston Rockets, Vancouver Grizzlies
Forward

High school: Federal Way (Seattle, Wash.)
College: University of Arizona
Draft: Selected in the first round by the Houston Rockets in the 1998 draft

Highlights

1997: Member, National Championship team
1998: Averaged 18 points a game for Arizona for the second straight year

Salvation

While a sophomore at Arizona, Dickerson got involved in Athletes in Action. He realized that he needed to have a reality check after being such a big star in high school. "I didn't think I had any need for Jesus," he says of his stardom. But under the direction of the AIA people, Dickerson saw his need and put his trust in Christ.

Family: Single

MARK EATON

Retired after the 1994 season
Utah Jazz
Center

High school: Westminster (Calif.) High
College: Cyprus Junior College, UCLA

Highlights

1984: Voted NBA Defensive Player of the Year
1984, 1985, 1987, 1988: Led NBA in blocked shots
1985: Set NBA records for highest blocked-shots-per-game average in one season (5.56)

Salvation

At the age of sixteen, Mark Eaton made a startling discovery. He was not a Christian. He had been baptized. He had gone to church. But it took a friend telling him all that didn't matter to get his attention. The friend explained that he needed to trust Jesus as his Savior. "I thought, this is the missing link." Eaton trusted Christ then and has "been trying to develop a closer walk with the Lord" ever since.

Family and personal: Wife, Marcie; and two sons, Nicholas and Douglas. Mark's hobby is working on cars. He was trained to do that before he realized he might become a pro basketball player.

TYUS EDNEY

Sacramento Kings, Boston Celtics
Guard

High school: Long Beach (Calif.) Poly
College: UCLA
Draft: Selected in the second round by the Sacramento Kings in the 1995 draft

Highlights

1995: ESPY award for Most Outstanding College Basketball Player
1996: NBA All-Rookie second team; averaged 12 ppg. in the play-offs

Salvation

Tyus accepted Jesus Christ as his Savior when he was in the second grade. His spiritual growth began in earnest when he was at UCLA, where he played for assistant coach Lorenzo Romar. Romar, Tyus says, "helped make me stronger in the Word and in the Lord."

Family: Single

CRAIG EHLO

Retired after the 1997 season
Houston Rockets, Cleveland Cavaliers, Atlanta Hawks, Seattle Sonics
Forward/Guard

High school: Lubbock (Tex.) High
College: Washington State University
Draft: Selected in the third round by the Houston Rockets in the 1983 draft

Highlights

1983: Led Pacific 10 in league-game assists (99)
1991, 1993: Played in all 81 games for the Cavaliers
1994: Recorded career-best 136 steals

Salvation

When Ehlo was a member of the Cleveland Cavaliers, one of his teammates and friends was Mark Price. Price took it upon himself to witness to Ehlo. He did it, though, with his life more than with his words. One evening Mark and his wife Laura invited Craig and Jani over their house. Mark asked Craig the question he had been dreading, "Do you know if you are going to heaven if you die?" Craig said he didn't, and Mark had the opportunity to lead him to faith in Christ that evening.

Family: Wife, Jani; and two children, Erica and Austin

TODD FULLER

Golden State Warriors, Utah Jazz, Charlotte Hornets
Center

High school: Charlotte (N.C.) Christian High
College: North Carolina State
Draft: Selected in the first round by the Golden State Warriors in the 1995 draft

Salvation

Todd Fuller became a Christian when he was just nine years old. "My family and I would always go to church on Sunday," he says. "I had Sunday school teachers and pastors who showed me what it was like to have a relationship with Christ. In 1983, I made that decision and committed my life to Jesus." Todd's high school coach was former NBA star Bobby Jones.

Family: Single

ARMEN GILLIAM

Phoenix Suns, Charlotte Hornets, Philadelphia 76ers, New Jersey Nets, Milwaukee Bucks, Orlando Magic
Forward

High school: Bethel Park Senior High (Pa.)
College: UNLV
Draft: Selected in the first round by the Phoenix Suns in the 1987 draft

Highlights

1987: All-America second team
1988: NBA All-Rookie team

Salvation

Growing up in a Christian home, it was not surprising that he trusted Jesus Christ as his Savior at a young age.

Family: Single

A. C. GREEN

Los Angeles Lakers, Phoenix Suns, Dallas Mavericks, Lakers
Forward

High school: Benson Polytechnic (Portland, Ore.)
College: Oregon State
Draft: Selected twenty-third by the L.A. Lakers in the 1985 draft

Highlights

1987, 1988: Member of NBA champion L.A. Lakers
1990: Selected to NBA All-Star Game
1998: Extended the all-time NBA record for most consecutive games played (1,028)

Salvation

A. C. Green was on his way to college. But he knew he wasn't on his way to heaven. As he and a bunch of friends sat in a church service between his senior year of high school and his freshman year at Oregon State, Green felt the clear leading of God to go forward during the invitation and trust Jesus Christ. Even though the peer pressure was great, he walked right past his friends and down to the front of the church, where he prayed to trust Jesus Christ that day.

Family and personal: Single. When A. C. spoke at a 3-on-3 tournament in the mid-90s as the Sunday chapel speaker, he gave an invitation for people to come forward and trust Christ. More than twenty people, mostly teenagers, answered the call and became Christians that day.
Ministries: A. C. Green Foundation for Youth

TOMMY HAMMONDS

Washington Bullets, Charlotte Hornets, Denver Nuggets, Minnesota Timberwolves
Forward

High school: Crestview (Fla.) High
College: Georgia Tech
Draft: Selected in the first round by the Washington Bullets in the 1989 draft

Highlights

1992: Averaged a career-high 11 ppg for Washington
1997–98: Went over the 2,000 rebound plateau

Salvation

Tommy's grandfather was instrumental in leading him to Christ. "My grandfather was a pastor," Hammond says. "He gave me something to hold on to. He helped me with the biggest part of my life—my personal relationship with Jesus Christ."

Family and personal: Wife, Carolyn; and two sons, Tommy Jr. and Keelan. Races stock cars in the off-season

HERSEY HAWKINS

Philadelphia 76ers, Charlotte Hornets, Seattle Sonics, Chicago Bulls
Guard

High school: Westinghouse Vocational High (Chicago)
College: Bradley University (Peoria, Ill.)
Draft: Drafted in the first round by the Los Angeles Clippers in the 1988 draft

Highlights

1988: Named the college basketball Player of the Year
1989: Named to NBA All-Rookie first team
1999: Named winner of NBA Sportmanship Award

Salvation

When Hersey Hawkins was a young Philadelphia 76er, he met Bruce McDonald, the former small-college All-American basketball and baseball player who serves as the team chaplain. Bruce took him out to a Friday's restaurant and told him about Christ. And he told Hersey he'd be there when he needed him. Four years later, Hawkins was unhappy with the way his life was going. He remembered his conversation with McDonald. Hawkins, whose wife had become a Christian, turned his life over to Jesus Christ. "It was the best decision I ever made in my life," he says.

Family: Wife, Jennifer; and three children, Brandon, Corey, and Devon
Ministries: Jammin' Against the Darkness

MARK JACKSON

New York Knicks, Los Angeles Clippers, Indiana Pacers, Denver Nuggets, Pacers
Guard

High school: Bishop Loughlin Memorial High (Brooklyn, N.Y.)
College: St. John's University (Jamaica, New York)
Draft: Selected in the first round by the New York Knicks in the 1987 draft

Highlights

1987: All-American second team
1988: NBA Rookie of the Year
1989: Selected to play in the NBA All-Star Game
1997: Led NBA with 11.4 assists per game and with 935 for the season

Salvation

Mark Jackson was a third-year pro with the New York Knicks when a woman named Desiree entered his life. She made no pretensions about what was important to her—she told Mark about her faith in Jesus Christ on their first date. It was a brand-new idea to him, but it made sense. "I accepted Christ as my Savior. It was a true blessing."

Family: Wife, Desiree; and two children, Mark II and Heavyn

AVERY JOHNSON

Seattle Sonics, Denver Nuggets, San Antonio Spurs, Houston Rockets, Spurs, Golden State Warriors, Spurs
Guard

High school: St. Augustine High (New Orleans)
College: New Mexico Junior College, Cameron, Southern University
Draft: Signed as a nondrafted free agent by the Seattle Sonics in 1988

Highlights

1987–88: Set the all-time NCAA record for assists per game (13.3)
1998: Won the NBA Sportsmanship Award
1998: Averaged 17 ppg in the play-offs

Salvation

As a kid growing up in a God-fearing, Christian family, it was a natural thing for Avery to trust Jesus Christ as a youngster. Yet it wasn't until after he had played one year in the NBA that he really began to take his faith seriously. It was the summer of 1989, and it's when, as Avery says, he became, "fully committed to Him every day" after he heard a pastor preach on the subject.

Family and personal: Wife, Cassandra; and two children, Christiane and Avery Jr. Avery designed his own home.
Ministries: Jammin' Against the Darkness; Avery Johnson Foundation

KEVIN JOHNSON

Retired after the 1998 season
Cleveland Cavaliers, Phoenix Suns
Guard

High school: Sacramento (Calif.) High
College: University of California
Draft: Selected in the first round by the Cleveland Cavaliers in the 1987 draft

Highlights

1989: Named NBA's Most Improved Player
1989–91, 1994: All-NBA second team
1993: Played most minutes ever in one game of the Finals (62)
1998: Set record for assists for Suns all-time (6,494)

Salvation

In his junior year of high school, Kevin trusted Christ as Savior. A friend had begun telling him about Jesus, and KJ grew curious. He went to church a few times to hear more about it, but before long, Kevin placed his faith in Jesus Christ.

Family and personal: Single. KJ received a Point of Light Award from President George Bush.
Ministries: Founded a kid-help organization called St. Hope Academy

BOBBY JONES

Retired after the 1986 season
Denver Nuggets, Philadelphia 76ers
Forward

High school: South Mecklenburg (Charlotte, N.C.)
College: University of North Carolina

Highlights

1972: Played for the U.S. Olympic team
1977–84: Selected All-Defensive first team in the NBA
1983: Received the NBA Sixth-Man Award

Salvation

While a student at North Carolina, Bobby met Tess. They fell in love, and he asked her to marry him. However, between their meeting and this question, Tess had become a Christian. She told Bobby that she could not marry him because he wasn't a believer. Although Bobby knew about Jesus Christ, he was afraid to make that big decision; he was afraid being a Christian would hurt his chances in basketball. Might make him soft, he thought. Finally, Bobby saw that he needed to stop worrying and start trusting. Soon, he put his faith in Jesus Christ.

Family and personal: Wife, Tess; and three children, Eric, Matthew, and Meredith. Bobby is a high school basketball coach. Several years ago his school, Charlotte Christian, won a state title with Todd Fuller in the middle.
Ministries: Bobby has traveled widely to speak about his faith in Christ.

CLARK KELLOGG

Retired after the 1986 season
Indiana Pacers

High school: St. Joseph (Cleveland, Oh.)
College: Ohio State University
Draft: Selected in the first round by the Indiana Pacers in the 1982 draft

Highlights

1982: Selected MVP in the Big Ten
1983: Named to NBA All-Rookie team
1983–85: Led Pacers in scoring and rebounding

Salvation

In 1986, Kellogg suffered a knee injury that would end his career. While still with the Pacers, though, he attended chapel services. There he heard chaplain Brian Chapman challenge him to trust Jesus Christ. Also, his wife, Rosey, was trying to edge him that way. Finally, he decided they were right, and he put his faith in Christ. Other Christians, including Wayman Tisdale, were an encouragement to him.

Family: Wife, Rosey; and three children, Talisa, Alex, and Nicholas. Clark has been a college basketball analyst for ESPN and CBS television.
Ministries: Kellogg has done some work with Sports Spectrum Radio.

ANDREW LANG

Phoenix Suns, Philadelphia 76ers, Atlanta Hawks, Milwaukee Bucks, New York Knicks
Center

High school: Dollarway High (Pine Bluff, Ark.)
College: University of Arkansas (business administration degree)
Draft: Selected in the second round by the Phoenix Suns in the 1988 draft

Highlights

1991, 1992: Blocked 201 shots
1996: Best offensive year; averaged 11.7 points per game
Has pulled down more than 3,300 career rebounds

Salvation

When Andrew, or Drew, as his friends called him, was thirteen, he felt the Holy Spirit tugging at his heart while at his home church, Missionary Baptist Church, in Pine Bluff, Arkansas. He went forward during the invitation, and he prayed to trust Jesus as Lord and Savior.

Family: Wife, Bronwyn; and two children, Andrew III and Alexander

JERRY LUCAS

Retired after the 1973 season
Cincinnati Royals, San Francisco Warriors, New York Knicks
Center

High school: Middletown (Ohio) High
College: Ohio State University
Draft: Selected by the Cincinnati Royals in the 1962 draft

Highlights

1961, 1962: College basketball Player of the Year
1964: NBA Rookie of the Year
1965, 1966, 1968: All-NBA first team
1965: NBA All-Star Game Most Valuable Player

Salvation

The remarkable salvation story in Jerry Lucas's life has to do with his parents. Lucas himself became a Christian after his college years. Later, his parents divorced. Jerry continued to witness to them as they remarried other people and continued their lives. Much later, after Jerry's stepfather died, the former Knick led the funeral service. In attendance was his dad—who accepted Christ that day. His second wife had died, so after becoming a Christian, the elder Lucas and Jerry's mother were remarried.

Family and personal: Cheri; and five children, Matt, Jeff, Julie, J. J., and Canaan. Lucas is a memory expert.

PETE MARAVICH

Retired after the 1980 season
Died: January 5, 1988
Atlanta Hawks, New Orleans/Utah Jazz, Boston Celtics
Guard

High school: Daniels High (Clemson, S.C.); Needham Broughton (Raleigh, N.C.); Edwards Military Institute (Salemburg, N.C.)
College: Louisiana State University
Draft: Selected in the first round by the Atlanta Hawks in the 1970 draft

Highlights

1970: Became top scorer in college basketball history
1970: College basketball Player of the Year
1986: Named to Basketball Hall of Fame
1996: Selected to NBA 50th Anniversary All-Time Team

Salvation

When he was a teenager, Pete attended a Christian camp. While there, he was confronted with the gospel and had an opportunity to trust Jesus Christ. He didn't do it. Instead, he went through his entire stellar college career and NBA career without Christ in his life. His unhappiness with life led him to pursue all kinds of avenues, looking for purpose. Drinking, the occult, UFOs—he tried looking everywhere. Finally, one night a few years after he retired, he felt the Lord calling him while he was in bed. Immediately, he got down on his knees and trusted Jesus as Savior. From then until his early death at the age of forty, Pete Maravich was on fire for Jesus, studying Scripture and preaching the gospel whenever he could.

Family and personal: Wife, Jacquelyn; and two children, Josh and Jaeson. Pete died of a heart attack while playing basketball with Dr. James Dobson and former UCLA player Ralph Drollinger.

ANTHONY PARKER

Philadelphia 76ers, Orlando Magic
Guard

High school: Central High (Naperville, Ill.)
College: Bradley University
Draft: Selected in the first round by the New Jersey Nets in the 1997 draft

Highlights

1998: Appeared in 37 games for the 76ers despite injuries

Salvation

While playing basketball at Bradley University, Anthony Parker met two people who exuded the love of Christ. One was head coach Jim Molinari, and the other was team chaplain Dick Belsley. Through their influence, Anthony trusted Christ as Savior while at Bradley. They then challenged Anthony to study the Bible and to take a stand for Jesus Christ.

Family: Single

ELLIOT PERRY

Los Angeles Clippers, Charlotte Hornets, Phoenix Suns, Milwaukee Bucks, New Jersey Nets
Guard

High school: Treadwell High (Memphis, Tenn.)
College: University of Memphis
Draft: Selected in the second round by the L.A. Clippers in the 1991 draft

Highlights

1995, 1997: Played in all 82 games for his team
1996, 1998: Played in 81 games each year
1998: Shot .844 from the free-throw line

Salvation

As a kid, Elliot Perry wasn't much of a churchgoer. While he was a student at the University of Memphis, a friend named Michael Toney began urging Elliot to go to church with him. He liked what he heard, and he kept going back until finally, he realized he needed to trust Christ. Perry calls that decision "the best move I ever made in my life."

Family: Single

BRENT PRICE

Washington Bullets, Houston Rockets, Vancouver Grizzlies
Guard

High school: Enid (Okla.) High
College: University of South Carolina, University of Oklahoma
Draft: Selected in the second round by the Washington Bullets in the 1992 draft

Highlights

1990: Scored 56 points in 1 game at Oklahoma
1996: Made 13 straight 3-pointers to tie an NBA record
1996-97: In an abbreviated season, hit all 21 of his free throws

Salvation

The Denny Price family of Enid, Oklahoma, is known far and wide as a Christian clan. So it is no wonder that when Brent was just nine years old, he went to his parents and said he wanted to become a Christian. "I told them I wanted to accept Jesus Christ as my Savior," he recalls. That day, he and his parents knelt by his bed, and he trusted Christ.

Family and personal: Wife, Marcie; and one child, Madison. Price does a very good impersonation of Elvis Presley.
Ministries: Works with an Oklahoma-based group that produces a series of Brent Price basketball skills videos with a Christian message

MARK PRICE

Retired after the 1998 season

Cleveland Cavaliers, Washington Bullets, Golden State Warriors, Orlando Magic

Guard

High school: Enid (Okla.) High

College: Georgia Tech

Draft: Selected in the second round by the Dallas Mavericks in the 1986 draft

Highlights

1993, 1994: Won the NBA All-Star Game Three-Point Shootout

1992, 1993: Led NBA in free-throw shooting percentage

1993: Selected First Team All-NBA

Holds career NBA record for free-throw percentage (.907)

Holds career NBA record for play-off free-throw percentage (.944)

Salvation

The Dennis Price family loved basketball and singing. Mark, as one of the singing Price brothers, joined right in. The family would travel around the Oklahoma area, singing about their faith. One problem: when Mark was seventeen, he discovered that he had never really trusted Christ. To him, basketball was the top thing in life. So Mark went forward during an invitation at a youth rally and prayed to put his faith in Jesus.

Family and personal: Wife, Laura; and two daughters, Caroline and Brittany. He and Laura like to support right-to-life causes.

Ministries: Lifeline singing ministry

DAVID ROBINSON

San Antonio Spurs
Center

High school: Osbourn Park High (Manassas, Va.)
College: Naval Academy
Draft: Selected in the first round by the San Antonio Spurs in the 1987 draft

Highlights

Only person to play for the U.S. Olympic basketball team three times
1987: College Player of the Year
1990: NBA Rookie of the Year
1992: NBA Defensive Player of the Year
1995: NBA Most Valuable Player
1998: All-NBA second team

Salvation

In June 1991, Greg Ball, a man who ministers to pro athletes, visited David Robinson. He challenged him in his thinking about whether David truly loved God. Robinson realized that he didn't, and Ball explained to him what it meant to become a Christian. Robinson prayed and committed his life to Christ. From then on, he has been one of the sports world's most dedicated Christians.

Family and personal: Wife, Valerie; and three sons, David, Corey, and Justin. Has his own web site at www.theadmiral.com.
Ministries: Jammin' Against the Darkness—an outreach put on by pro athletes

BRYAN SKINNER

Los Angeles Clippers
Forward

High school: Temple (Tex.) High
College: Baylor University (Waco, Tex.)
Draft: Selected in the first round by the L. A. Clippers in the 1998 draft

Highlights

1997: Gold medalist in the World University Games
1998: Named honorable mention All-American at Baylor

Salvation

Brian's parents took him to church and taught him about the gospel when he was very little. When he was five years old, he trusted Jesus Christ as his Savior. He realizes that it's not a very exciting testimony, but he says, "I am grateful that I didn't have to go through heartache and pain."

Family and personal: Wife, Rebecca; and one daughter, Avery Alexis Ann. During the lockout of 1998, he coached varsity basketball at Southwestern Christian Academy in Houston.

CHARLES SMITH

Los Angeles Clippers, New York Knicks, San Antonio Spurs, Clippers
Forward

High school: Warren Harding High (Bridgeport, Conn.)
College: University of Pittsburgh
Draft: Selected in the first round by the Philadelphia 76ers in the 1988 draft

Highlights

1989: Named to NBA All-Rookie first team
1990: Had his best scoring season with 21.1 points a game
1995: Won the Mickey Mantle Community Service Award

Salvation

Life was a struggle for Charles Smith in 1991. First, he developed serious knee problems. Then, tragically, his father died. "I was at the point where I asked, 'When is it going to stop?'" The pain didn't stop, but Smith found Someone who could help him endure. He realized he needed to turn to Jesus Christ. "My conversion was like what happens to a lot of people who've had tragic circumstances," he says. Through Christ he found peace in the middle of trouble.

Family: Wife, Lisa; and one child, Charles D.
Ministries: Charles Smith Foundation

BRYANT STITH

Denver Nuggets
Guard

High school: Brunswick (Lawrenceville, Va.)
College: University of Virginia
Draft: Selected in the first round by the Denver Nuggets in the 1992 draft

Highlights

1992: MVP of the National Invitational Tournament championship game
1995–96: Only Nugget to appear in all 82 games
1999: Started the 1999–2000 season as the Nugget's eighteenth all-time leading scorer

Salvation

Bryant trusted Jesus Christ as his Savior when he was a young child. He recalls that he had a lot of people in his circle of influence who encouraged him to stay close to the Lord throughout his youth.

Family and personal: Wife, Barbara; and three children, Brandan, Broderick, and Bria. He was an assistant coach at his old high school during the 1998 lockout.
Ministries: Occasionally Bryant speaks in churches about his faith.

DAVID THOMPSON

Retired after the 1984 season
Denver Nuggets, Seattle Supersonics
Forward

High school: Shelby (N.C.) High
College: North Carolina State
Draft: Drafted in the first round by the Denver Nuggets in the 1975 ABA draft and by the Atlanta Hawks in the 1975 NBA draft

Highlights

1975: Selected College basketball Player of the Year
1976: Named ABA Rookie of the Year
1978: Scored 73 points in one game against the Detroit Pistons
1979: Named MVP of the NBA All-Star team

Salvation

David Thompson, basketball superstar, had hit rock bottom. He had landed in jail for attacking his wife after destroying his career through drug abuse and wrong living. While in jail, he was visited by a pastor. The preacher shared the gospel with David, and he trusted Jesus as Savior. It was the same gospel he knew about because he had grown up going to church back in North Carolina. Finally, it had hit home.

Family: Wife, Cathy; and two daughters, Brooke and Erika
Ministries: David speaks often to young people about how Christ rescued him from the mess he had made of his life.

REX WALTERS

New Jersey Nets, Philadelphia 76ers, Miami Heat
Guard

High school: Piedmont Hills and Independence (San Jose, Calif.)
College: Northwestern, (Kans.)
Draft: Selected in the first round by the New Jersey Nets in the 1993 draft

Highlights

1995: Finished second on the 76ers in 3-point percentage (.362)
1997: Scored a career-high 27 points (January 22 against the Celtics)

Salvation

Rex trusted Christ as Savior while attending a Philadelphia 76ers chapel service.

Family: Wife, Deanna

CHARLIE WARD

New York Knicks
Guard

High school: Thomasville (Ga.) High
College: Florida State
Draft: Drafted by the Milwaukee Brewers in 1993; did not sign. Selected in the first round by the New York Knicks in the 1994 draft

Highlights

1993: Won college football's Heisman Trophy
1998: Played 2,317 minutes for the Knicks, most ever in his career
1998: Shot .805 from the free-throw line

Salvation

Charlie Ward grew up hearing the gospel, so it was no surprise that he became a Christian as a young child. He says, "The Lord gives me an inner peace that a lot of people are missing."

Family and personal: Wife, Tonja. Tonja and Charlie have worked with children who need adult role models.
Ministries: Charlie has a book out that details his life and his faith. It's called *Winning By Grace.*

PAUL WESTPHAL

Retired after the 1984 season
Player: Boston Celtics, Phoenix Suns, Seattle Sonics, New York Knicks
Guard
Head coach: Phoenix Suns, Seattle Sonics

High school: Aviation High (Redondo Beach, Calif.)
College: University of Southern California

Highlights

1978: Averaged 25.2 points per game with Phoenix
1983: Comeback Player of the Year
A four-time All-Star with the Phoenix Suns

Salvation

Westphal trusted Jesus Christ at an early age. His biggest influence in making that decision was his father, who lived out his faith in front of Paul and his brother Bill. Paul says he was six or seven years old when he prayed something like this: "I believe You, Lord, when You say we're sinners and that we need You to come into our hearts and cleanse us from sin. Please forgive me, Jesus."

Family and personal: Wife, Cindy; and two children, Victoria and Michael. Began his coaching career with Southwestern and Grand Canyon, two Christian colleges.

BUCK WILLIAMS

Retired after the 1998 season
New Jersey Nets, Portland Blazers, New York Knicks
Forward

High school: Rocky Mount (N.C.) High
College: University of Maryland
Draft: Selected in the first round by the New Jersey Nets in the 1981 draft

Highlights

1980: Member of U.S. Olympic team
1982: NBA Rookie of the Year
1990, 1991: NBA All-NBA defensive first team
1997–98: Played in his 1300th NBA game

Salvation

"I grew up attending church, and I had a friend who would take me to church each Sunday. We rarely missed a Sunday service. It was always a part of my life. One Sunday I knelt and gave my life to Christ. From that day on, I've tried to live the Christian life. I read the Bible and am faithful in prayer."

Family and personal: Wife, Mimi; and two children, Julien and Malek. A geneology buff, Williams has traced his roots back to 1795.

SCOTT WILLIAMS

Chicago Bulls, Philadelphia 76ers, Milwaukee Bucks
Forward

High school: Woodrow Wilson High (Los Angeles)
College: University of North Carolina
Draft: Never drafted. Signed as a free agent with the Chicago Bulls in 1990.

Highlights

1991, 1992, 1993: Was a member of NBA champs in each of his first three years in the league
1995: Grabbed 20 rebounds against Golden State Warriors (February 20)
1998: Crossed the 2,000-point plateau in career scoring

Salvation

"The 1996 season was a tremendous year for me because it was the first year I had a relationship with Jesus Christ. I had religion before, but now I have a relationship. It's been a big difference for me. I let Christ guide me in all walks of my life. It was a tremendous feeling when I finally said the words, 'I've accepted Christ as my Lord and Savior.' "

Family and personal: Wife, Lisa. Has been mentored closely in his spiritual life by 76ers chaplain Bruce McDonald.

DAVID WOOD

Chicago Bulls, Houston Rockets, San Antonio Spurs, Detroit Pistons, Golden State Warriors, Phoenix Suns, Dallas Mavericks, Milwaukee Bucks
Forward

High school: Hudson's Bay High (Vancouver, Wash.)
College: Skagit Valley College (Wash.)
Draft: Not drafted by the NBA

Highlights

1991, 1993: Played in the NBA play-offs
1998: Played for U.S. in World Games

Salvation

David Wood really wanted to be saved. He wanted it so bad that he used to ask Jesus to come into his heart every day. That began when he was about three. He continued this pattern until he was eight and found out that he had to trust Jesus just one time. He has been a powerful witness for Jesus ever since.

Family and personal: Wife, Angie. Considers himself a missionary to the NBA
Ministries: Jammin' Against The Darkness

WOMEN'S BASKETBALL

RHONDA BLADES

New York Liberty, Detroit Shock
Guard

High school: Parkway High (Kans.)
College: Vanderbilt University

Highlights

1997: Hit first 3-point shot in WNBA history
1998: Was first pick by the Detroit Shock in the 1998 WNBA expansion draft

Salvation

Tony and Gail Blades led their daughter Rhonda to faith in Christ when she was a preteen, and they continued to raise her as a churchgoing kid. Yet her love for sports pulled her attention from Christ for a while. After her freshman year at Vanderbilt, Rhonda went to Kannakuk Kamp in Missouri, and there she rededicated her life to serving Christ. She's used her success as an athlete as a platform to talk about her love for Jesus Christ.

Family and personal: Husband, Parke. The Blades live in Nashville, where Parke owns a couple of businesses.

RUTHIE BOLTON-HOLIFIELD

Sacramento Monarchs
Guard

Hometown: Gainesville, Fla.

Highlights

1988: Named to NCAA Final Four All-American team
1991: USA Basketball Female Athlete of the Year
1997: WNBA first team All-Star
1999: Scored 34 points (against Mystics) for third time in career

Salvation

It might be easy to get ignored in a big family like Ruthie's. After all, Linwood and Leola Bolton had twenty children to keep track of. However, there was one thing Rev. Bolton (Ruthie's dad was a pastor) made sure he knew—and that was that his children knew how to become Christians. For Ruthie, that day came early. "I was saved when I was seven years old," she says.

Family and personal: Husband, Mark. Ruthie's brothers have recorded a gospel CD.

CHARLOTTE SMITH

Colorado Xplosion, Long Beach Sting Rays, and Seattle Reign of American Basketball League; Charlotte Sting
Forward

Hometown: San Jose, Calif.
College: University of North Carolina

Highlights

1994: Only second woman to dunk basketball (occurred during NCAA title game)
1994: Hit shot to win the NCAA tourney for North Carolina; named tournament MVP
1998: Selected to ABL All-Star team

Salvation

As a teenager, fifteen-year-old Charlotte Smith was no stranger to the gospel. Her dad, Ulysses, was a pastor, and her uncle, David Thompson, had been saved after his NBA career self-destructed. Charlotte's grandma kept telling her that life was uncertain and that she needed to get things squared away with God. "You never know when Jesus is coming back," Grandma would say. That finally got Charlotte's attention. She prayed and said, "Lord, I'm sorry I'm a sinner. Please forgive me. I trust You."

Family: Single

NANCY LIEBERMAN-CLINE

Phoenix Mercury, player
Center
Detroit Shock, general manager and coach

High school: Far Rockaway High (N.Y.)
College: Old Dominion University

Highlights

Played in four professional women's leagues: WBL, WABA, USBL, and WNBA
1996: Voted to the Naismith Memorial Basketball Hall of Fame
1997: Selected first coach of the WNBA Detroit Shock

Salvation

Nancy Lieberman was a tough, streetwise Jewish girl who grew up in New York City playing against guys on the playground. When she went to Old Dominion University as the best women's college basketball player in the land, she was in for a surprise when an Athletes in Action basketball team visited the campus and she heard someone explain what it means to follow Jesus Christ. Nancy liked what she heard and she prayed to accept Jesus as Savior. Her faith lay dormant, though, for several years, and she struggled to keep Christ at the center of her life. Things changed when she met Tim Cline while both of them were playing for the Washington Generals, the team that accompanies the Harlem Globetrotters. Nancy's marriage to him and later friendships with other Christians have strengthened her faith.

Family and personal: Husband, Tim; and one son, T. J. Nancy has written two books: *Magic: The Nancy Lieberman-Cline Story*, an autobiography; and *Basketball for Women*, with ESPN/ABC commentator Robin Roberts.

JANE ALBRIGHT-DIETERLE

Head Coach, University of Wisconsin women's basketball; former coach, Northern Illinois

Hometown: Graham, N.C.
College: Appalachian State University

Highlights

1991: Illinois Basketball Coaches Association Coach of the Year
1993: Mid-Continent Conference Coach of the Year
1995: Big Ten Coach of the Year

Salvation

Long before she became a famous basketball coach, Jane Albright came to faith in Jesus Christ. In her hometown of Graham, North Carolina, she attended an evangelistic crusade at a movie theater when she was in the seventh grade. That day, she accepted Christ as her Savior. Later, in 1984, she took another positive step in her Christian journey. "I had always understood that Jesus was my Savior, that He died for my sins. I didn't quite understand the Lord part." So, while a young coach, she dedicated her life to putting Jesus as Lord of her life.

Family: Husband, David Dieterle
Ministries: Habitat for Humanity, Salvation Army, personal notes to people who are hurting

KAY YOW

Head Coach, North Carolina State women's basketball

High school: Gibsonville High (N.C.)
College: East Carolina

Highlights

1986: Coached the women's U.S. team at the World Championships
1988: Coached U.S. team at the Olympic Games
Has coached the U.S. team at the Goodwill Games

Salvation

Kay grew up in a churchgoing family, but she didn't make any personal decisions about the faith while at home. More than a decade after graduating from college, in 1975, after Kay was named head coach at North Carolina State, one of the first visitors in her office was a young woman who wanted to start a Bible study for the basketball team. Reluctantly, Kay allowed her to do so. At the very first meeting, Kay herself prayed to put her faith in Jesus Christ. From that beginning, she has become a strong voice for the Lord in college women's sports.

Family and personal: Single. Kay battled breast cancer in the late 1980s.
Ministries: Popular speaker at civic and church functions

FOOTBALL (NFL)

BILL BATES

Retired after the 1997 season
Safety
Dallas Cowboys (15 years with same team)
Coach, Dallas Cowboys (beginning with 1998 season)

High school: Farragut High (Knoxville, Tenn.)
College: University of Tennessee
Draft: Selected by New Jersey Generals in the 1983 USFL draft; signed as a free agent by the Dallas Cowboys in April 1983

Highlights

1984: Selected to the NFC Pro Bowl team
1992, 1993, 1995: Played on Super Bowl-winning team

Salvation

While a high school student, Bill attended a sports camp in North Carolina, sponsored by the Fellowship of Christian Athletes. While there, he heard speakers talk about a relationship with Jesus Christ. Bill had grown up in the church and had heard about Jesus, but this was different. By the end of the week, Bill knew he needed to trust Jesus as his Savior, and he did.

Family and personal: Wife, Denise; and five children, Graham, Hunter, Brianna, Tanner, and Dillon. Bill and Denise particularly appreciate the March of Dimes; that organization helped them in 1989 when their triplets were born.

DON BEEBE

Retired after the 1997 season
Buffalo Bills, Carolina Panthers, Green Bay Packers
Special teams, wide receiver

High school: Kaneland High (Maple Park, Ill.)
College: Western Illinois, Aurora (Ill.), Chadron State (Nebr.)
Draft: Selected in the third round by the Buffalo Bills in the 1989 draft

Highlights

1991: Had four touchdown receptions in one game (against Pittsburgh)
1992, 1993, 1994, 1997, 1998: Played in five Super Bowls
1996: Had 11 receptions in one game (10–14 vs. San Francisco)

Salvation

For as long as Don Beebe can remember, he wanted to be someone special in sports. But he adds, "Any attention I receive is about Don Beebe, the guy living for Christ." At age seven, Beebe gave his life to Jesus Christ.

Family: Wife, Diana; and three children, Amanda, Makayla, and Chad

---

TONY BOSELLI

Jacksonville Jaguars
Offensive tackle

High school: Fairview High (Boulder, Colo.)
College: University of Southern California
Draft: Selected in the first round by the Jacksonville Jaguars in the 1995 draft

Highlights

1996–99: Played in four consecutive Pro Bowls
1998: Named to All-Pro teams by eight print and broadcast media and by NFL Films

Salvation

Tony Boselli was led to faith in Christ after he joined the Jaguars. His teammate and good friend Mark Brunell explained the gospel to him, and he was saved.

Family and personal: Wife, Angi; and one child, Andrew. Formed the Boselli Foundation in 1995 to help children "become champions at home, school, and on the playing field."
Ministries: Safe Harbor Boys Home, a Christian group home for boys; Champions for Christ

---

KYLE BRADY

New York Jets, Jacksonville Jaguars
Wide receiver

High school: Cedar Cliff High (Camp Hill, Pa.)
College: Penn State
Draft: Selected in the first round by the New York Jets in the 1995 draft

Highlights

1994: Named to *The Sporting News* All-America second team
1995: Had 5 receptions in a game against Jacksonville

Salvation

When Kyle's parents were divorced during his seventh-grade year, his church attendance tailed off, and matters of faith were no longer very important. When Kyle went to Penn State to play football for the Nittany Lions, his roommate was a strong Christian. "He introduced me to what it is to have a personal relationship with Jesus Christ and to accept Him into your heart as your Savior," Kyle says. When an injury made Kyle wonder about his place in the world, he decided his roommate was right, and he trusted Jesus as Savior. "God has a perfect will for my life," Kyle says.

Family and personal: Single. Kyle is a Civil War buff who enjoys visiting old battlefields.

CORWIN BROWN

New England Patriots, New York Jets
Safety

High school: Percy L. Julian High (Chicago, Ill.)
College: University of Michigan
Draft: Selected in the fourth round by the New England Patriots in the 1993 draft

Highlights

1993: Started 12 games as a rookie
1996: Played in Super Bowl XXXI
1997: Named Pro Bowl first alternate

Salvation

Problems surfaced for Corwin Brown when he got into the NFL because he had drifted away from the faith his parents had taught him about. Anger, materialism, and a bad attitude typified his life. Then he realized that he needed to grow up as 1 Corinthians 13:11 describes. He recognized that he needed to put his faith in Jesus Christ, which he did. Now he says, "Only when you live with the Lord can you understand His peace."

Family and personal: Wife, Melissa; and one son, Corwin Jr. Brown has served as a volunteer assistant with Boston University.

ISAAC BRUCE

St. Louis Rams
Wide receiver

High school: Dillard High (Ft. Lauderdale, Fla.)
College: Memphis State
Draft: Selected in the second round by the then-Los Angeles Rams in the 1994 draft

Highlights

1995: Gained 1,781 receiving yards, the second best in league history
1996, 1999: Played in the Pro Bowl
1997: In one game, Isaac had 233 yards on 10 receptions vs. Atlanta
1998: Caught 21 passes in first two games of season

Salvation

Isaac's mom was the guiding light in his life in relationship to his faith in Christ. She made sure he and his fourteen brothers and sisters were in church each time the door opened. And she was the one who pointed Isaac toward his faith in Jesus Christ. "She planted the seed," he says. "And it just grew and grew."

Family and personal: Single. Plans to be a minister when his career is over

---

MARK BRUNELL

Green Bay Packers, Jacksonsville Jaguars
Quarterback

High school: St. Joseph High (Santa Maria, Calif.)
College: University of Washington
Draft: Selected in the fifth round by the Green Bay Packers in the 1993 draft

Highlights

1996–99: Selected to four straight Pro Bowls
1997: Led AFC in passing; Pro Bowl Game Most Valuable Player
1998: Selected as the first alternate quarterback for the Pro Bowl

Salvation

A churchgoing background in high school didn't translate into dedicated Christianity for Mark. It wasn't until he was at the University of Washington and a visiting speaker, Tom Sirotnak, came to challenge the football team, that Brunell turned his life over to Jesus Christ. Not until then did he put his faith in Christ. "It was a total turnaround," Brunell says.

Family and personal: Wife, Stacy; and two children, Caitlin and Jacob. Mark hosts the Mark Brunell Charity Golf Tournament each year.
Ministries: Champions for Church; home church

EARNEST BYNER

Retired after the 1997 season
Cleveland Browns, Washington Redskins, Browns, Baltimore Ravens
Running back

High school: Baldwin High (Milledgeville, Ga.)
College: University of East Carolina
Draft: Selected in the tenth round by the Cleveland Browns in the 1984 draft

Highlights

1990, 1991: Played in the Pro Bowl
1991: Member of Super Bowl championship team

Salvation

When Byner played for the Washington Redskins, his teammate Tim Johnson quoted 2 Corinthians 5:17 to Byner. Earnest had been doing some heavy thinking in the days before that, and when Johnson talked to him about being "a new creation," it hit home. Soon, Byner knew he had to trust Jesus Christ. "Hearing that verse was something God had planned," Byner says.

Family: Wife, Tina; and four daughters, Semeria, Adriana, Brani, and Kyara

GILL BYRD

Retired in 1994
San Diego Chargers
Safety

High school: Baldwin High (Milledgeville, Ga.)
College: San Jose State (Calif.)
Drafted: Selected in the first round by the San Diego Chargers in 1993

Highlights

1984: Returned a pass interception 99 yards against Kansas City
All-time leader in interceptions by a San Diego Charger

Salvation

Gill's journey to Jesus began when his girlfriend Marilyn began to talk to him about Jesus Christ. Later, when he was first with the Chargers, a teammate, Sherman Smith, showed Byrd that being a Christian was not a cop-out, but the way to be a real man. During the 1983 season, Byrd accepted Jesus Christ on an airplane as the team was making its way back from a road trip.

Family and personal: Wife, Marilyn; and two children Gill II and Jarius. Has his own website at www.gillbyrd.com
Ministries: His ministry is called Heart of a Champion.

CRIS CARTER

Philadelphia Eagles, Minnesota Vikings
Wide receiver

High school: Middletown (Ohio) High
College: Ohio State University
Draft: Selected in the fourth round by the Philadelphia Eagles in the 1987 draft

Highlights

1993–99: Played in seven consecutive Pro Bowls
1998: Totaled 101 career TD receptions, second in NFL history
Holds numerous Minnesota Vikings receiving records

Salvation

When Eagles teammates Keith Byars and Reggie White led Cris Carter to the Lord in 1988, Carter did not immediately toss away some of the junk of his pre-Christ days. When he became a member of the Minnesota Vikings, team chaplain Tom Lamphere recruited some of the Christians on the team to pray for Cris and some of his bad lifestyle habits. It worked. He became dedicated to his faith in Christ and recognized, "I have a purpose in life . . . to use the platform I've been given so that God's name might be glorified."

Family and personal: Wife, Melanie; and two children, Duron and Monterae. In 1996 was ordained as a minister of the gospel
Ministries: Along with William White, founded the Carter-White Foundation

BOB CHRISTIAN

Chicago Bears, Carolina Panthers, Atlanta Falcons
Running back

High school: McCluer High (Florissant, Mo.)
College: Northwestern University
Draft: Selected in the 12th round by the Atlanta Falcons in the 1991 draft

Highlights

1997: Second on Falcons in special teams tackles with 11
1997: Twice named as offensive player of the game by the coaching staff because of his blocking

Salvation

"I'm thankful to think being a Christian and belonging to Christ are more important than my last name. I'm thankful I have a heavenly Father and His Son, Jesus Christ."

Family and personal: Single. In 1998 traveled to South Africa for a missions trip
Ministries: Fellowship of Christian Athletes, Athletes in Action

RANDALL CUNNINGHAM

Philadelphia Eagles, Minnesota Vikings
Quarterback

High school: Santa Barbara High (Calif.)
College: UNLV
Draft: Selected in the second round by the Philadelphia Eagles in the 1985 draft

Highlights

1988: Named outstanding player of Pro Bowl
1990: Played in third consecutive Pro Bowl
1990, 1998: NFL Player of the Year
1992: Comeback Player of the Year
1998: Led NFL in passing efficiency rating (106.0)

Salvation

Before Randall Cunningham's first retirement in 1996, he had put his faith on the back burner and himself on the front. Two years later, when he recalled that time away, Cunningham said, "My time away from football got me back in line with what God would have me do. As a Christian, I think God has put me here [in Minnesota during the 1998 season] for a purpose. I have to make sure I stay in His will."

Family and personal: Wife, Felicity; and two children, Randall II and Vandi. Donated $100,000 to St. John's Baptist Church in New Jersey in 1990
Ministries: Champions for Christ

TRENT DILFER

Tampa Bay Buccaneers
Quarterback

High school: Aptos High (Santa Cruz, Calif.)
College: Fresno State
Draft: Selected in the first round by the Tampa Bay Buccaneers in the 1994 draft

Highlights

1997: Played in the Pro Bowl
1998: Started all 16 games for fourth straight year

Salvation

Trent Dilfer's spiritual life was an up-and-down prospect for a long time. Enough people thought he was a Christian that he even attended a Christian sports camp as a counselor. However, while at that camp, he observed the way the real Christians acted. Their love for each other and for the Lord were so impressive that Trent decided that he should become a true believer. He trusted Christ as Savior at that camp.

Family and personal: Wife, Cassandra; and two children, Madeline and Trevin. Trent has won several off-season golf tournaments.
Ministries: Fellowship of Christian Athletes, Hardy's Huddle, Athletes in Action

---

TONY DUNGY

Retired after the 1979 season
Defensive back, quarterback

Player: Pittsburgh Steelers, San Francisco 49ers
Head coach: Tampa Bay Buccaneers

High school: Parkside High (Jackson, Mich.)
College: University of Minnesota
Draft: Signed with Pittsburgh as a free agent in 1977

Highlights

1997: Selected Professional Coach of the Year (Maxwell Football Club)

Salvation

Grandpa was a pastor, so Tony Dungy was no stranger to matters of faith. Because his earliest memories were related to Bible reading and worship at church, Dungy knew as a youngster that he had to put his faith in Jesus Christ. His spiritual growth stalled a bit when he went to the University of Minnesota to play football, but as a member of the NFL Pittsburgh Steelers, he was encouraged by teammate Donnie Shell to make his faith a higher priority in his life.

Family and personal: Wife, Lauren; and three children, Tiara, James, and Eric. Lauren is a widely respected volunteer in the Tampa area.
Ministries: Fellowship of Christian Athletes, Athletes in Action

---

IRVING FRYAR

Retired after the 1998 season
New England Patriots, Miami Dolphins, Philadelphia Eagles, Washington Redskins
Wide receiver

High school: Rancocas Valley Regional High (Mount Holly, N.J.)
College: University of Nebraska; degree in divinity from South Florida Bible College
Draft: Selected in the first round by the Chicago Blitz in the 1984 USFL draft; signed by the New England Patriots in 1984

Highlights

1985: Played in Super Bowl XX
1985, 1993, 1994, 1996, 1997: Played in five Pro Bowl games
1997: Played in his 200th NFL game

Salvation

Irving Fryar's NFL life before he became a Christian was mostly trouble. He had family squabbles and team difficulties. In 1989, though, he accepted Jesus as his Savior. Still, it would be a while before his faith made a real difference in his life. "When I first confessed my faith," he says, "three years went by and nothing happened. I was saved but I really didn't know what I was doing." He got into a spot of trouble again because he went where he shouldn't have gone. At that point he said, "All I can do is live for the Lord." Since then he's been a strong witness for Christ.

Family and personal: Wife, Jacqueline; and four children, Londen, Irving Jr., Adrianne, and Jacqueline
Ministries: Fryar Foundation, set up to help at-risk youth

CHAN GAILEY

Head coach: Dallas Cowboys

High school: Americus High (Ga.)
College: University of Florida

Highlights

1984: Coached Troy State to NCAA Division II national title

Salvation

When he was eleven years old, Chan Gailey trusted Christ as his Savior. When he was nearly thirty, he rededicated his life to Jesus, vowing to live his faith each day—and to continue to build on his relationship with Christ.

Family: Wife, Laurie; and two sons, Tate and Andrew

KENT GRAHAM

New York Giants, Detroit Lions, Arizona Cardinals, Giants
Quarterback

High school: Wheaton North (Ill.)
College: Notre Dame, Ohio State
Draft: Selected in the eighth round by the New York Giants in the 1992 draft

Highlights

1996: Started 8 games at quarterback for the Arizona Cardinals
1998: Went 5–1 in final 6 games as starter, lifting the Giants to .500 for the season

Salvation

Kent trusted Jesus as Savior when he was five or six years old. "God has a plan for our lives," he says, "and that plan was for His Son to come and die for us 2,000 years ago to give us a chance to deal with the sin in our lives."

Family and personal: Wife, Courtney; and three children, Taylor, Lauren, and Cassidy. Kent and Courtney have known each other since junior high school.

DARRELL GREEN

Washington Redskins
Safety

High school: Jesse H. Jones Senior High (Houston, Tex.)
College: Texas A & I
Draft: Selected in the tenth round by the Denver Gold in the USFL 1983 draft; selected in the first round by the Washington Redskins in the 1983 NFL draft

Highlights

1984, 1986, 1987, 1990, 1991, 1996, 1997: Played in seven Pro Bowl games
1988: Returned a punt for a touchdown in NFC championship game
1991: Selected to *The Sporting News* All-Pro team
1998: Tied Sammy Baugh and Monte Coleman for Redskins seasons (16)

Salvation

Darrell Green came to grips with his own sinfulness while a student at Texas A & I. He attended a Bible study with other college students and was shocked at what he discovered. "When I first heard the gospel," he says, "I said, 'I'm as wicked as anybody else.'" He felt that he was okay by his own standards, but by Christ's standards he realized, as he says, "I nailed Him to the cross." These revelations soon led to his conversion. Green has been one of the top Christians in the NFL since he first entered the league.

Family and personal: Wife, Jewell; and three children, Jarrel, Jared, and Joi. At one time Green was known as the NFL's Fastest Man.
Ministries: Darrell Green Youth Life Foundation; Fellowship of Christian Athletes

ARCHIE GRIFFIN

Retired after the 1982 season
Cincinnati Bengals
Running back

High school: Eastmoor High (Columbus, Ohio)
College: Ohio State University
Draft: Selected in the first round by the Cincinnati Bengals

Highlights

Won back-to-back Heisman Trophies while at Ohio State
Rushed for 2,800 yards in seven seasons with the Bengals

Salvation

Archie trusted Jesus Christ as Savior when he was thirteen years old. He says of his remarkable career and the accompanying attention: "It used to bother me when someone would praise me, because this is something God has given me. And if anyone should be praised, it's Him."

Family and personal: Wife, Bonita; and three sons, Anthony, Andre, and Adam. Archie is an assistant athletic director at Ohio State University.

HOWARD GRIFFITH

Buffalo Bills, San Diego Chargers, Los Angeles Rams, Carolina Panthers, Denver Broncos
Running back

High school: Percy L. Julian High (Chicago, Ill.)
College: University of Illinois
Draft: Selected in the ninth round by the Indianapolis Colts in the 1991 draft

Highlights

1996: Played in NFC championship game
1997, 1998: Member of Super Bowl champion Broncos teams

Salvation

Griffith says he has been a Christian since he was in junior high school.

Family: Wife, Kim; and one child, Howard II

JASON HANSON

Detroit Lions
Kicker

High school: Mead High (Spokane, Wash.)
College: University of Washington
Draft: Selected in the second round by the Detroit Lions in the 1992 draft

Highlights

1992: Voted Offensive Rookie of the Year in the NFL
1993: Selected to *The Sporting News* All-Pro team
1993: Led NFC in scoring (130 points)
1997, 1999: Named to Pro Bowl team

Salvation

From a churchgoing family, Hanson discovered at age eleven that he needed to make his own decision about faith. "It was made clear to me that just because I went to church or because my parents were Christians didn't mean I was going to heaven. I decided I wanted to accept Christ. I wanted to be forgiven."

Family and personal: Wife, Kathleen; and one child, Ryan. Growing up, Jason was a soccer star with aspirations of being the next Péle.
Ministries: Speaking to young people

JIM HARBAUGH

Chicago Bears, Indianapolis Colts, Baltimore Ravens, San Diego Chargers
Quarterback

High school: Ann Arbor (Mich.) Pioneer High
College: University of Michigan
Draft: Selected in the first round by the Chicago Bears in the 1987 draft

Highlights

1995: Played in the Pro Bowl
1995: Played in AFC championship game

Salvation

Jim Harbaugh put his faith in Christ in 1990. He was in training camp, and he was feeling empty. He had reached his goal of playing pro football, but he was not satisfied. He had been attending Bible studies with Mike Singletary and other Bears, and his brother had been praying for him to accept Christ. Although no one prompted him, Harbaugh says "I got down on my knees and asked Jesus to come into my life."

Family and personal: Wife, Miah; and two sons, Jay and James. Is a part owner of an Indy race car team

CHAD HENNINGS

Dallas Cowboys
Defensive lineman

High school: Benton Community High (Van Horne, Iowa)
College: United States Air Force Academy
Draft: Selected in the 11th round by the Dallas Cowboys in the 1988 draft; because of military obligations, did not play until 1992

Highlights

1993, 1994, 1996: Member of three Super Bowl champion Cowboy teams

Salvation

A strong church background gave Chad Hennings a good grounding in knowledge of the Bible. But it wasn't until he was serving his active-duty hitch after four years at the Air Force Academy that Hennings made faith in Christ personal. A military chaplain made the gospel clear to him while he was stationed overseas, and he trusted Christ at that time.

Family and personal: Wife, Tammy; and two children, Chase and Brenna. Flew multiple missions over Iraq for the U.S. Air Force after the Persian Gulf War. He has written *It Takes Commitment* (Multnomah), telling of his faith and life.

MIKE HOLMGREN

Head coach: Green Bay Packers, Seattle Seahawks

High school: Lincoln High (San Francisco, Calif.)
College: University of Southern California

Highlights

1997: Led the Green Bay Packers to a Super Bowl win

Salvation

In 1960, the Holmgren family attended a Billy Graham Crusade in San Francisco. At the meetings, twelve-year-old Mike trusted Christ. However, he put his faith on the back burner for several years until he became a high school teacher and coach. During that time, through the influence of friends, Holmgren's faith grew to become an integral part of his life.

Family: Wife, Kathy; and four daughters, Calla, Jenny, Emily, and Gretchen

JEFF HOSTETLER

Retired after the 1998 season
New York Giants, Los Angeles Raiders, Oakland Raiders, Washington Redskins
Quarterback

High school: Conemaugh Valley High (Johnstown, Pa.)
College: Penn State, West Virginia
Draft: Selected by the Pittsburgh Marauders in the 1984 USFL draft; selected in the third round by the New York Giants in the 1984 NFL draft

Highlights

1990: Member of Super Bowl championship team
1994: Played in the Pro Bowl

Salvation

It was at a summer tent revival as a teenager that Jeff, whose parents raised him in a strong Christian family, trusted Christ as Savior. Ironically, Jeff had not wanted to go to the revival meetings, wishing instead he and his friends could play. "Sure enough, that's when I opened my heart up to the Lord."

Family and personal: Wife, Vicki; and three children, Jason, Tyler, and Justin. Jeff and his brother Ron have written a book called *What It Takes* (Multnomah).

BROCK HUARD

Seattle Seahawks

High school: Puyallup (Wash.) High
College: University of Washington
Draft: Selected in the third round by the Seattle Seahawks in the 1999 draft

Highlights

1997: Academic All-American
1997: Set a school record for passing with 2,790 yards in one season

Salvation

A youth pastor in Puyallup, Scott Sears, took a special interest in Brock. He and others of Brock's friends would get together for Bible study each Wednesday. After reading and understanding the gospel, Brock accepted Christ as Savior in 1993 while a high school student.

Family: Single

MICHAEL HUSTED

Tampa Bay Buccaneers, Oakland Raiders
Kicker

High school: Hampton (Va.) High
College: University of Virginia
Draft: Signed as a nondrafted free agent by the Tampa Bay Buccaneers in 1993

Highlights

1997: Led Buccaneers in scoring for fifth straight year
1998: Became all-time Buccaneers scoring leader

Salvation

Michael's mom gave him a good background in matters of faith, but it wasn't until he was a high school junior that "everything started to click for him," as his sister Suzanne describes it. That year he gave his heart and life to Jesus Christ.

Family and personal: Wife, Cassie. He married Cassie during the 1998 season.
Ministries: Kicks for Kids

QADRY ISMAIL

Minnesota Vikings, Green Bay Packers, Baltimore Ravens
Wide receiver

High school: Elmer L. Meyers (Wilkes-Barre, Pa.)
College: Syracuse University
Draft: Selected in the second round by the Minnesota Vikings in the 1993 draft

Highlights

1995: Had 7 receptions versus the Bears in one game
1998: Averaged 29.3 yards on four kickoff returns against Colts (Sept. 27)

Salvation

As kids, Qadry and his brother Rocket (Raghib) were raised as Muslims. However, the godly influence of the grandmother, a Christian, could not be denied. Qadry says he saw her faith and her dependence on prayer, and he was impressed. "I knew Jesus was the answer," he says. "I wanted to have the relationship my grandmother had." So Qadry trusted Christ as Savior.

Family: Wife, Holly; and one daughter, Qalea

ANTHONY JOHNSON

Indianapolis Colts, New York Jets, Chicago Bears, Carolina Panthers
Running back

High school: John Adams High (South Bend, Ind.)
College: University of Notre Dame
Draft: Selected in the second round by the Indianapolis Colts in the 1990 draft

Highlights

1996: Played in the NFC championship game
1998: Entered season as career rushing leader in Panthers history

Salvation

Anthony trusted Jesus as Savior at age eight under the influence of his mother. While he was in college, he rededicated his life to Jesus.

Family and personal: Wife, Shelly; and two children, Taylor and Kylie. Anthony has established the Johnson Family Foundation.
Ministries: Speaks to groups; works with Crisis Pregnancy Centers

---

BRENT JONES

Retired after the 1997 season
San Francisco 49ers
Tight end

High school: Leland High (San Jose, Calif.)
College: University of Washington
Draft: Selected in the fifth round by the Pittsburgh Steelers in the 1986 draft

Highlights

1992–95: Played in five consecutive Pro Bowl games
1988, 1989, 1994: Member of Super Bowl champion 49ers teams

Salvation

While a sophomore at Leland High, young Brent Jones followed some friends to Young Life meetings. He enjoyed the fun of the meetings, including games and skits, but he zoned out when the leaders talked about Jesus Christ. But he couldn't avoid the Holy Spirit's promptings. Before long, he could zone out the gospel no longer. Before the school year was over, he had accepted Jesus as Savior.

Family and personal: Wife, Dana; and two daughters, Rachel and Courtney. Brent joined the CBS football broadcast team in 1998 after retiring from the game.
Ministries: Each year hosts a Young Life golf tournament to benefit a Bay Area Christian ministry

---

TONY JONES

Cleveland Browns, Baltimore Ravens, Denver Broncos
Offensive tackle

High school: Franklin County High (Carnesville, Ga.)
College: Western Carolina University
Draft: Not drafted. Signed as a free agent by the Cleveland Browns in 1988

Highlights

1998: Named to the Pro Bowl team
1998, 1999: Member of Super Bowl champion Denver Broncos

Salvation

Twice, Tony Jones thought he was dead. The first time was when he was being operated on for an elbow problem. Something happened, and he suffered a massive heart attack. He was, for all purposes, dead. The doctors were able to revive him, though. Later, his football team's flight experienced trouble, and death stalked him again. Not long after that, he took the advice of a teammate and put his faith and trust in Jesus Christ.

Family and personal: Wife, Kamilla; and one child, Tony Jr. Tony has headed a drive to promote adoption by minorities.

DANNY KANELL

New York Giants, Atlanta Falcons
Quarterback

High school: Westminster Academy (Fort Lauderdale, Fla.)
College: Florida State
Draft: Selected in the fourth round by the New York Giants in the 1996 draft

Highlights

1997: Began game seven and compiled 7-2-1 record during rest of the season
1998: Completed 53.5% of passes in first ten games for Giants

Salvation

Danny became a Christian when he was nine years old. He was attending a Christian family camp at which Chuck Swindoll was the speaker. The kids at the camp stayed in an Indian-type village. "When I prayed to receive Jesus Christ," Danny says, "I was inside a teepee." Jokingly, he says that was God's way of telling him he was going to be a Florida Seminole.

Family and personal: Single. Danny's dad is team physician for the New York Yankees. Danny was drafted by the Milwaukee Brewers in 1992 but stayed at Florida State to complete 529 passes and break Charlie Ward's FSU record.
Ministries: Speaking to Christian groups

JOHN KASAY

Seattle Seahawks, Carolina Panthers
Kicker

High school: Clarke Central High (Athens, Ga.)
College: University of Georgia
Draft: Selected in the fourth round by the Seattle Seahawks in the 1991 draft

Highlights

1996: Played in the Pro Bowl
1996: Set NFL single-season record for most field goals made (37)
1998: Hit career-best 56-yard field goal against Green Bay

Salvation

The question was too hard for John Kasay to answer. He was working at a camp in South Carolina when an Athletes in Action counselor named Charles Collins asked John to tell him about his relationship with Jesus Christ. As Kasay tells it, "I was stuck." His attempt to sound like a Christian didn't work, and Collins saw right through it. Even before that happened, Kasay had noticed how peaceful and calm the Christians were at this camp. He realized it came from their faith in Christ. It wasn't long until John was praying to accept Jesus as his Savior.

Family: Wife, Laura; and two children, Steven and Caroline
Ministries: Pro Athletes Outreach

NAPOLEON KAUFMAN

Oakland Raiders
Running back

High school: Lompoc (Calif.) High
College: University of Washington
Draft: Selected in the first round by the then-Los Angeles Raiders in the 1995 draft

Highlights

1996: Led NFL with 5.8 yards per rush average
1997: Rushed for 1,294 yards, including team record 227 rushing yards in 1 game

Salvation

In August 1966, Napoleon Kaufman finally took care of business. He had begun his NFL career and was successful, but he felt empty. "The Lord was calling me," he says. Finally realizing what he had to do, he knelt and prayed, "Lord, I want to repent. Please forgive me." He says that "ever since, I've been dedicated to serving God."

Family: Married and has one son

JEFF KEMP

Retired after the 1991 season
Los Angeles Rams, San Francisco 49ers, Seattle Seahawks, Philadelphia Eagles
Quarterback

High school: Winston Churchill (Potomac, Md.)
College: Dartmouth

Highlights

1987: Had a 137.1 passing rating (13 games)
1991: Completed 151 passes for 1,753 yards

Salvation

Jeff Kemp was afraid of commitment to God, afraid of what God might ask him to do if he trusted Him. Although he knew the truth of God's Word and the story of salvation from growing up in a Christian home, like many athletes he thought it best to do what Jeff Kemp wanted to do. When he was a twenty-one-year-old college student, he says, he finally "decided to say yes to God." Now he says, "My security is in knowing Christ. As a Christian, I know I have power that will carry me through all circumstances."

Family and personal: Wife, Stacy; and three children, Kyle, Kory, and Kolby. Helped his dad, Jack, run for U.S. vice president in 1996

STEVE LARGENT

Retired after the 1989 season
Seattle Seahawks
Wide receiver

High school: Putnam City High (Oklahoma City, Okla.)
College: University of Tulsa
Draft: Selected in the fourth round by the Houston Oilers in the 1976 draft

Highlights

1976: First team All-Rookie NFL team
1988: NFL Man of the Year
1989: Retired as NFL's top receiver of all time (819 receptions)
1994: Inducted into the Pro Football Hall of Fame

Salvation

An illustration from a preacher led to Steve Largent's understanding of the gospel. The speaker said there is a wall separating us from God, but that God loved us enough to put a door in the wall. Jesus Christ, he was told, is the Door, and He's the only way to reach God. On that day, Largent, then a high school student, trusted Jesus. "I passed through the wall," he says.

Family and personal: Wife, Terry; and four children, Kyle, Casie, Kelly, and Kramer. Terry and Steve's fourth child, Kramer, was born with spina bifida.
Ministries: As a member of the U.S. House of Representatives, Largent sees his work as a ministry to God as he serves people and tries to make a difference for good.

NEIL LOMAX

Retired after the 1988 season
St. Louis Cardinals, Phoenix Cardinals
Quarterback

High school: Lake Oswego (Ore.) High
College: Portland State University
Draft: Selected in the second round by the St. Louis Cardinals in the 1981 draft

Highlights

1984: Had a 92.5 passer efficiency rating
1987: Led the NFL in attempts (463), competitions (275), and yards (3,387)

Salvation

As a kid, Neil was totally uninitiated into Christianity. He didn't go to church, and he had no idea who God or Jesus is. But when his brother came back from attending a Christian camp, Neil noticed that "his life was drastically changed." Eventually, Neil attended the camp, and he too saw his life transformed when he trusted Jesus as Savior.

Family: Wife, Lori; and three children, Nicholas, Alexandra, and Jack
Ministries: Neil Lomax Charity Quarterback Shootout, a golf tournament that benefits Young Life and Fellowship of Christian Athletes

---

RYAN LONGWELL

Green Bay Packers
Kicker

High school: Bend (Ore.) High
College: University of California (B.A. in English)
Draft: Signed as a nondrafted free agent by the San Francisco 49ers in 1997; claimed off waivers by the Green Bay Packers on April 29, 1997

Highlights

1997: Ranked third in NFL scoring (120 points); played in Super Bowl XXXI
1997–98: Scored at least one field goal in 14 consecutive games, a Packers record

Salvation

Ryan trusted Jesus Christ as Savior while a high school student in Bend, Oregon. He attended Young Life meetings, where he was exposed to the gospel and understood how simple it is to trust Jesus Christ. After becoming a believer in high school, his stay with the Packers led him to a stronger faith. With the Pack, he says, "I incorporated Christ into my everyday life."

Family and personal: Single. After the 1997 season, the Packers honored Ryan with the Lee Remmel Sports Award for professional achievement.
Ministries: Young Life and Athletes in Action

CURTIS MARTIN

New England Patriots, New York Jets
Running back

High school: Allderdice High (Pittsburgh, Pa.)
College: University of Pittsburgh
Draft: Selected by the New England Patriots in the third round of the 1995 draft

Highlights

1995: Named the NFL Rookie of the Year
1996: Played in the Pro Bowl game (after rookie season)
1999: Rushed for more than 1,000 yards for fifth consecutive year

Salvation

Curtis Martin grew up on the mean streets of Pittsburgh. As a high school kid, he realized how fortunate he was to be alive among the crime and violence of his neighborhood. That gratitude drove him to church, where he heard the gospel. "It became something I wanted to be committed to. I wanted to serve God, so I got saved. I accepted Christ as my Lord and Savior."

Family: Single

RUSSELL MARYLAND

Dallas Cowboys, Oakland Raiders
Linebacker

High school: Whitney-Young High (Chicago, Ill.)
College: University of Miami (Fla.), (degree in psychology)
Draft: Selected in the first round by the Dallas Cowboys in the 1991 draft

Highlights

1993: Played in the Pro Bowl
1992, 1993, 1995: Member of Super Bowl champion Cowboys teams
1997: Named Raiders True Value Man of the Year

Salvation

On the first day of 1984, Russell Maryland prayed to accept Jesus as his Savior. He was in his church in Chicago—the one his parents made sure he attended. He was baptized by his 94-year-old pastor, Reverend Augustus Johnson.

Family: Married with one daughter

BRUCE MATTHEWS

Houston Oilers, Tennessee Oilers/Titans
Guard/Center

High school: Arcadia (Calif.) High
College: University of Southern California (degree in industrial engineering)
Draft: Selected by the Los Angeles Express in the 1983 USFL draft; selected in the first round by the Houston Oilers in the 1983 NFL draft

Highlights

1988–99: Played in 12 straight Pro Bowls at 2 positions (8 guard, 4 center)
1988–90, 1992, 1993: Named to *The Sporting News* All-Pro team
1999: Played in 17th season as an Oiler/Titan

Salvation

Growing up in a football family, it was natural for Bruce to feel that the sport was everything. However, during his first NFL season, he realized that there was a void in his life that only God could fill. So, during that rookie year back in 1983, Bruce turned his life over to Jesus Christ.

Family and personal: Wife, Carrie; and five children, Steven, Kevin, Jacob, Michael, and Marilyn. Both his father (Clay Sr.) and brother (Clay Jr.) played in the NFL.

CADE McNOWN

Chicago Bears
Quarterback

High school: West Lynn (Ore.) High
College: UCLA
Draft: Selected in the first round by the Chicago Bears in the 1999 NFL draft

Highlights

1997: Led NCAA in passing efficiency

1999: First Bears rookie to pass for more than 300 yards (301) in 28–10 win over Detroit

Salvation

Cade trusted Jesus Christ as his Savior when he was young. Later, while in college, his relationship with Christ grew—leading him to be vocal in speaking out to youth groups and others about his faith.

Family: Single

PETE METZELAARS

Retired after the 1997 season
Seattle Seahawks, Buffalo Bills, Carolina Panthers, Detroit Lions
Tight end

High school: Central High (Portage, Mich.)
College: Wabash (Ind.) College
Draft: Selected in the third round by the Seattle Seahawks in the 1982 draft

Highlights

1991–1994: Played in four straight Super Bowls with Buffalo Bills

Salvation

For Pete, as it has been for a number of pro athletes, attending a Pro Athletes Conference was his spiritual turning point. While attending the 1987 football PAO conference, Pete found out about the importance of putting his faith in Christ. "After being introduced to Christ and finding out about Him, I said, 'That's what I want.' "

Family: Wife, Barb; and two sons, Anthony and Jonathan

JOHN MICHELS

Green Bay Packers, Philadelphia Eagles
Offensive tackle

High school: La Jolla (Calif.) High
College: University of Southern California
Draft: Selected in the first round by the Green Bay Packers in the 1996 draft

Highlights

1995: Named All-Pac 10 first team
1996: Named to All-Rookie team of *Pro Football Weekly;* played in Super Bowl

Salvation

When he was a sophomore in high school, Michels was invited by a friend to attend a church youth group. There he found out for the first time about Jesus Christ. It wasn't long before John had put his faith in Christ. "I decided to give my life to Christ," John says.

Family and personal: Wife; Melissa; and one child, Lauren. Drafted to replace Ken Ruettgers on the offensive line, Michels became his close friend as Ruettgers ended his career and retired.
Ministries: Leap of Faith ministry (Green Bay); The Gathering youth ministry (San Diego)

GLYN MILBURN

Denver Broncos, Detroit Lions, Green Bay Packers, Chicago Bears
Wide receiver, kick returner

High school: Santa Monica (Calif.) High
College: University of Oklahoma, Stanford University (Calif.)
Draft: Selected in the second round by the Denver Broncos in the 1993 draft

Highlights

1995: Played in the Pro Bowl
1996: Selected to *The Sporting News* All-Pro team
1997–99: Selected to Pro Bowl as kick returner three consecutive years

Salvation

"Christ and salvation give you such a peacefulness about life—that you know where your eternity is. That you know your life is not based on performance—it's based on the grace of God and His mercy. My life has made many changes, many uniform changes, but that's only the exterior. The constant in my life has been Jesus Christ. His love, ever since I accepted Him, has been the same."

Family and personal: Single. Glyn loves reading Christian books.
Ministries: Athletes in Action, Champions for Christ

ANTHONY MUÑOZ

Retired after the 1993 season
Cincinnati Bengals, Tampa Bay Buccaneers
Lineman

High school: Chaffey High (Ontario, Calif.)
College: University of Southern California
Draft: Selected in the first round by the Cincinnati Bengals in the 1980 draft

Highlights

Named to the Pro Bowl 11 consecutive seasons
1998: Inducted into the Pro Football Hall of Fame

Salvation

Anthony and his wife, DeeDee, were led to Christ by her sister and his brother-in-law. The sister asked them if they had ever thought of asking Christ to be their Savior. Neither had. DeeDee at first protested that she had been too bad for God to accept her. Soon, though, both she and Anthony put their faith in Christ to save them.

Family and personal: Wife, DeeDee; and two children, Michael and Michelle. His son gave his presentation speech when Anthony was inducted into the Pro Football Hall of Fame.

HARDY NICKERSON

Tampa Bay Buccaneers
Linebacker

High school: Verbum Dei (Los Angeles, Calif.)
College: University of California
Draft: Selected in the fifth round by the Pittsburgh Steelers in the 1987 draft

Highlights

1993: Named to *The Sporting News* All-Pro team
1993, 1996–99: Selected to play in five Pro Bowl games
1997: Associated Press All-Pro team

Salvation

Church was a family thing for Hardy Nickerson. His parents made sure that the lessons of the church were taught at home—including the importance of trusting Jesus Christ. As a teenager, their teaching bore fruit as Hardy prayed to be saved during his high school years.

Family and personal: Wife, Amy; and three children, Ashleigh, Hardy, and Haleigh. Hardy has received the NFL Players' Association Whizzer White Award for humanitarism.
Ministries: Hardy Nickerson Foundation to help at-risk young people

JOHN OFFERDAHL

Retired after 1998 season
Miami Dolphins
Linebacker

High school: Fort Atkinson (Wisc.) High
College: Western Michigan University
Draft: Selected in the second round by the Miami Dolphins in the 1986 draft

Highlights

1986–90: Named to five consecutive Pro Bowl teams

Salvation

"A personal relationship with Jesus Christ is the only thing that will last beyond our lives on earth." John Offerdahl can say that because he accepted Jesus as his Savior after being ministered to by folks in the Fellowship of Christian Athletes and Campus Crusade for Christ.

Family: Wife, Lynn; and one child, Alexandra

BRYCE PAUP

Green Bay Packers, Buffalo Bills, Jacksonville Jaguars
Outside linebacker

High school: Scranton (Iowa) High
College: Northern Iowa (degree in business)
Draft: Selected in the sixth round by the Green Bay Packers in the 1990 draft

Highlights

1994–97: Selected to play on four Pro Bowl teams
1995: Named AFC Most Valuable Player

Salvation

It's hard to imagine Bryce Paup as a four-year-old, but that's how old he was when he trusted Jesus as his Savior. "A lot of people don't think you know what you're doing [at that age], but I knew exactly what I was doing! I knew I needed Christ." So, he prayed to asked Jesus to forgive him of his sins.

Family and personal: Wife, Denise; and three children, Alex, Nathan, and Rachel. Bryce is involved in the Make A Wish Foundation.

DOUG PEDERSON

Miami Dolphins, Green Bay Packers, Philadelphia Eagles
Quarterback

High school: Ferndale (Wash.) High
College: Northeast Louisiana University
Draft: Signed as a nondrafted free agent by the Miami Dolpins in 1991

Highlights

1996: Member of Super Bowl champion Packers team

Salvation

You might think someone who was given the job of restoring a winning tradition in Philadelphia might be a bit nervous. After all, Eagles fans aren't the most forgiving. But Doug Pederson can handle it. "I sleep well at night because I know God sent His Son to die for me." Pederson grew up in a Christian family, so he knew the way to Christ at an early age.

Family and personal: Wife, Jeannie; and two children, Drew and Josh. Doug works with the Cerebral Palsy Telethon.

TODD PETERSON

New England Patriots, Arizona Cardinals, Seattle Seahawks
Kicker

High school: Valdosta (Ga.)High
College: The Naval Academy, University of Georgia
Draft: Selected in the seventh round by the New York Giants in the 1993 draft

Highlights

1995: Selected AFC Special Teams Player of the Week (week 14)
1996: Scored a franchise record 111 points for Seattle
1998: Made 41 straight PATs for perfect 149 of 149 in first five seasons

Salvation

When Todd and his girlfriend attended a Christian retreat while he was a student at Georgia, he found out that he couldn't be good enough to earn God's favor. He realized that only Jesus Christ could give him the goodness he needed. So, after fighting what he knew was right for a long time, Todd trusted Christ. "I'm not the person in control here," he says. "God is."

Family and personal: Wife, Susan. Todd donates money for each field goal to several groups.
Ministries: Young Life; Seattle/King County Leadership Prayer Breakfast

---

DOUG PELFREY

Cincinnati Bengals
Kicker

High school: Scott High (Covington, Ky.)
College: University of Kentucky (dental studies)
Draft: Selected in the eighth round by the Cincinnati Bengals in the 1993 draft

Highlights

1996: At the end of the season, stood with a 81.25 percent field goal accuracy, which at the time was the best all-time mark in league history

Salvation

A star athlete growing up in the shadows of Riverfront Stadium, Doug thought he knew what success was all about—winning trophies. When he was a sophomore at the University of Kentucky, though, he asked Jesus to come into his life to be his Lord. "I now know that it is more important to care what God thinks than what people think," he says.

Family: Wife, Carla
Ministries: Kicks for Kids

FRANK REICH

Retired after the 1998 season
Buffalo Bills, Carolina Panthers, Detroit Lions

High school: Cedar Crest (Lebanon, Pa.)
College: University of Maryland
Draft: Selected by the Tampa Bay Bandits in the 1985 USFL draft; selected in the third round by the Buffalo Bills in the 1985 draft

Highlights

1991–94: Played in 4 straight Super Bowls with Buffalo Bills
1992: Led Bills to score 35 consecutive points and eventual comeback win in NFL play-off game

Salvation

"I had a conversion experience when I was a senior in college," Frank says. "But I don't like to tell people that I got saved then. I usually tell people that I was saved 2,000 years ago when Jesus died on the cross for my sins. Then I accepted that forgiveness when I was in college."

Family and personal: Wife, Linda; and two daughters, Lia and Aviry. Frank works with Crosswalk.com, on the Sports Channel.

MEL RENFRO

Retired after the 1977 season
Dallas Cowboys
Wide receiver

High school: Jefferson High (Portland, Ore.)
College: Stanford University
Draft: Selected in the second round by the Dallas Cowboys in the 1964 draft

Highlights

1964: Led NFL in punt returns (32), yards (418), kickoff returns (40), and yards (1,017)
1996: Inducted into the Pro Football Hall of Fame

Salvation

In 1980, Mel knew he needed to get back to the basics. He had trusted Christ as a kid, but he knew he wasn't living for Him. So, he recommited his life to God. That decision, though, was not backed up by action. He still held on to some of the destructive habits that had driven him from God. Finally, in 1994, he got serious—asking God to give him the strength to stop drinking, which was the vice that he knew was stopping his spiritual progress cold. That was the beginning of a new life of service for Mel.

Family: Single
Ministries: Mel Renfro Foundation, which supports inner-city youth

---

ALLEN RICE

Retired after the 1991 season
Minnesota Vikings, Green Bay Packers
Running back

High school: Klein High (Tex.)
College: Baylor University
Draft: Selected in the fifth round by the Minnesota Vikings in the 1984 draft

Highlights

1986: Averaged 13 yards per reception
1988: Rushed for a career-high 322 yards

Salvation

While at Baylor, Allen Rice thought he could run his own life. Trouble was, he wasn't enjoying it. Finally, he called on the God his parents had taught him about. He gave his life to Jesus, gave up all the desires that had been dragging him down, and discovered that he had never had so much fun in his life.

Family: Wife, Cheryl; and one daughter, Fallon

JAY RIEMERSMA

Buffalo Bills
Tight end

High school: Zeeland (Mich.) High
College: University of Michigan
Draft: Selected by the Buffalo Bills in the 1996 draft

Highlights

1997: Scored a touchdown on his NFL reception
1998: Scored 6 touchdowns to tie Bills' single season record for TDs by a tight end

Salvation

Growing up in a Christian family in a predominately Christian community, Jay trusted Jesus as his Savior "when I was really, really young," as he puts it.

Family and personal: Wife, Cara. Before each game, Jay prays, telling the Lord, "I want all those people in the stands and the people I'm playing with to know that I'm a Christian."
Ministries: Athletes in Action

EUGENE ROBINSON

Seattle Seahawks, Green Bay Packers, Atlanta Falcons
Safety

High school: Weaver High (Hartford, Conn.)
College: Colgate University (Hamilton, N.Y.)
Draft: Selected by the New Jersey Generals in the USFL draft; signed as a nondrafted free agent by the Seattle Seahawks in 1985

Highlights

1992, 1996, 1998: Selected to the Pro Bowl team
1997: Member of Super Bowl champion Packers team

Salvation

Eugene Robinson knows he can't reach God by himself. He lists all of his great accomplishments as a pro football player—including winning a Super Bowl ring—and concludes that they mean nothing in the long run. They don't add up to the perfection God requires. He knows this because he came to that conclusion while a college student. In 1984, after his girlfriend helped him see his need for Jesus, Robinson put his faith in Christ. Today, he is an outspoken messenger for the Lord.

Family and personal: Wife, Gia; and two children, Brittany and Brandon. Eugene was selected Seattle's Man of the Year four times as a Seahawk.
Ministries: Pro Athletes Outreach

KEN RUETTGERS

Retired during the 1996 season
Green Bay Packers
Offensive tackle

High school: Garces Memorial High (Bakersfield, Calif.)
College: University of Southern California
Draft: Selected in the first round by the Green Bay Packers in the 1985 draft

Highlights

1995: Played in NFC championship game
1996: Retired during the Packers' championship season

Salvation

Before 1992, Ken Ruettgers knew who Jesus was, but he had never trusted Him as Savior. It wasn't until Ken got together with a group of Christian men who modeled Christlike behavior did he begin to understand how to put his faith in Jesus Christ. "My friends led me to Jesus. It changed my life."

Family and personal: Wife, Sheryl; and three children, Matt, Katherine, and Susan. In 1995, Ken published his book *Home Field Advantage,* which is dedicated to talking about role models.

DEION SANDERS

Atlanta Falcons, San Francisco 49ers, Dallas Cowboys
Cornerback, wide receiver

High school: North Fort Myers (Fla.) High
College: Florida State
Draft: Selected in the first round by the Atlanta Falcons in the 1989 draft

Highlights

1991–96: *The Sporting News* All-Pro team
1991–94, 1997–99: Named to the Pro Bowl team
1997: NFC Defensive Back of the Year

Salvation

It was during the baseball season of 1997, when Deion was toiling for the Cincinnati Reds, that everything seemed to come apart for him. He realized that all the fame, money, and stuff in his life failed to bring him happiness. He had been reading some Christian books and had been meeting with several Christians who told him how to be saved. Finally, during the middle of the night, while alone in his room, Deion put his trust in Jesus Christ to be his Savior.

Family and personal: Single. Only person to play in both the World Series and the Super Bowl. Also, only athlete in modern history to score an NFL touchdown and hit a major league home run in the same week; in 1989 he blasted a home run for the New York Yankees five days prior to his first NFL game, when he returned an interception for a TD.
Ministries: Gave the proceeds of his book, *Power, Money, & Sex: How Success Almost Ruined My Life* to Potter's House in Texas

MARK SCHLERETH

Washington Redskins, Denver Broncos
Guard

High school: Robert Service High (Anchorage, Ala.)
College: Stanford University
Draft: Selected in the tenth round by the Washington Redskins in the 1989 draft

Highlights

1997: Winner of the Halas Award
1998: Member of Super Bowl champions Broncos team

Salvation

"Just because you accept Christ doesn't mean everything will go smoothly," he says. "I'm very thankful that there's a place for me in heaven."

Family and personal: Wife, Lisa; and three children, Alex, Avery, and Daniel. First native-born Alaskan to play in the NFL
Ministries: Holds Monday night Bible studies at his home for teammates

JUNIOR SEAU

San Diego Chargers
Linebacker

High school: Oceanside (Calif.) High
College: University of Southern California
Draft: Selected in the first round by the San Diego Chargers in the 1990 draft

Highlights

1994: Played in Super Bowl XXIX
1995: Led Chargers in tackles with 129
1991–97: Played in seven consecutive Pro Bowls

Salvation

"My family didn't have a lot of money," Seau says, "but we did have a lot of love: love for one another and a strong love and faith in our Lord Jesus Christ." He also credits his chaplain at USC, Tom Sirotnak, with guiding him and helping him develop a closer walk with Christ.

Family and personal: Wife, Gina; and two children, Sydney and Jake. Junior was chosen the NFL Man of the Year in 1994.
Ministries: Junior Seau Foundation

HEATH SHULER

Washington Redskins, New Orleans Saints, Oakland Raiders
Quarterback

High school: Swain County High (Bryson City, N.C.)
College: University of Tennessee
Draft: Selected in the first round by the Washington Redskins in the 1994 draft

Highlights

1993: Finished second in Heisman Trophy voting
1997: Completed 52 percent of his passes

Salvation

Heath Shuler was very young when he became a Christian. "I trusted Christ at Camp Livingwater when I was just seven years old. It was twenty-five years to the day after my dad made his decision to trust Jesus—at the same camp." Before his pro career began, Shuler said, "There's nothing more important than the Lord and His Word."

Family and personal: Wife, Nikol. Heath works with Boys and Girls Clubs.

MICHAEL SINCLAIR

Seattle Seahawks
Defensive end

High school: Charlton-Pollard High (Beaumont, Tex.)
College: Eastern New Mexico
Draft: Selected in the sixth round by the Seattle Seahawks in the 1991 draft

Highlights

1992: Named to All-World League team
1996–98: Played in three consecutive Pro Bowls

Salvation

When he was a first-year player in Seattle, Michael Sinclair and his wife Betty began to recognize that their lives were incomplete. It was at that time that Michael understood that although he had "made a decision for Christ" when he was ten years old, he needed now to make Jesus the Lord of his life. During Michael's rookie year, he and Betty committed their lives to Jesus Christ.

Family and personal: Wife, Betty; and four children, Michael, Johnnie, Glenn, and Michaela. Michael is training to become an ordained minister.
Ministries: On multiple occasions, Michael has traveled overseas on missions trips. He has gone to Kenya and Costa Rica to spread the gospel.

MIKE SINGLETARY

Retired after the 1992 season
Chicago Bears
Middle linebacker

High school: Evan E. Worthing High (Houston, Tex.)
College: Baylor University (Tex.)
Draft: Selected in the second round by the Chicago Bears in the 1981 draft

Highlights

1984–93: Named to 10 straight Pro Bowls
1990: NFL Man of the Year
1998: Inducted into the Pro Football Hall of Fame

Salvation

When he was thirteen, Mike Singletary trusted Jesus as Savior. Yet his faith didn't grow for a long time. Not until he was married and in the NFL did Singletary realize that even though he was saved, he needed to get into the Bible and grow spiritually. It was in 1985 that Singletary began to give his whole life to Christ.

Family and personal: Wife, Kim; and seven children, Kristen, Jill, Mathew, John, Jaclyn, Brooke and Becky. In 1998, published *Daddy's Home at Last* (Zondervan).

JACKIE SLATER

Retired after the 1995 season
Los Angeles Rams
Offensive tackle

High school: Wingfield High (Jackson, Miss.)
College: Jackson State University (Jackson, Miss.)
Draft: Selected in the third round by the Los Angeles Rams in the 1976 draft

Highlights

1981: Appeared in the Super Bowl
1985–90: Selected six straight years to the Pro Bowl team

Salvation

In 1974, Jackie Slater was a college student. He met a girl named Anne. She told him about Jesus Christ and what He could do for Jackie. Two weeks later, Slater says, "I asked Jesus Christ to come into my heart and forgive me of my sins and make me the man He wanted me to be." A little over a year later, Anne and Jackie were married.

Family: Wife, Anne; and two children, Matthew and David

DARRIN SMITH

Dallas Cowboys, Seattle Seahawks
Linebacker

High school: Norland High (Miami, Fla.)
College: University of Miami (Fla.)
Draft: Selected in the second round by the Dallas Cowboys in the 1993 draft

Highlights

1993, 1995: Member of Super Bowl champion Cowboys teams

Salvation

As a youngster, Darrin Smith learned from his mother the importance of trusting Christ. When he got to the University of Miami, though, he began to drift away from going to church, praying, and reading the Bible. When he found himself struggling, he realized that he was not leaning on the power of God as he should have been. So, in the middle of his freshman year, he rededicated his life to Christ and began looking for opportunities to share with others about Jesus' love.

Family: Wife, Kimberly
Ministries: Fellowship of Christian Athletes

STEVE STENSTROM

Chicago Bears, San Francisco 49ers
Quarterback

High school: El Toro (Calif.) High
College: Stanford University
Draft: Selected in the fourth round by the Kansas City Chiefs in the 1995 draft

Highlights

1994: Set career passing record at Stanford (10,531 yards), surpassing John Elway
1997: Completed 57 percent of his passes in three games
1998: Started 7 games, again completing 57 percent of his passes
In college, broke or tied 11 Stanford records

Salvation

The family went to church, and they knew about God, but Steve knew he didn't have a personal relationship with Jesus. As a freshman at Stanford, he began to attend fellowship meetings with other football players. There, he heard his teammates talk about a personal relationship with Christ. He liked what he heard, and during his sophomore year, Steve "accepted the Lord in my heart, and He has become my best friend."

Family and personal: Wife, Lori; and one daughter, Brooke. Lori was an NCAA champion swimmer at Stanford.

MATT STOVER

New York Giants, Cleveland Browns, Baltimore Ravens
Kicker

High school: Lake Highlands High (Dallas, Tex.)
College: Louisiana Tech (degree in marketing, 1991)
Draft: Selected in the 12th round by the New York Giants in the 1990 draft

Highlights

1995: Set Browns all-time record with 29 field goals
1998: Entered the season as Ravens' all-time top scorer

Salvation

When he joined the NFL, Matt Stover found immediate success. In his first year, his team won the Super Bowl. But he was not fulfilled. Not long after that, he attended a Professional Athletes Outreach conference. While there, someone shared from Mark 8:35–36. When he heard, "What shall it profit a man, if he shall gain the whole world, and lose his own soul?" (KJV) Matt knew what he was missing. So, in February 1992, Stover trusted Christ as Savior. He now has peace.

Family and personal: Wife, Debbie; and two children, Jenna and Jacob. Jenna and Jacob are exactly one year apart in age.
Ministries: Fellowship of Christian Athletes

DAVE SZOTT

Kansas City Chiefs
Guard

High school: Clifton (N.J.) High
College: Penn State (degree in political science)
Draft: Selected in the seventh round by the Kansas City Chiefs in the 1990 draft

Highlights

1993: Played in the 1993 AFC championship games
1997: Named to the All-Madden team
1997: Selected All-Pro by several magazines

Salvation

A "chance" meeting with a girl he went to elementary school with changed everything for Dave. Her name was Andrea, and she began to let Dave know that he needed to examine the claims of Christ. It was because of Andrea's influence that Dave trusted Jesus as Savior. They've been married since the early '90s.

Family and personal: Wife, Andrea; and two children, Shane and Joshua. Dave and Andrea's son Shane has cerebral palsy.
Ministries: Szott's Tots, an outreach that helps visually impaired kids

---

STEVE TASKER

Retired after the 1997 season
Houston Oilers, Buffalo Bills
Wide receiver

High school: Wichita County High (Leoti, Kans.)
College: Dodge City CC (Kans.); Northwestern University
Draft: Selected in the ninth round by the Houston Oilers in the 1985 draft

Highlights

1987, 1990–95: Selected to seven Pro Bowl games
1992: Named Outstanding Player of the Pro Bowl
1990–94: Played in four Super Bowl games

Salvation

"My faith in Christ is the most important thing in my life," he says. "I asked God to take control of my life in 1978, and He has never failed me. All of my major decisions in life are based on my faith and my belief in God."

Family: Wife, Sarah; and four children, Deacon, Lucas, Gabriel, and Annelise

---

ADAM TIMMERMAN

Green Bay Packers, St. Louis Rams
Guard

High school: Washington High (Cherokee, Iowa)
College: South Dakota State
Draft: Selected in the seventh round by the Green Bay Packers in the 1995 draft

Highlights

1997: Did not miss a play the entire season at right guard
1997: Member of Super Bowl champion Packers team

Salvation

After spending some time with the Christians on the Packers, Timmerman realized that although he thought he knew about matters of faith, he really never had a personal relationship with Jesus Christ. Now he strives to keep growing in his faith.

Family and personal: Wife, Jana. Two players from South Dakota State are in the NFL—Timmerman and Adam Viniateri of the Patriots. They played against each other in 1998 in Super Bowl XXXII.
Ministries: Athletes in Action

ADAM VINATIERI

New England Patriots
Kicker

High school: Rapid City (S. D.) Central High
College: South Dakota State
Draft: Signed as a free agent by the New England Patriots on June 28, 1996

Highlights

1996: Played in the Super Bowl for the New England Patriots
1998: Scored 127 points; hit a 55-yard field goal

Salvation

"I grew up in a family that always led me toward Christ, but it was never real personal." That didn't happen until he was a senior in college. After that, his growth in Christ was spurred on by his teammates on the Patriots.

Family: Single
Ministries: Fellowship of Christian Athletes, Athletes in Action

---

HERSCHEL WALKER

Retired after the 1997 season
Dallas Cowboys, Minnesota Vikings, Philadelphia Eagles, New York Giants, Cowboys
Running back

High school: Johnson County High (Wrightsville, Ga.)
College: University of Georgia
Draft: Selected by the New Jersey Generals in the USFL in 1983; selected in the fifth round by the Dallas Cowboys in the 1984 NFL draft

Highlights

1985: USFL Player of the Year
1987, 1988: Played in the Pro Bowl
1994: Only player in NFL history to have a run from scrimmage, a pass reception, and a kickoff return of more than 90 yards in one season

Salvation

As a teenager, Herschel made a profession of faith in Jesus Christ. However, his real growth as a Christian came much later. During his career in the NFL, he discovered the importance of discipleship, Bible study, and the Christian disciplines.

Family: Wife, Cindy

STEVE WALLACE

Retired after the 1996 season
San Francisco 49ers, New Orleans Saints, Carolina Panthers
Offensive tackle

High school: Chamblee (Ga.) High
College: Auburn University
Draft: Selected by the Birmingham Stallions of the USFL in 1986 draft; selected in the fourth round by the San Francisco 49ers in the 1986 NFL draft

Highlights

1988, 1989, 1994: Member Super Bowl champions 49ers team
1992: Played in the Pro Bowl

Salvation

Steve Wallace was a high school student when he accepted Jesus Christ as his Savior.

Family: Wife, Vassar; and three children, Baron, Ella, and Xaia

KURT WARNER

St. Louis Rams
Quarterback

High school: Regis High (Cedar Rapids, Ia.)
College: Northern Iowa
Draft: Selected as a free agent by the St. Louis Rams, 1997

Highlights

1999: Led NFL in passing efficiency (109.2) and pass completions (65.1%)
1999: Selected NFL Most Valuable Player

Salvation

Kurt Warner put his faith in Jesus Christ after college and before he became an NFL star. When asked the secret of his success, he says, "It's my faith in Jesus Christ."

Family: Wife, Brenda; and two children, Zachary and Jesse

DANNY WUERFFEL

New Orleans Saints
Quarterback

High school: Ft. Walton Beach (Fla.) High
College: University of Florida
Draft: Selected in the fourth round by the New Orleans Saints in the 1997 draft

Highlights

1996: Won the Heisman Trophy
1998: Passed for 278 yards against New England Patriots

Salvation

"My faith in God is not a reflection of what I've done for Him. Rather, it is a reflection of my countless experiences with the living God. And, after all, that's what being a Christian is all about: not a formula or a feeling, but a true experience with Jesus Christ."

Family: Single
Ministries: Works with a local, inner-city ministry in New Orleans

---

REGGIE WHITE

Retired after the 1998 season
Memphis Showboats (USFL), Philadelphia Eagles, Green Bay Packers
Defensive end

High school: Howard High (Chattanoga, Tenn.)
College: University of Tennessee
Draft: Selected by the Memphis Showboats in the 1984 USFL draft; selected in the first round by the Philadelphia Eagles in the 1984 NFL draft

Highlights

1991, 1995: NFC Defensive Player of the Year
1996: NFL Extra Effort Award winner
1997: All-NFC team
1998: Selected to the Pro Bowl for the 12th time
Has recorded the most sacks in NFL history

Salvation

Reggie was thirteen years old when he trusted Jesus Christ as Savior. White was especially impressed by the love and compassion of the pastor of his church, and he wanted to have what the preacher had. Upon understanding that it was faith in Jesus Christ that set him apart, Reggie too trusted Jesus as his Savior.

Family and personal: Wife, Sara; and two children, Jeremy and Jecolia. White has opened Reggie White Studios to produce family-safe movies.
Ministries: Holy Land tours, several books, an inner-city bank

---

WILLIAM WHITE

Retired after the 1998 season
Detroit Lions, Kansas City Chiefs, Atlanta Falcons
Strong safety

High school: Lima (Ohio) High
College: Ohio State University
Draft: Selected in the fourth round by the Detroit Lions in the 1988 draft

Highlights

1989–93: Started every game for the Lions
1990: Snagged 5 interceptions
1992: Named Detroit's Man of the Year
1997: Had a career-high 119 tackles

Salvation

James and Carline White raised William in a Christian home. Yet the big guy says he didn't "seek a relationship with Christ until I was in high school." As a college student, he used his faith to protect himself against the troubles that come from alcohol and drugs.

Family: Wife, Nikol
Ministries: Speaks to kids during the off-season about substance abuse

---

AENEAS WILLIAMS

Arizona Cardinals
Wide receiver

High school: Fortier High (New Orleans)
College: Southern University (Baton Rouge, La.)
Draft: Selected in the third round by the Phoenix Cardinals in the 1991 draft

Highlights

1994–98:Played in five straight Pro Bowls
1995: Named to *The Sporting News* All-Pro team

Salvation

"I get the most fulfillment leading my teammates and friends throughout the league to the Lord and discipling them," Aeneas says. "I am still in awe of what the Lord has done in my life. My heart's desire is to disciple young believers, and to give them the heart I've been given."

Family: Wife, Tracy; and one daughter, Saenea

GOLF
PROFESSIONAL GOLFERS ASSOCIATION

PAUL AZINGER

First year on the tour: 1981

Hometown: Bradenton, Fla.
College: Brevard Junior College, Florida State
Highlights

1988: Won first tournament, the Phoenix Open
1993: Best year in winnings with $1,459,000, second on the PGA Money List
1993: Won the PGA championship
1998: Won the AT&T Pebble Beach Tournament and the National Pro-Am

Salvation

Paul's quote about faith, in relation to his bout with cancer in 1993: "The only way you will ever have true contentment is in a personal relationship with Jesus Christ. I know I'll spend eternity with God."

Family and personal: Wife, Toni; and two children, Sarah and Josie. Azinger battled lymphoma and came back to continue playing on the PGA Tour. Wrote a book, *Zinger,* about his experiences

---

BOB ESTES

First year on the tour: 1988

Hometown: Graham, Tex.
College: University of Texas

Highlights

1988: College Player of the Year
1994: Won the Texas Open

Salvation

Bob grew up in a Christian home going to church. So, it was natural that at a young age, eleven, he trusted Christ as Savior. While at the University of Texas, Bob spent so much time on golf and school that he let his relationship with the Lord move to the back burner. He realizes now that his mistake was not finding a church right away to attend. Ironically, the church he attends now that he is back in strong fellowship with God is just a block from the apartments he lived in while in college.

Family: Single

JIM GALLAGHER JR.

First year on the tour: 1983

Hometown: Greenwood, Miss.
College: University of Tennessee

Highlights

1990: First tour win, the Greater Milwaukee Open
1993: The Tour Championship
1995: Won two championships, earned more than $1 million
1998: Won the MasterCard Colonial

Salvation

Two people were working on Jim Gallagher. He knew something had to change in his life, and so did his wife, Cissye, and a local pastor, Jim Phillips. Both had been trying to influence Jim to trust Christ, but they knew they had to wait for Jim to be ready. Finally, he told his wife, "I'm ready to talk to Jim." They went to see the pastor, and Jim Gallagher trusted Christ that day. "It was really a great feeling," he says.

Family: Wife, Cissye; and three children, Mary, James, and Kathleen

---

STEVE JONES

First year on the tour: 1981

Hometown: Phoenix, Ariz.
College: University of Colorado

Highlights

1988: Won first tournament: AT&T Pebble Beach National Pro-Am
1989: Won MONY Tournament of Champions
1996: Won the U.S. Open; won $810,644 for the year
1998: Won the AT&T Pebble Beach Tournament and the National Pro-Am

Salvation

In November 1984, a friend invited Steve to attend an evangelistic meeting where Lehman Strauss was preaching. When Strauss told the audience that each of them was either a son of God or a son of Satan, Steve took the words seriously. Knowing that he would rather be with God, he received Jesus Christ as Savior that day.

Family: Wife, Bonnie; and two children, Cy, and Stacey

BERNHARD LANGER

First year on the tour: 1976

Hometown: Anhausen, Germany

Highlights

1985, 1993: Won the Masters Tournament

Salvation

After finding success on both sides of the ocean as a golfer, Bernhard felt empty. He was winning lots of tournaments and earning lots of money, but he knew something was missing. Fellow golfer Bobby Clampett challenged Langer to think about the claims of Christ. Also, Larry Moody, who has led PGA Bible studies over the years, got together with Bernhard to study the Bible. Eventually, Langer accepted Jesus as Savior and soon became a leader among golfers.

Family: Wife, Vicki

Ministries: Langer was among those who began the European PGA Bible study in 1989.

TOM LEHMAN

First year on the tour: 1982

Hometown: Scottsdale, Ariz.

College: University of Minnesota

Highlights

1994: Won first PGA victory at Memorial Tournament

1995: Played in Ryder Cup

1996: Won more than $1.7 million on the Tour

1996: Won the British Open; PGA Player of the Year

Salvation

The highs and lows of high school sports were getting to Tom Lehman. So when he attended a Fellowship of Christian Athletes meeting and his football coach talked about how Jesus Christ could give meaning to his life, Tom listened. He understood his need, for he felt a huge burden of guilt on his shoulders. Once he understood God's grace through Christ, though, he readily trusted Jesus as his Savior. "I felt like a different person," he says.

Family: Wife, Melissa; and three children, Rachael, Holly, and Thomas

LARRY MIZE

First year on the tour:1980

Hometown: Columbus, Ga.
College: Georgia Tech

Highlights

1983: Captured first tour win: Danny Thomas-Memphis Classic
1987: Won the Masters; played in Ryder Cup
1993: Had best money year on tour, $724,000
1998: Finished second in the Canon Greater Hartford Open

Salvation

Larry was twelve years old when he trusted Jesus as Savior. "My parents are Christians, and they brought me up in a Christian manner," says Larry. "I was taught to know and love Christ at an early age." As he got going on the golf scene, though, he misplaced his priorities. He put golf first, even before his relationship with God. On the day of his first son's birth, though, he sat holding him in the hospital and rededicated his life to Christ.

Family: Wife, Bonnie; and three sons, David, Patrick, and Robert

LARRY NELSON

First year on the tour: 1971
First year on Seniors Tour: 1997

Hometown: Marietta, Ga.
College: Kennesaw (Ga.) Junior College

Highlights

1979: Won first tournament: Jackie Gleason-Inverrary Classic
1979, 1981, 1987: Played on the Ryder Cup team
1987: Had best money year on tour, $500,000

Salvation

While in a hotel and looking for something to do between golf tournaments, Larry Nelson picked up the hotel Gideon Bible and read it. It was through that Bible that Nelson learned about salvation and trusted Jesus as his Savior.

Family: Wife, Gayle; and two children, Drew and Josh

DAVID OGRIN

First year on the tour: 1980

Hometown: Garden Ridge, Tex.
College: Texas A & M

Highlights

1994: Won the Peru Open, an international victory (not PGA)
1996: Won his first tournament, the LaCantera Texas Open
1999: Won the GTE Classic and Bruno Memorial Classics (Seniors)

Salvation

When Texas A & M took a golfing trip to Guadalajara, Mexico, in 1980, David Ogrin had no idea how that excursion would change his life. While at the tournament, someone shared with him the importance of trusting Jesus for forgiveness from sin. David spent some time thinking about the gospel, and one night in Mexico he trusted Jesus.

Family: Wife, Sharon; and four children, Amy, Jessica, Dana, and Clark
Ministries: Has written several columns for the *Linksletter*

COREY PAVIN

First year on the tour: 1982

Hometown: Orlando, Fla.
College: UCLA

Highlights

1984: Won his first tournament, the Houston Coca-Cola Open
1991: Finished first on the Money List, earning $1.3 million
1991, 1993, 1995: Played on the Ryder Cup team
1995: Won the U.S. Open
1998: Won Players Championship while setting course record (66) in Australia

Salvation

"I grew up in a Jewish home, and I knew some of the Old Testament stories. I received a book called *Jesus Was A Jew,* and I was amazed. I kept reading that little book and thinking, 'This is obvious.' So, through reading that book, which kept referring me back to the Bible, it really opened my eyes." Through the help of that book and some players in the PGA Tour Bible study, Pavin became a Christian in the early 1990s.

Family and personal: Wife, Shannon; and two children, Ryan and Austin. Pavin's good friend David Robinson named his second son after Corey.

LOREN ROBERTS

First year on the tour: 1975

Hometown: Germantown, Tenn.
College: Cal Poly San Luis Obispo (Calif.)

Highlights

1994: Captured first PGA title, the Nestlé Invitational
1995: Won the Nestlé Invitational again
1996: Won the Greater Milwaukee Open and the MCI Classic
1999: Won the GTE Byron Nelson Classic

Salvation

Loren Roberts trusted Jesus as his Savior in 1983. His further growth in Christ he credits to some discussions with Larry Moody, the PGA Tour Bible study leader, and former PGA player Wally Armstrong.

Family: Wife, Kimberly; and two children, Alexandria and Addison

---

TED SCHULZ

First year on the tour: 1984

Hometown: Louisville, Ky.
College: University of Louisville

Highlights

1989: Won the Southern Open
1991: Won the Nissan Los Angeles Open

Salvation

During Ted's first year on the tour, he and his wife began attending the PGA Tour Bible studies. After attending several of those meetings, Ted realized that although he believed in God, he didn't have a personal relationship with Jesus Christ. Diane came to the same conclusion for herself, so they both prayed to trust Christ as Savior.

Family: Wife, Diane; and one child, Samuel

SCOTT SIMPSON

First year on the tour: 1977

Hometown: San Diego, Calif.
College: University of Southern California

Highlights

1980: First win was at the Western Open
1987: Won the U.S. Open; played in the Ryder Cup
1993: Won the GTE Byron Nelson Classic
1998: Won the Buick Invitational

Salvation

When Scott Simpson started playing on the PGA Tour, he was very skeptical about Christianity. In fact, he kept asking questions of one Christian golfer because he was trying to prove how wrong the other golfer was. When the tour Bible study leader, Larry Moody, suggested that Scott investigate the Bible, Simpson discovered that it was true. In 1984, he was convinced that he needed a Savior, and he prayed to ask Jesus to save him.

Family: Wife, Cheryl; and two children, Brea and Sean

PAUL STANKOWSKI

First year on the tour: 1991

Hometown: Irving, Tex.
College: University of Texas-El Paso

Highlights

1996: Won his first tournament, the BellSouth Classic
1997: Won the United Airlines Hawaiian Open

Salvation

Golf took Paul Stankowski to the University of Texas at El Paso, but it was Jesus Christ who helped him make it through school. Before his March 1990 conversion, Paul hung around with some guys, and did some things with them he's not proud of now. But his new faith in Christ and his new friends in the UTEP Fellowship of Christian Athletes chapter helped change his friends and outlook on life.

Family: Wife, Regina

PAYNE STEWART

First year on tour: 1979
Died October 25, 1999

Hometown: Orlando, Fl.
College: Southern Methodist University (Dallas, Tex.)

Highlights

1982: first win on Tour: the Quad City Classic
1991: Won the U.S. Open
1999: Won U.S. open; played on Ryder Cup team
1999: Third on PGA Money List for year, $1.8 million

Salvation

Always popular on the PGA tour, Payne Stewart began to feel uneasy about his life in the mid-1990s. His wife and two children influenced him to consider the claims of Christ, and in 1998 he finally did. He trusted Christ as his Savior and began attending First Baptist Church in Orlando with his family. During the final months of his life he was discipled by Byron Nelson, golf statesman.

Family and personal: Wife, Tracey; and two children, Chelsea and Aaron.
Payne died at age forty-two when a private jet carrying the golfer and four others crashed enroute to the PGA Tour Championship. The PGA later created the Payne Stewart Award, which each year honors a player "who best represents the ideals" of Stewart: "professionalism, personal presentation, character, community work, and charity."

GOLF
LADIES PROFESSIONAL GOLF ASSOCIATION

LAURIE BROWER

First year on the tour: 1991

Hometown: Villa Park, Calif.
College: Texas Tech University

Highlights

1983–85: All Southwestern Conference Player of the Year
1996: Had her best year on the tour, finishing 62nd and winning almost $100,000
1998: Won the Australian Ladies Masters

Salvation

It was January 1992 when Laurie put her faith in Jesus as Savior. While getting therapy for an injured wrist, she noticed that a therapist wore a pin that read, "Happy Birthday, Jesus." When she commented on it and the two began to talk, the therapist suggested she read a book by Josh McDowell. She did, and she understood what it meant to become a Christian—which is what she did. "It's been the toughest thing I've ever done," she says, "and the most rewarding."

Family and personal: Single. Her degree from Texas Tech is in handicap recreation.

BARB BUNKOWSKY-SCHERBAK

First year on the tour: 1983

Hometown: West Palm Beach, Fla.
College: Florida State University

Highlights

1991: Had her best year on the tour, finishing 28th with a 72.89 scoring average
1994: Biggest money year with more than $167,000
1997: Hit a hole-in-one at the du Maurier Classic

Salvation

Early in her LPGA career, in 1986, Barb was fed up with the lifestyle she was living. Knowing nothing better, she was involved in drinking and other destructive behavior. Friends on the tour had been writing her notes and talking to her about Jesus Christ. While in Hawaii, she finally decided they were right, and she gave her life to the Lord.

Family: Husband, Mark

JACKIE GALLAGHER-SMITH

First year on the tour: 1994

High school: Marion (Ind.) High
College: Louisiana State University

Highlights

1989: NCAA All-American
1995: Recorded career-low score of 68 in HEALTHSOUTH Inaugural
1998: Won career-best $122,425 on the tour
1999: Won Grant Eagle LPGA Classics

Salvation

After Jackie and her husband, Eddie Smith, were married, he began attending Bible studies. This made Jackie think about matters of faith. "I had grown up in the church," she says, "but I didn't have a relationship with Christ." After a period of time passed, Jackie began attending the studies, and one night she accepted Christ as her Savior.

Family and personal: Husband, Eddie. During 1998, Jackie's caddie was Nate Hair, the husband of Wendy Ward.

KATHY GUADAGNINO

First year on the tour: 1983

Hometown: Boca Raton, Fla.
College: University of Tulsa (Okla.), South Florida Bible College

Highlights

1980: Won Western Amateur
1982: Captured NCAA National Championship
1985: Won the U.S. Woman's Open
1988: Won the Konica San Jose Classic
1994: Recorded career-low score of 66 in McCall's Classic

Salvation

When Kathy Baker was a freshman at the University of Tulsa, a girl in the dorm stopped by her room and asked her some questions about her faith. She couldn't answer the questions well because she was not a Christian. The survey, though, got her thinking. Later, a member of the Tulsa football team explained the gospel to her. Before her freshman year was over, Kathy prayed to receive Jesus Christ as her Savior.

Family and personal: Husband, Joe Guadagnino; and three children, Nikki, Megan, and Joseph. Kathy's husband is a pastor.

BETSY KING

First year on the tour: 1977

Hometown: Limekiln, Pa.
College: Furman University (Greenville, S.C.)

Highlights

1984: Captured first career win: the Kemper Open
1984: Rolex Player of the Year
1984–95: Won 30 tournaments to gain entrance into the LPGA Hall of Fame
1997: Won the Nabisco Dinah Shore tournament
1998: Finished six tournaments in the top 10

Salvation

Early in her stellar career, Betsy became a Christian through the fellowship group that meets on the LPGA Tour. In 1979, she was invited to attend a conference organized by LPGA Tour chaplain Margie Davis. While there, Betsy heard Bruce Wilkinson from Walk Through The Bible. He asked the people in attendance if they wanted to trust Jesus as Savior. Betsy prayed along with Bruce and his invitational prayer, and she became a new creature in Christ.

Family: Single
Ministries: Has traveled on several occasions with Extended Hand of Romania to that country to visit orphanages with other LPGA women. Also works with Fellowship of Christian Athletes and Habitat for Humanity

---

BARB MUCHA

First year on the tour: 1987

Hometown: Parma Heights, Ohio
College: Michigan State University

Highlights

1990: Won her first tournament: Boston Five Classic
1992: Won the first Oldsmobile Classic
1997: Tied career-low of 65 in Standard Register PING
1998: Won the Sara Lee Classic

Salvation

Christianity was nothing new to Barb as she made her way through Michigan State, but it wasn't until after she graduated that she did anything about her need for a Savior. Her brother and his wife invited her to a church service in December 1984. She was touched by the pastor's message on the book of John, and she prayed that night to accept Jesus Christ.

Family and personal: Single. Loves to bowl in her "spare" time. She also enjoys listening to Christian music.
Ministries: Has traveled to Romania to visit orphanages

ALISON NICHOLAS

First year on the tour: 1990

Hometown: Birmingham, England

Highlights

1990, 1992, 1994, 1996: Named four times to the European Solheim Cup team
1993: Won the Corning Classic LPGA event
1997: Won the U.S. Open
1999: Won the Hawaiian Ladies Open

Salvation

In 1989, Alison Nicholas observed that some of the women on the European Tour had "something special" in their lives. She attended their Bible studies, studied the Bible on her own, and concluded that what they had was right for her. Soon after, she trusted Jesus as Savior.

Family and personal: Single. As a kid, Alison played tennis and soccer, but not much golf.
Ministries: Extended Homes ministry to Romanian orphanages

SUZANNE STRUDWICK

First year on the tour: 1993

Hometown: Stafford, England

Highlights

1989: Won the French Open

1993: Named the LPGA Rookie of the Year

1994: Recorded her career-low score of 66 at the State Farm Rail Classic

1998: Average career-low 72.47 scoring average

Salvation

A fellow golfer, an American, told Suzanne about Jesus Christ. One of the reasons Strudwick wanted to join the American Tour was to have fellowship with Christian golfers whom she knew in the United States.

Family: Single

WENDY WARD

First year on the tour: 1996

Hometown: San Antonio, Tex.
College: Arizona State University

Highlights

1993–95: Selected to first team All-American three straight years

1994: United States Women's Amateur Champion

1997: Won her first tournament: the Fieldcrest Cannon Classic

1998: Best money year at $342,500

Salvation

Wendy, the product of a Christian home, trusted Jesus when she was a young child. However, her faith stayed somewhat in the background until she was encouraged in her faith by her golf coach, Lori Brock. She asked Wendy to attend an FCA meeting on campus. Wendy was energized by that, and she felt that the Holy Spirit was guiding her to live more completely for Jesus.

Family and personal: Husband, Nate Hair. Nate has competed on the Nike Tour in the past.

BARB WHITEHEAD

First year on the tour: 1983

Hometown: Scottsdale, Ariz.
College: University of Tulsa

Highlights

1980: Named All-American at Tulsa
1982: Finished third in NCAA championship
1997: Member of LPGA Executive Committee
1998: Recorded two holes in one

Salvation

Although she grew up in a Christian home, Barb's faith didn't become a personal thing until she was in college. A college teammate, Kathy Baker, stopped by one day after church and told her about a question the pastor had offered that day. Kathy told her the pastor said, "If you were to die today, do you know that you'd go to heaven?" Barb wasn't sure she could answer that question in the affirmative, so that night Kathy helped guide her to a saving faith in Jesus Christ. Kathy Baker-Guadagnino and Wendy see each other regularly as fellow LPGA golfers.

Family: Husband, Trent
Ministries: Has been involved with other LPGA golfers on missions trips to Romania

NATIONAL HOCKEY LEAGUE

BOB BASSEN

Chicago Blackhawks, St. Louis Blues, Dallas Stars, Calgary Flames
Rightwing

High school: Sir Winston Churchill (Calgary, Ala.)

Highlights

1986–88: Played in 125 straight NHL games
1994: Had a three-game goal-scoring streak

Salvation

At a summer camp, Bob Bassen became a follower of Christ. Counselors explained to Bob and his campmates that although they came from Christian homes, they had to make a decision to trust Christ on their own. "I did that because I didn't want to miss eternal life."

Family and personal: Wife, Holly. Bob's dad, Hank, tended goal for Chicago, Pittsburgh, and Detroit in the NHL.
Ministries: Hockey Ministries International

LAURIE BOSCHMAN

Retired after the 1994 season
Toronto Maple Leafs, Edmonton Oilers, Winnipeg Jets, New Jersey Devils
Center

Hometown: Major, Saskatchewan
Draft: Selected in the first round by the Toronto Maple Leafs in the 1979 draft

Highlights

1979: Member of WHL All-Star team
1984-85: Scored a career-high 32 goals for the Jets

Salvation

Boschman accepted Christ as Savior as a rookie in the NHL after he was impressed by the peace of fellow Maple Leaf player Ron Ellis. The veteran Ellis invited Boschman to a Bible study led by Mel Stevens. Boschman was intrigued by what he heard, and by the time the evening was over, he had prayed to trust Jesus. "I don't know how many times I've said to my wife," Boschman says, "how fortunate I am that God revealed Himself to me at that time."

Family: Wife, Nancy; and two children, Brent and Mark

KEITH BROWN

Retired after the 1995 season
Chicago Blackhawks, Florida Panthers
Defenseman

Hometown: Corner Brook, Newfoundland
Draft: Selected in the first round of the 1979 entry draft by the Chicago Blackhawks

Highlights

1978: WHL Rookie of the Year
1991: Scored 300th career point
1994: Nominated for the Nill Masterton trophy

Salvation

Keith did not grow up in a Christian family, and he thought hockey was everything. Until 1983. That's when he realized that "there has to be more to life than hockey." So that year, soon after he and his wife attended a church in Elmhurst, Ill., and heard the gospel, he trusted Jesus. "How it changed my life is incredible," he says.

Family: Wife, Debbie; and one child, Christy
Ministries: Hockey Ministries International Christian Athlete Hockey Camps

ADAM BURT

Hartford Whalers/Carolina Hurricanes
Defenseman

Hometown: Detroit, Mich.
Draft: Selected in the second round by the Hartford Whalers in the 1987 draft

Highlights

1991–92: Had best scoring season with 24 points
1994–95: Led as captain of the Hartford Whalers

Salvation

When Adam was a preteen, his parents divorced. His mom, searching for meaning in her life, began attending a church. There, she accepted Christ as her Savior. She began taking her children to that church. One night, after Adam had viewed a movie about the end of the world from a Christian perspective, he accepted the pastor's invitation to be saved.

Family: Wife, Susan; and two daughters, Cassandra and Elizabeth

SHANE DOAN

Winnipeg Jets/Phoenix Coyotes
Rightwing

Hometown: Eston, Saskatchewan
Draft: Selected in the first round by the Winnipeg Jets in the 1995 draft

Highlights

1994–96: Won Stafford Smyth Trophy (WHL)
1995–96: Scored 17 points in his rookie season
1995–96: Named Winnipeg Jets Rookie of the Year

Salvation

Shane grew up in a family that ran a church camp in Canada. He trusted Jesus Christ as his Savior as a youngster.

Family and personal: Single. Shane's cousin is married to Catriona Le May Doan, Canadian Gold Medal speedskater.

JOHN DRUCE

Washington Capitals, Winnipeg Jets, Los Angeles Kings, Philadelphia Flyers
Rightwing

Hometown: Peterborough, Ontario
Draft: Selected in the second round by the Washington Capitals in the 1985 draft

Highlights

1991–94: Scored hat tricks each year
1990, 1991: Scored career-high 58 points

Salvation

When John played for the Los Angeles Kings, one of the people who influenced him in matters of faith was Peter Millar, the team trainer. Others also talked to John about Jesus Christ. Finally, a friend realized that John knew everything he needed to know; he needed to trust Christ. So, when he asked John to pray and put his faith in Jesus, John did so.

Family: Wife, Chantel; and two daughters, Courtney and Natalie

MIKE EAGLES

Quebec Nordiques, Chicago Blackhawks, Winnipeg Jets, Washington Capitals
Center

Hometown: Sussex, New Brunswick
Draft: Selected in the sixth round by the Quebec Nordiques in the 1981 draft

Highlights

1986–87: Scored a career-high 19 goals
1997–98: Scored two points in the play-offs for the Capitals

Salvation

"I try to live my life as if Jesus was living inside me. I try to make the choices He would make. I know that's not going to happen all the time. But the person I'm trying to model myself after is not just any person—it's Jesus."

Family and personal: Wife, Anne Marie; and two sons, Matthew and Christopher. Mike enjoys cycling, wind surfing, and tennis.
Ministries: Hockey Ministries International Christian Athlete Hockey Camps

MIKE GARTNER

Retired after the 1998 season
Washington Capitals, Minnesota North Stars, New York Rangers, Toronto Maple Leafs, Phoenix Coyotes
Rightwing

Hometown: Ottawa
Draft: Selected in the first round by the Washington Capitals in the 1979 draft

Highlights

1980, 1985,1986, 1990, 1993, 1996: Played in 6 NHL All-Star Games
1993: Named All-Star Game Most Valuable Player
1979–94: Set NHL record for most consecutive 30-goal seasons (15)

Salvation

Like Ryan Walter, Mike Gartner came to faith in Jesus Christ through the leadership of Jean Pronovost of the Washington Capitals. While playing with the Caps, Gartner felt that his life, although successful, was missing something. Pronovost guided Gartner and Walter through a Bible study, and Mike understood the gospel. Soon Gartner had trusted Jesus as his Savior.

Family: Wife, Colleen; and three children, Joshua, Dylan, and Natalie
Ministries: Hockey Ministries International Christian Athlete Hockey Camps

STU GRIMSON

Calgary Flames, Chicago Blackhawks, Anaheim Mighty Ducks, Detroit Red Wings, Hartford Whalers/Carolina Hurricanes, Mighty Ducks
Leftwing

Hometown: Kamloops, British Columbia
College: University of Manitoba
Draft: Selected in the tenth round by the Detroit Red Wings in 1983

Highlights

1991: Scored his first NHL goal off Mike Vernon on October 24
1998: Played in his 500th NHL game on April 11

Salvation

Growing up in Kamloops, Stu and his parents attended church. He says he had heard about Jesus Christ and about Bible stories, but he didn't really understand the importance of Jesus' death on the Cross. When Grimson went to his first pro hockey camp, he was given a copy of *Breakaway,* a collection of profiles of hockey players. Through reading the book, he recognized that he needed to trust Jesus Christ as his Savior. He soon prayed to put his faith in Jesus.

Family: Wife, Pam; and three children, Erin, Hannah, and Kristjan
Ministries: Hockey Ministries International Christian Athlete Hockey Camps

MARKUS NASLUND

Pittsburgh Penguins, Vancouver Canucks
Leftwing

Hometown: Harnosand, Sweden
Draft: Selected in the first round by the Pittsburgh Penguins in the 1991 draft

Highlights

1995-96: Scored career-high 52 points in 66 games
1995-96: Had his lone career hat trick

Salvation

The product of a Christian home, Naslund trusted Christ as his Savior as a youngster growing up in Sweden.

Family and personal: Wife, Lotta. Favorite book of the Bible is Proverbs, or as it is known in his native homeland of Sweden: "Advice for Young Men."
Ministries: Works with Hockey Ministries International in their hockey camps

MARK OSBORNE

Retired after the 1994 season
Detroit Red Wings, New York Rangers, Toronto Maple Leafs, Winnipeg Jets, Maple Leafs

Hometown: Toronto, Ontario
Draft: Selected forty-sixth by the Detroit Red Wings in the 1980 entry draft

Highlights

1981, 1982: Scored a career-high 26 goals for Detroit
1993: Played in 19 play-off games for Toronto

Salvation

The death of his uncle in a car wreck led Mark to begin wondering about his own fate. "I wondered what would happen to me if I died," he says. About a year later, a Billy Graham staff member spoke at Mark's church. He made it clear to the teenager that he was a sinner and that he needed to get things straight with God. "I knew the Holy Spirit was knocking at my heart," Osborne says. "It wasn't easy to step forward" at the time of the invitation, but he did. He was saved that day.

Family: Wife, Madolyn; and one child, Abigail
Ministries: Hockey Ministries International Christian Athlete Hockey Camps

CHICO RESCH

Retired after the 1986 season
New York Islanders, Colorado Rockies, New Jersey Devils, Philadelphia Flyers
Goaltender

Hometown: Moosejaw, Saskatchewan
Draft: Played before the draft era

Highlights

1976, 1977, 1984: Selected to three NHL All-Star teams
1980: Member of the Stanley Cup champion New York Islanders

Salvation

The first seed of interest in Jesus Christ was planted in Chico's life early in his career when a minor-league teammate, Don Liesemer (now head of Hockey Ministries International) invited Resch to listen to Billy Zeoli, a noted sports chapel speaker. A few years later, Chico and his wife Diane attended a Pro Athletes Outreach conference. There the two of them accepted Jesus Christ as Savior.

Family and personal: Wife, Diane; and one child, Holly. Chico now is a coach in the NHL.
Ministries: Hockey Ministries International

JOHN VANBIESBROUCK

New York Rangers, Florida Panthers, Philadelphia Flyers
Goalkeeper

Hometown: Detroit, Mich.
Draft: Selected in the fourth round by the New York Rangers in the 1981 draft

Highlights

1985–86: Won the Vezina Trophy, named to All-Star first team
1994, 1995, 1996: Played in three consecutive All-Star Games

Salvation

First, his wife trusted Jesus after attending church soon after the Vanbiesbroucks moved to Florida so John could play for the Panthers. Not long after that, Roger Neilson, the Panthers' coach, helped Steve Debardelaben establish chapel. While attending chapel and listening to chaplain Steve, John too trusted Christ.

Family and personal: Wife, Rosalinde; and three children Ian, Benjamin, and Nicholas. John is a big Detroit Tigers fan.

RYAN WALTER

Retired after the 1993 season
Washington Capitals, Montreal Canadians
Center/Leftwing

Hometown: New Westminster, British Columbia
Draft: Selected first by the Washington Capitals in the 1978 draft

Highlights

1978: WHL Most Valuable Player
1978: WHL Player of the Year
1992: NHL Man of the Year

Salvation

When young Ryan was sent to the Washington Capitals, he was warned to keep an eye on Jean Pronovost because he was one of those "born-again Christians." So, Ryan watched him. He was not repulsed. He was impressed. Pronovost and Walter began discussing matters of faith. Ryan was an up-and-coming star in the NHL, but he had fears about what would happen to him if he were to die. Pronovost calmly shared the gospel with Ryan, and before the season was over, Walter was praying in a hotel room in Edmonton, asking Jesus to forgive him and save him.

Family and personal: Wife, Jennifer; and three children, Benjamin, Christiana, and Ryan Jr. Ryan owns a company that builds indoor ice rinks.
Ministries: Hockey Ministries International Christian Athlete Hockey Camps

NASCAR

JEFF GORDON

Dupont No. 24

Hometown: Pittsboro, Ind.

Highlights

1994: Won his first Winston Cup race
1995, 1997, 1998: Finished first in Winston Cup
1997: Won more than $6 million
1998: Won his third points championship

Salvation

Belief in God was nothing new to Jeff Gordon when he met Brooke, now his wife but then Miss Winston. He had even been an occasional Bible reader. But Brooke, along with Motor Racing Outreach director Max Helton, showed Jeff that he needed more. They showed him that he needed to make a personal commitment to Jesus Christ, which he did in the early part of his NASCAR career.

Family: Wife, Brooke
Ministries: Motor Racing Outreach

BOBBY HILLIN

No. 8

Hometown: Midland, Tex.

Highlights

1982: Drove at North Wilkesboro NASCAR race at age seventeen

1986: Won Talladega 500 at age twenty-two

Salvation

As a teenager, Bobby Hillin was convinced that he was a pretty good guy. After all, his dad had taught him not to lie. But when Hillin began attending Young Life meetings at his high school, he began to learn about the Bible and about the gospel. He discovered that no matter how good he was, it wasn't good enough. "I learned that I still had a sin nature. I knew I wasn't right in God's eyes." Hillin didn't become a Christian then, but a few years later, in 1985 while attending a Bible study with other drivers, he accepted Christ as his Savior.

Family and personal: Wife, Kim; and two children, Luke and Stephanie. Drives a car sponsored by major league baseball players

Ministries: Motor Racing Outreach

ERNIE IRVAN

Retired during the 1999 season
Skittles No. 36

Hometown: Salinas, Calif.

Highlights

1990: Won first Winston Cup race

1991: Went over $1 million in earnings for first time

1996: Came back from a serious injury to finish 10th on the earnings list

Salvation

Max Helton has led many Sunday chapel services at NASCAR races. But one of them is extra special to Ernie Irvan. It's the one after which Ernie pulled Max aside and asked him to tell him more about this idea of accepting Jesus as Savior. Max explained, and Ernie drank it in. "I gave myself to Christ," Ernie says. "It was the biggest thing I ever did."

Family: Wife, Kim; and one child, Jordan

DALE JARRETT

Ford Quality Care No. 88

Hometown: Hickory, N.C.

Highlights

1993, 1996: Won the Daytona 500
1997: Finished second in Winston Cup
1997: Won seven races

Salvation

Growing up in a Christian family, Dale Jarrett readily accepted the teachings of his parents. It wasn't until he was married and under the spiritual influence of Joe Gibbs that he made a personal decision to trust Jesus Christ and commit his life to Him. That was in 1992. "We decided once and for all that this is the way it was going to be—that God had led us in this direction for a reason."

Family: Wife, Kelley; and four children, Jason, Natalee, Karsyn, and Zachary

---

NED JARRETT

Retired in 1966 from racing
TV announcer, former NASCAR champion driver

Hometown: Newton, N.C.

Highlights

1961: NASCAR points champion
1965: NASCAR points champion

Salvation

"I grew up in a Christian family. Dad and Mom took us to church every Sunday and they tried to teach us right from wrong. But there comes a time in your life when you need to make a personal commitment to the Lord." For Ned, that came in 1959 while he was out for his daily jog. "I just stopped right in the street and prayed. Jesus came into my life and gave me direction."

Family and personal: Wife, Martha; and three children, Glenn, Dale, and Patti Makar (wife of NASCAR crew chief Jimmy Makar). One highlight of Ned's announcing career was the opportunity he had to broadcast Dale's first victory at the Daytona 500.
Ministries: DARE and other public-speaking opportunities

MARK MARTIN

Valvoline No. 6

Hometown: Batesville, Ark.

Highlights

1990: Finished second in standings ($1,300,000)
1993: Won five Winston Cup races
1997: Won more than $2.5 million

Salvation

The death of a member of the larger NASCAR family sent Mark Martin on a soul-searching mission. He wanted to make sure that if anything happened to him, he would be ready. Because Martin had a church background, the idea of accepting Christ as Savior was not new. However, he had doubts that he truly had been saved. Therefore, he made sure of his commitment to Jesus Christ. At the same time, he realized that his closer relationship with Christ was what he needed to deal with other aspects of his life. Martin says his relationship with Christ makes "the tough times, the hard times more manageable."

Family: Wife, Arlene; and four children, Heather, Rachel, Stacy, and Matthew
Ministries: Motor Racing Outreach

LAKE SPEED

No. 9

Hometown: Jackson, Miss.

Highlights

1985: Best finish, tenth place in point standings
1988: Captured his lone Winston Cup victory
1994: Had 9 Top Ten finishes and won $832,000

Salvation

Lake Speed trusted Jesus Christ as his Savior in 1983 in his hometown of Jackson, Mississippi. "I went to a church, and I could tell that the people were joyful. I turned my life over to Jesus that day."

Family and personal: Wife, Reesa; and three children, Chambers, Sara Ann, and Maurie. Along with Darrell and Stevie Waltrip, Bobby and Kim Hillin, Lake and Reesa are founding couples of Motor Racing Outreach.
Ministries: Motor Racing Outreach

DARRELL WALTRIP

Big K No. 66

Hometown: Owensboro, Ky.

Highlights

1985: Finished atop the Winston Cup point standings

1989, 1990: Voted NASCAR's most popular driver

Salvation

It was a Wednesday night Bible study that caught Darrell Waltrip's spiritual attention. The year was 1983, and his wife was concerned that her hubby had his priorities all wrong. When Darrell attended the Bible study of Dr. Cortez Cooper, he found out she was right. "He was the first minister in my life who could make the Bible come alive." The night of that Bible study, Waltrip prayed to accept Christ as his Savior. He's been a witness in NASCAR ever since.

Family: Wife, Stevie; and three children, Jessica, Leigh, and Sarah
Ministries: Helped start Motor Racing Outreach

OLYMPIC SPORTS

CATRIONA LE MAY DOAN

Olympic speedskating

Hometown: Saskatoon, Saskatchewan

Highlights

1988, 1994: Raced for Canada in the Olympics Games

1996: Captured the World Championship

1998: Won Olympic gold at Nagano by setting a world record of 38.21 in the 500 meters

Salvation

While in Lillehammer for the 1994 Olympics, Catriona saw a sign for Athletes In Action. Thinking it was for her because she was an athlete, she went to the meeting and met Harold Cooper, a fellow Canadian. Harold explained the gospel to Catriona, and she trusted Jesus as her Savior.

Family and personal: Husband, Bart Doan. When Catriona met Bart, he was the Zamboni driver for the arena where she was training.
Ministries: Athletes in Action

BOB CTVRTLIK

Volleyball

Hometown: Long Beach, Calif.

Highlights

1986: Member, U.S. team, World Cup champs
1987: Member, U.S. team, Pan Am champs
1988: Member, U.S. Olympic team, Gold medal
1992, 1996: Member, U.S. Olympic team

Salvation

Volleyball Olympian Bob was brought up as a churchgoer, but he never really took the idea of the gospel to heart until 1988, when he was the youngest member of the U.S. team. During that time, though, faced with a great amount of pressure, he began earnestly reading the Bible. He discovered that his main need was to trust Jesus as Savior. He did, and he's been an eager witness for Christ since.

Family: Wife, Cosette; and two sons, Josef and Erik

JOSH DAVIS

Swimming

High school: Churchill High (San Antonio, Tex.)
College: University of Texas

Highlights

1996: Captured a gold medal in 400-meter freestyle medley at the Olympics Games in Atlanta
1996: Won Olympic gold medal in 800-meter freestyle medley

Salvation

Mike and Joan Davis had brought Josh up to understand the importance of morality and living right. But as an underclassman at the University of Texas, Josh thought it would be better for him to be a fence-sitter in matters of conviction. As his freshman year wound down, though, Josh became ill. He had time to think about what he was doing. "I had to look up to God. I was able to listen to Him," he says. "I responded to the truth that Jesus is who He says He is." Josh placed his faith in Jesus Christ.

Family: Wife, Shantel; and one child, Caleb

ROSALYNN SUMNERS

Figure skating

Hometown: Edmonds, Wash.

Highlights

1988: Won the Bronze medal in the Olympics
1996: Named Professional Skater of the Year

Salvation

While growing up, Rosalynn became a Christian at a young age. She stayed true to her faith—even journaling her faith journey leading up to the Olympics. Yet when she failed to win the gold medal in the 1988 Games, she became frustrated with God. For the next few years, she tried to make it on her own. "Looking back, I know that's a joke, because I was very unhappy." Things changed, though, when she and a friend listened to a CD by a group named Stryper. She noticed that the name of the group came from the verse that says, "By His stripes we are healed." She suddenly realized what Christ had done for her and how wrong she was to turn her back on Him. She rededicated her life to Jesus Christ that day.

Family and personal: Single. Rosalynn loves to read Christian books and pray. "I could do twenty-four hours of prayer."
Ministries: Has participated with Michael W. Smith and Paul Wylie in ministry efforts

SHEILA TAORMINA

Swimming

Hometown: Livonia, Mich.
College: University of Georgia

Highlights

1996: Won Olympic gold in 4 by 200 freestyle relay

Salvation

It took six years of interest in God's Word and the witness of friends before Sheila trusted Christ. Just one year before her Olympic gold-medal-winning performance, she met with a pastor who clearly explained the gospel to her. During that meeting, Sheila trusted Christ.

Family: Single

PAUL WYLIE

Retired after the 1998 season
Figure skating

College: Harvard

Highlights

1988: Competed for the U.S. in the Olympics in Calgary
1992: Captured the silver medal at the Olympics Games in Albertville
1992: Received Clairol Personal Best Award at the Olympics
1993–98: Skated with Discover Stars on Ice

Salvation

While attending a church service while a student at Harvard, Wylie was touched by a concept presented by the pastor. The preacher explained that God really heard and answered prayer. Wylie was touched by this idea because he knew he needed God. He knew he was lost. "I realized that for Christ to truly live in me and me in Him, I had to accept His gift of spiritual birth." His new faith was spurred on by the surprising number of fellow Christians he found on the Harvard campus.

Family: Single
Ministries: Has been involved with the Billy Graham Crusades

SOCCER

MICHELLE AKERS

Hometown: Orlando, Fla.
College: Central Florida University

Highlights

1985–88: All-American at Central Florida
1988: Hermann Trophy (Best college soccer player)
1991: Leading scorer at World Cup
1996: Member Olympic gold medal
1998: Awarded FIFA Medal of Merit

Salvation

A high school teacher led Michelle to faith in Christ when she was a teenager. Between then and twelve years later, after she had conquered the soccer world, she didn't grow spiritually. She knew, though, that her life was a mess. So, with the help of some friends and after spending some time of solitude in a cabin in the Cascade Mountains, Michelle rededicated her life to Jesus Christ. She has become a key figure in the sports world among those who are trying to evangelize through sports.

Family and personal: Single. During the 1996 Olympics, Michelle was suffering from chronic fatigue syndrome and had little energy with which to perform. Yet she never stopped working to help the United States win.
Ministries: Michelle's web site is a ministry tool: http://www.michelleakers.com

---

BRIAN McBRIDE

Columbus Crew

High school: Arlington Heights (Ill.) High
College: St. Louis University
Draft: Selected in the 1995 MLS draft

Highlights

1993: Became St. Louis University's all-time leading scorer (184)
1998: Played for U.S. National team in the World Cup
1999: Became all-time leading scorer in Crew history

Salvation

"I don't play for myself, I play for the Lord. Being a Christian has helped me be a better person."

Family: Single.

MIKE LAPPER

Columbus Crew

High school: Huntington Beach (Calif.) High
College: UCLA
Draft: Allocated to the Crew in June 1997

Highlights

1991: First team All-American
1994: Played on the U.S. World Cup team
1995–96: Played for Southend, First Division, England

Salvation

Lapper trusted Christ as a boy growing up in Southern California. "I put God first and leave my frustrations on the field."

Family and personal: Single. Missed much of the 1998 season and part of 1999 because of a serious knee problem

ROY LASSITER

Tampa Bay Mutiny, D.C. United

High school: Raleigh (N.C.) High
College: North Carolina State
Draft: Not available

Highlights

1995: Scored his first goal for U.S. National team
1995: Costa Rica, First Division, Foreigner of the Year
1996: Played in MLS All-Star Game

Salvation

In 1995, after establishing himself as a star soccer player, Lassiter turned to Christ through the influence of his mother. "I was in church with her when the Holy Spirit convicted me, and I received Jesus as my Savior."

Family: Wife, Wendy; and one son, Ariel Daniel

CLAUDIO TAFFAREL

Brazilian national team
Goalkeeper

Hometown: Belo Horizonte, Brazil

Highlights

1988: Won a silver medal in the Olympics
1994: Stopped Baggio in a shootout as the Brazilians won the World Cup
1998: Was Brazil's goalkeeper as they finished second to France in the World Cup

Salvation

As a professional soccer player in Brazil, Claudio Taffarel had fulfilled his childhood dream in 1984. While playing in Brazil's Junior League, he was introduced to the gospel through a Bible study he attended with other players. "After hearing about Jesus, I understood that only He could give me the satisfaction I had dreamed of," Taffarel says. It wasn't long until, as he explains, "I accepted His death for me as the only way to salvation."

Family: Wife, Andrea; and two children, Catherine and E. Claudio
Ministries: Atleticas de Cristo

TENNIS

NICOLE ARENDT

Hometown: Somerville, N.J.
College: University of Florida

Highlights

1997: Reached the third round of Wimbledon
1997: Won 13 doubles tournaments; reached No. 3 ranking in doubles

Salvation

It wasn't until Nicole became a pro tennis player that she turned her life over to Jesus Christ. She was facing numerous difficulties, and she knew she didn't have the answers. "There was such an emptiness," she says. Finally, she turned her heart over to Jesus. "If you don't have faith in Jesus," she says, "it's difficult to deal with things."

Family: Single

MARGARET COURT

Retired in 1976
Australia

Highlights

1961–75: Ranked in the world's Top Ten
1970: Won tennis's Grand Slam (Wimbledon, French Open, U.S. Open, Australian Open)
1970: Won all three Wimbledon titles (singles, doubles, mixed doubles)

Salvation

In 1973, a close friend on the pro tennis tour studied the Bible with Margaret and gave her some Christian literature to read. Through that influence, Margaret gave her life to Jesus Christ that year. About five years later, a serious heart problem got her attention, and she got really serious about her faith—even going to a Bible college to learn more.

Family: Husband, Barry; and four children, Daniel, Marika, Theresa, and Lisa
Personal: Margaret's life story was told in the book *A Winning Faith,* published in 1993.

MICHAEL CHANG

Hometown: Hoboken, N.J.

Highlights

1987: Became youngest winner of a main draw match at the U.S. Open
1989: Became the youngest winner of the French Open
1996: Reached the No. 2 ranking in the world

Salvation

Michael became a Christian when he was fifteen years old. His grandparents had given him a Bible, and he dug into it to see what it said. As he looked up some words in it, words such as friendship and love, Michael was impressed with Jesus' love for people. That led to his putting his faith in Jesus Christ as his Savior.

Family: Single

Ministries: Michael's web site contains a gospel presentation at www.mchang.com

---

MARY JOE FERNANDEZ

Hometown: Miami, Fla.

Highlights

1985: Won a U.S. Open match at the age of fourteen
1992, 1994: Won Olympic gold in doubles
1997: Won German Open

Salvation

When she realized that the faith of her parents was not enough to get her through life and that she needed a faith of her own, Mary Joe turned to the Bible. A friend recommended the gospel of John, which she read. Also, a book called *Power for Living,* which quoted celebrities talking about their faith, influenced her. "It hit me that I needed to make a commitment to Christ," which is what she did. Now, she says, "Everything I do is for His glory."

Family: Single

MEREDITH McGRATH

Hometown: Midland, Mich.
College: Stanford University

Highlights

1989: Was 26–0 for Stanford in singles
1990: Named pro tennis's Rookie of the Year by *Tennis* magazine
1994: Selected WTA Comeback Player of the Year

Salvation

While on a rehabilitation stint during the early years of her career, Meredith met a woman named Maggie Charlton. Maggie and Meredith became friends, even to the point that Meredith moved into the Charlton home with Maggie, her husband, and their three children. There Meredith was introduced to Christianity. "Jesus was the center of everything," she says. It wasn't long until Meredith put her faith in Christ too.

Family and personal: Single. Injuries have hampered Meredith in her attempts to make it big on the pro tennis circuit.

KERI PHEBUS

Hometown: Newport Beach, Calif.
College: UCLA

Highlights

1995: Won NCAA singles and doubles titles
1997: Won the ITF/Woodland Tournament, Texas

Salvation

"I grew up in a Christian home. I was surrounded by Christian people. But it wasn't until college that I had to decide if I was going to walk with the Lord or live for myself." When she attended an Athletes in Action camp while in college, however, she participated in an activity that impressed upon her the significance of Jesus' sacrifice on the Cross. Finally, she prayed to give her life to Jesus.

Family: Single

STAN SMITH

Retired after the 1983 season

Hometown: Pasadena, Calif.
College: University of Southern California

Highlights

1968, 1974, 1978, 1980: Won the U.S. Open doubles championship
1970: Won Australian Open doubles
1973: Ranked third in the world

Salvation

While a sophomore at USC, Stan began to hear from some of his friends about Jesus. This was a new, fresh idea to Stan, that a relationship with Jesus could change his life. That year, Stan put his faith in Jesus Christ.

Family: Wife, Margie; and four children, Ramsey, Trevor, and two daughters

---

DAVID WHEATON

Hometown: Lake Minnetoka, Minn.
College: Stanford University

Highlights

1988: Played No. 1 singles and doubles for Stanford's NCAA national championship team
1990: Won first tour singles title, Kiawah Island
1991: Had highest ranking: 17th in the world

Salvation

David was just six years old when he realized what the gospel meant, and he trusted Christ as his Savior. However, as the years went by and as his tennis career was moving upward, Wheaton lived a life of partial commitment to the Lord. When he was twenty-three, Wheaton realized that he was not making Jesus the Lord of his life, and he recommitted his life to Christ.

Family: Single

LINDA WILD

Hometown: Chicago, Ill.
College: University of Southern California

Highlights

1996: Highest ranking: 23rd in the world
1996: Won three tournaments on the Corel Tour

Salvation

As a high school student, Linda read the Bible, went to church, and even thought she was a Christian. However, when she went to USC, she felt that there was a hole in her life that nothing was filling. Her dad gave her a book by Josh McDowell, and at the end of the book, she read a sinner's prayer that would guide the reader to a personal relationship with Jesus Christ. Linda prayed that prayer, asking God to forgive her sins and to accept her through what Jesus did for her on the cross. "When Christ came into my life," she says, "I felt at peace."

Family: Single

TRACK AND FIELD

KRISS AKABUSI

Track

Hometown: Southhampton, England

Highlights

1984: Won the silver medal as part of the 4 x 400 team for Great Britain
1987: Won the World Games Silver medal in the 4 x 400 relay
1990: Set British record in the 400-meter hurdles

Salvation

As a successful young athlete, Kriss discovered that each goal he achieved only left him empty for something more. He began his search for meaning by taking ten months to study what Jesus said in the Bible. He grew convinced of the truth of Jesus' teachings and that Jesus died on the cross for the sins of mankind. In 1987, Kriss prayed to trust Christ as Savior and he understood that God had given him meaning in life.

Family and personal: Wife, Monica; and two children, Ashani and Shakira. When not training and running, Kriss is a warrant officer in the Army Physical Training Corps in England.
Ministries: Christians in Sports

JEAN DRISCOLL

Wheelchair marathon

Hometown: Champaign, Ill.
College: University of Illinois, Champaign-Urbana

Highlights

1990: Goodwill Games gold medalist
1990–96: Won the Boston Marathon seven straight years
1998: Finished second in the Boston Marathon

Salvation

Jean Driscoll, who was born with spina bifida, has used a wheelchair since she was a teenager. Her situation has meant several hospital stays. During one hospitalization, at a time when she was depressed about the problems she faced, she met a nurse named Lori O'Brien. Lori invited Jean to live in her home to help with Lori's children. When Jean did that, Lori explained to Jean what it means to become a Christian. Jean liked what she heard and prayed to trust Christ. Nothing much happened spiritually, for a while. In 1992, six years later, she met a woman named Debbie Richardson who was organizing a special day for Jean in Champaign, Illinois. She too was a Christian, and she invited Jean to church, where Jean rededicated her life to Christ. Since then, she has taken her faith seriously.

Family and personal: Single. When Jean finished second in the 1998 Boston Marathon after being ahead up until the final seconds, she said, "I thought Jesus would carry me to victory, but I discovered that He was going to carry me through the defeat." She was able to witness through her calm demeanor after the disappointing defeat.

JONATHAN EDWARDS

Triple jump
Great Britain

Highlights

1988, 1992, 1996: Competed in three consecutive Olympic Games
1995: Set the world record in the triple jump

Salvation

The son of a British pastor, or vicar, Jonathan knew about faith in Christ from an early age. He noticed the difference Christ made in his parents' lives, and that influenced him to trust Jesus too.

Family: Wife, Alison; and two sons, Samuel and Nathan
Ministries: Christians in Sports

DAVE JOHNSON

Decathalon

Hometown: Corvallis, Ore.

Highlights

1987: Won World University Games decathlon
1992: Captured the bronze medal in the Olympics in decathlon

Salvation

While a high school student in Corvallis, Oregon, Dave Johnson was a hotshot athlete who often got into trouble. One of his teammates, though, caught Dave's attention because he was different from the others. He didn't involve himself with the usual vices of high school kids, and Dave was impressed with that. His name was Matt Hirte, and he was not ashamed to talk to Dave about Jesus Christ. The more Dave heard and saw of Matt, the more he thought about his own life and his spiritual needs. It wasn't long before Dave too trusted Jesus Christ as Savior.

Family: Wife, Sheri

ELANA MEYER

Marathon
South Africa

College: Stellenbosch University (South Africa)

Highlights

1991: Set South Africa record for 3,000 meters (8 min. 32 seconds)
1992: Olympic silver medalist in the 10,000 meters

Salvation

Elana accepted Jesus Christ as her Savior during her first year of high school. However, she struggled to be assured of her relationship. She felt that when she let God down, she had to accept Christ again. While in college, she began to have fellowship with some Christians who showed her that she could have assurance of salvation. She realized that once she had trusted Christ, she was His child.

Family: Husband, Michael

MADELINE MIMS

800 meters

Hometown: Tulsa, Okla.
College: Tennessee State University

Highlights

1968: Won the 800 meters gold medal

Salvation

Madeline's mother made sure she was in church each Sunday, and it paid off. When she was just six years old, after watching her Sunday school teacher show her a picture of Jesus holding a small, black lamb, Madeline asked if Jesus could hold her in the same way. Assured that Jesus would, Madeline prayed and accepted Him as her Savior. Her childlike faith has brought her through more than forty-five years of trusting in Him.

Family: Husband, Roderick; and two children, John and Lana
Ministries: Friendship Fellowship (see Chapter 6 "Resources")

JIM RYUN

Mile

Hometown: Wichita, Kans.
College: University of Kansas

Highlights

1964: Ran a sub-4-minute mile at age seventeen; ran for U.S. in the summer Olympics
1968: Won a silver medal at the Olympic Games in Mexico
1972: Appeared in third Olympics Games

Salvation

When Jim Ryun failed to win the gold medal at the Olympics the first two times, he disappointed a lot of people. Struggling to find peace of mind, he and his wife Anne began reading the Bible and investigating Christianity. He found acceptance in Jesus Christ, for he felt that Christ was saying, "I love you because I love you, not because of the athletic achievements." Three months before competing in his third Olympics in Munich, Jim and Anne Ryun trusted Christ as Savior.

Family and personal: Wife, Anne; and four children, Heather, Ned, Drew, and Catharine. Jim recently won a seat in the U.S. House of Representatives.

MISCELLANEOUS

JEREMY BAYE

Snowboarding

Highlights

1996: Named Best Snowboarder by *Hudson Valley Magazine*
1997: Finished second in the Japan Open

Salvation

"I grew up in a Christian home," Jeremy says. He also says that he trusted Jesus as his Savior when he was eight years old. Prayer has been an important part of his life. "Ever since I was little, God has really shown Himself to me through prayer," he says.

Family: Single

CHRISTY CARLSON

Jet-Ski champion

Hometown: Chicago, Ill.

Highlights

1989–93, 1996: National Jet-Ski champion
1989–92, 1996: World Champion Jet-Ski racer

Salvation

When Christy Carlson's mom became a Christian, she grew concerned about her teenage daughter and sons. When she found out about a get-together for Christian teens, she sent Christy and her brothers. The speaker told them that if they didn't put their faith in Christ, they couldn't go to heaven. As churchgoing kids who thought they were all right, this was a revelation. "By the end of the weekend," Christy says, "all of us were stricken about our condition by the Holy Spirit." All in the same evening, the Carlson kids accepted Christ's sacrifice for their sins.

Family and personal: Husband, Leon Wolek. After conquering the jet-ski world, Christy also tried her hand at auto racing.

CLAY O'BRIEN COOPER

Rodeo (team roping)

Hometown: Phoenix, Ariz.

Highlights

1985: Cooper, teaming with partner Jake Barnes, recorded the fastest time ever for a roping (4.3 seconds).

Salvation

As a teenager, Clay accepted Jesus as his Savior with his dad doing the leading. Later, while in the early years of his rodeo career, he realized that he had lost some of his spiritual fervor. Through the people at the Pro Rodeo Ministry, he got back on track with God. "The closer I get to Jesus and the more I get to know Him, the more it changes my perspective on life," he says.

Family: Wife, Beth; and two children, Bailey and Quinn

TONY MUSE

In-line skating

Hometown: Des Moines, Iowa

Highlights

1985–96: Won gold medal in World Games
1985–87, 1990, 1991, 1994: Won gold medal in Olympic Festival
1987, 1991, 1995: Captured gold medal in Pan American Games

Salvation

In the mid-1990s, Tony Muse accepted Christ as his Savior through the influence of his wife, Cassandra. Although he was saved, he wasn't gung ho about his faith until his wife gave him another assist. When he was getting ready to skate for a world title, she slipped a dcTalk tape into his Walkman. The tape contained the song "Free At Last." Tony was a self-professed fence-straddling Christian at that point in his life. The tape encouraged him to put Christ first in his life.

Family and personal: Wife, Cassandra; and three children, Gabrielle, Rachel, and Antony. "I no longer skate for myself," Tony says. "I skate for Christ."

DAVE SADOWSKI

Motorcyling

Hometown: Bethseda, Md.

Highlights

1986: Won the National Endurance Championship
1990: Captured the Daytona 200
1990: Crowned the AMA 600 Supersport champion

Salvation

He had recently won the prestigious Daytona 200, but Sadowski was troubled by the fact that although he was somewhat religious, he wasn't a Christian. A friend, David Frederick, invited Sadowski to church. There, the motorcycle champ heard about the importance of accepting Jesus Christ as Lord and Savior. "I realized that Jesus had died and shed His blood for me," Sadowski says of his coming to faith.

Family: Wife, Beverly; and two sons, Matthew and Davey

Chapter 4

ATHLETE BIRTHDAYS

Like noses, everybody has one. Birthdays, that is. That's one reason we are so interested in knowing when other people celebrate their births. For sports fans, there is something special about sharing a birthday with a favorite athlete. In some small way, that fact gives fans a connection with athletes.

As you look over this listing of athletes' birthdays, perhaps you will find your own day and discover that you share it with someone you already know about. But even if you don't, you can put this information to good use. You could send cards to your favorite athletes as their birthdays approach. Or you could use this list as a prayer reminder, giving you a pattern to follow as you pray for God to protect, guide, and bless the chosen athletes. It's no secret that they need God's help as they try to live for Him.

JANUARY

January 1, 1973
Justin Armour
National Football League

January 2, 1963
Edgar Martinez
Major League Baseball

January 3, 1962
Darren Daulton
Major League Baseball

January 5, 1965
Mark Dewey
Major League Baseball

January 6, 1960
Paul Azinger
Professional Golfers' Association

January 9, 1959
Mark Martin
NASCAR

January 13, 1959
Ernie Irvan
NASCAR

January 14, 1972
Kyle Brady
National Football League

January 15, 1969
Adam Burt
National Hockey League

January 17, 1948
Lake Speed
NASCAR

January 19, 1969
Junior Seau
National Football League

January 20, 1968
Nick Anderson
National Basketball Association

January 21, 1946
Johnny Oates
Major League Baseball

January 22, 1961
Barb Whitehead
Ladies Professional Golf Association

January 25, 1966
Mark Schlereth
National Football League

January 27, 1968
Matt Stover
National Football League

January 29, 1968
Aeneas Williams
National Football League

January 31, 1968
Michael Sinclair
National Football League

Doug Pederson
National Football League

FEBRUARY

February 1, 1966
Michelle Akers
Soccer

February 1, 1973
Andrew DeClecq
National Basketball Association

February 5, 1947
Darrell Waltrip
NASCAR

February 10, 1970
Bobby J. Jones
Major League Baseball

February 11, 1971
Linda Wild
Tennis

February 12, 1963
Brent Jones
National Football League

February 13, 1966
John Druce
National Hockey League

February 13, 1968
Matt Mieske
Major League Baseball

February 14, 1973
Tyus Edney
National Basketball Association

February 15, 1960
Darrell Green
National Football League

February 15, 1964
Mark Price
National Basketball Association

February 19, 1959
Tim Burke
Major League Baseball

February 19, 1966
William White
National Football League

February 19, 1971
Glyn Milburn
National Football League

February 22, 1972
Michael Chang
Tennis

February 29, 1968
Bryce Paup
National Football League

MARCH

March 2, 1962
Terry Steinbach
Major League Baseball

March 3, 1962
Herschel Walker
National Football League

March 4, 1966
Kevin Johnson
National Basketball Association

March 5, 1961
Steve Ontiveros
Major League Baseball

March 6, 1962
Alison Nicholas
Ladies Professional Golf Association

March 7, 1959
Tom Lehman
Professional Golfers' Association

March 7, 1960
Joe Carter
Major League Baseball

March 7, 1963
Mike Eagles
National Hockey League

March 8, 1960
Buck Williams
National Basketball League

March 12, 1970
Rex Walters
National Basketball League

March 13, 1972
Trent Dilfer
National Football League

March 18, 1969
Sheila Taormina
Swimming

March 20, 1961
Kathy Guadagnino
Ladies Professional Golf Association

March 21, 1968
Scott Williams
National Basketball Association

March 22, 1966
Brad Edwards
National Football League

March 22, 1969
Russell Maryland
National Football League

March 22, 1973
Luther Elliss
National Football League

March 24, 1961
Jim Gallagher Jr.
Professional Golfers' Association

March 25, 1965
Avery Johnson
National Basketball Association

March 25, 1969
Travis Fryman
Major League Baseball
Scott Sanders
Major League Baseball
Dan Wilson
Major League Baseball

March 26, 1962
Kevin Seitzer
Major League Baseball

March 27, 1963
Randall Cunningham
National Football League

March 27, 1967
Tom Hammonds
National Basketball Association

March 28, 1967
Shawn Boskie
Major League Baseball

March 28, 1969
Elliot Perry
National Basketball Association

March 29, 1961
Mike Kingery
Major League Baseball

March 30, 1940
Jerry Lucas
National Basketball Association

APRIL

April 1, 1962
Rich Amaral
Major League Baseball

April 1, 1965
Mark Jackson
National Basketball Association

April 4, 1966
Darren Holmes
Major League Baseball

April 8, 1954
Gary Carter
Major League Baseball

April 10, 1962
Steve Tasker
National Football League

April 11, 1965
Turner Ward
Major League Baseball

April 13, 1964
Doug Strange
Major League Baseball

April 15, 1970
Darrin Smith
National Football League

April 15, 1971
Jason Sehorn
National Football League

April 17, 1972
Tony Boselli
National Football League

April 18, 1970
Rico Brogna
Major League Baseball

April 20, 1964
Rosalynn Sumners
Skating

April 20, 1973
Todd Hollandsworth
Major League Baseball

April 22, 1961
Jeff Hostetler
National Football League

April 25, 1966
Darren Holmes
Major League Baseball

April 25, 1970
Corwin Brown
National Football League

April 27, 1968
Patrick Lennon
Major League Baseball

April 28, 1971
Meredith McGrath
Tennis

April 29, 1971
Sterling Hitchcock
Major League Baseball

MAY

May 1, 1973
Curtis Martin
National Football League

May 1, 1974
Keri Phebus
Tennis

May 4, 1966
Randy Tolsma
NASCAR

May 5, 1970
LaPhonso Ellis
National Basketball Association

May 6, 1965
Bob Bassen
National Hockey League

May 6, 1973
Wendy Ward
Ladies Professional Golf Association

May 10, 1977
Amanda Borden
Gymnastics

May 12, 1935
Felipe Alou
Major League Baseball

May 15, 1956
Alice Miller
Ladies Professional Golf Association

May 15, 1967
John Smoltz
Major League Baseball

May 15, 1969
Emmitt Smith
National Football League

May 16, 1959
Bob Patterson
Major League Baseball

May 19, 1976
Brian Skinner
National Basketball Association

May 17, 1970
Hubert Davis
National Basketball Association

May 19, 1976
Brian Skinner
National Basketball Association

May 20, 1965
Stu Grimson
National Hockey League

May 24, 1960
Pete Metzelaars
National Football League

May 24, 1966
Tony Jones
National Football League

May 24, 1968
Jerry DiPoto
Major League Baseball

May 25, 1973
Todd Walker
Major League Baseball

May 26, 1977
Tara Snyder
Tennis

May 27, 1967
Ruthie Bolton-Holifield
Women's National Basketball Association

May 28, 1963
Eugene Robinson
National Football League

May 28, 1964
Armon Gilliam
National Basketball Association

May 31, 1960
Norm Johnson
National Football League

JUNE

June 2, 1969
David Wheaton
Tennis

June 4, 1965
Kurt Stillwell
Major League Baseball

June 6, 1961
Bill Bates
National Football League

June 9, 1964
Wayman Tisdale
National Basketball Association

June 15, 1948
Mike Holmgren
National Football League

June 15, 1957
Brett Butler
Major League Baseball

June 15, 1972
Andy Pettitte
Major League Baseball

June 16, 1970
Michael Husted
National Football League

June 17, 1970
Jason Hanson
National Football League

June 19, 1972
Brian McBride
Major League Soccer

June 19, 1975
Anthony Parker
National Basketball Association

June 20, 1970
Mike Grace
Major League Baseball

June 22, 1947
Pete Maravich
National Basketball Association

June 24, 1955
Lorne Roberts
Professional Golfers' Association

June 24, 1957
Doug Jones
Major League Baseball

June 28, 1966
Andrew Lang
National Basketball Association

June 30, 1962
Tony Fernandez
Major League Baseball

June 30, 1973
Markus Naslund
National Hockey League

JULY

July 1, 1958
Nancy Lieberman-Cline
Women's National Basketball Association

July 2, 1965
Steve Sparks
Major League Baseball

July 3, 1953
Frank Tanana
Major League Baseball

July 4, 1965
Suzanne Strudwick
Ladies Professional Golf Association

July 5, 1970
Doug Bochtler
Major League Baseball

July 6, 1966
Darrin Winston
Major League Baseball

July 7, 1968
Chuck Knoblauch
Major League Baseball

July 7, 1973
Napoleon Kaufman
National Football League

July 10, 1965
Buddy Groom
Major League Baseball

July 12, 1965
Mike Muñoz
Major League Baseball

July 16, 1942
Margaret Court
Tennis

July 16, 1959
Gary Anderson
National Football League

July 16, 1960
Terry Pendleton
Major League Baseball

July 16, 1965
Charles Smith
National Basketball Association

July 17, 1971
Calbert Cheaney
National Basketball Association

July 20, 1971
Charles Johnson
Major League Baseball

July 22, 1956
Scott Sanderson
Major League Baseball

July 25, 1974
Todd Fuller
National Basketball Association

July 26, 1962
Jody Reed
Major League Baseball

AUGUST

August 2, 1961
Danny Sheaffer
Major League Baseball

August 3, 1960
Sid Bream
Major League Baseball

August 4, 1971
Jeff Gordon
NASCAR

August 5, 1968
John Olerud
Major League Baseball

August 6, 1965
David Robinson
National Basketball Association

August 8, 1961
Bruce Matthews
National Football League

August 9, 1967
Deion Sanders
National Football League

August 9, 1971
Scott Karl
Major League Baseball

August 10, 1964
Andy Stankiewicz
Major League Baseball

August 10, 1971
Sal Fasano
Major League Baseball

August 11, 1961
Craig Ehlo
National Basketball Association

August 13, 1955
Betsy King
Ladies Professional Golf Association

August 14, 1971
Adam Timmerman
National Football League

August 15, 1964
Jeff Huson
Major League Baseball

August 15, 1966
Scott Brosius
Major League Baseball

August 16, 1975
Ryan Longwell
National Football League

August 19, 1958
Gary Gaetti
Major League Baseball

August 19, 1966
Woody Williams
Major League Baseball

August 19, 1971
Mary Joe Fernandez
Tennis

August 20, 1962
Ken Ruettgers
National Football League

August 20, 1967
Andy Benes
Major League Baseball

August 21, 1966
John Wetteland
Major League Baseball

August 22, 1956
Paul Molitor
Major League Baseball

August 23, 1973
Charlotte Smith
Women's National Basketball Association

August 24, 1968
Tim Salmon
Major League Baseball

August 26, 1964
Chad Krueter
Major League Baseball

August 26, 1969
Nicole Arendt
Tennis

August 28, 1970
Mike Lapper
Major League Soccer

SEPTEMBER

September 1, 1965
Hardy Nickerson
National Football League

September 2, 1960
Rex Hudler
Major League Baseball

September 4, 1963
John Vanbiesbrouck
National Hockey League

September 9, 1960
Alvin Davis
Major League Baseball

September 10, 1947
Larry Nelson
Professional Golfers' Association

September 10, 1963
Randy Johnson
Major League Baseball

September 15, 1962
Earnest Byner
National Football League

September 16, 1958
Orel Hershiser
Major League Baseball

September 17, 1955
Scott Simpson
Professional Golfers' Association

September 17, 1970
Mark Brunell
National Football League

September 22, 1970
Mike Matheny
Major League Baseball

September 23, 1957
Tony Fossas
Major League Baseball

September 23, 1958
Larry Mize
Professional Golfers' Association

September 25, 1970
Doug Pelfrey
National Football League

September 28, 1962
Irving Fryar
National Football League

September 29, 1966
Hersey Hawkins
National Basketball Association

OCTOBER

October 2, 1972
Grant Hill
National Basketball Association

October 3, 1966
Darrin Fletcher
Major League Baseball

October 4, 1963
A. C. Green
National Basketball Association

October 10, 1976
Shane Doan
National Hockey League

October 12, 1970
Charlie Ward
National Basketball Association

October 13, 1958
Barb Bunkowsky-Scherbak
Ladies Professional Golf Association

October 14, 1964
Joe Girardi
Major League Baseball

October 16, 1959
Brian Harper
Major League Baseball

October 20, 1931
Mickey Mantle
Major League Baseball

October 20, 1965
Chad Hennings
National Football League

October 20, 1975
J. D. Drew
Major League Baseball

October 29, 1959
Jesse Barfield
Major League Baseball

Mike Gartner
National Hockey League

October 29, 1969
John Kasay
National Football League

October 29, 1972
Rhonda Blades
Women's National Basketball Association

October 30, 1960
Dave Valle
Major League Baseball

October 31, 1968
Eddie Taubensee
Major League Baseball

NOVEMBER

November 1, 1968
Kent Graham
National Football League

November 5, 1973
Johnny Damon
Major League Baseball

November 6, 1968
Chad Curtis
Major League Baseball

November 8, 1970
Qadry Ismail
National Football League

November 10, 1964
Keith Lockhart
Major League Baseball

November 10, 1972
Isaac Bruce
National Football League

November 12, 1961
Greg Gagne
Major League Baseball

November 12, 1963
Laurie Brower
Ladies Professional Golf Association

November 14, 1968
Kent Bottenfield
Major League Baseball

Bob Christian
National Football League

November 16, 1959
Corey Pavin
Professional Golfers' Association

November 16, 1966
Jean Driscoll
Wheelchair Marathon

November 17, 1967
Howard Griffith
National Football League

November 18, 1969
Rocket Ismail
National Football League

November 21, 1973
Danny Kanell
National Football League

November 23, 1971
Vin Baker
National Basketball Association

November 24, 1962
Randy Velarde
Major League Baseball

November 24, 1967
Cal Eldred
Major League Baseball

November 25, 1966
Cris Carter
National Football League

November 26, 1956
Dale Jarrett
NASCAR

November 26, 1960
Harold Reynolds
Major League Baseball

November 28, 1963
Walt Weiss
Major League Baseball

November 28, 1971
Tracy Hanson
Ladies Professional Golf Association

November 29,1960
Howard Johnson
Major League Baseball

November 30, 1950
Paul Westphal
National Basketball Association

November 30, 1964
David Wood
National Basketball Association

DECEMBER

December 1, 1961
Greg McMichael
Major League Baseball

Barb Mucha
Ladies Professional Golf
Association

December 2, 1959
Patty Jordan
Ladies Professional Golf
Association

December 2, 1969
Paul Stankowski
Professional Golfers' Association

December 3, 1970
Paul Byrd
Major League Baseball

Lindsey Hunter
National Basketball Association

December 4, 1961
Frank Reich
National Football League

December 5, 1970
Kevin Haller
National Hockey League

December 7, 1972
Clay Shiver
National Football League

December 9, 1968
Brent Price
National Basketball Association

December 10, 1963
Doug Henry
Major League Baseball

December 10, 1970
Bryant Stith
National Basketball Association

December 11, 1965
Jay Bell
Major League Baseball

December 11, 1967
Jackie Gallagher-Smith
Ladies Professional Golf Association

December 12, 1967
Dave Szott
National Football League

December 13, 1963
Jim Harbaugh
National Football League

December 14, 1969
David Nilsson
Major League Baseball

December 18, 1951
Bobby Jones
National Basketball Association

December 18, 1964
Don Beebe
National Football League

December 19, 1961
Reggie White
National Football League

December 22, 1964
Mike Jackson
Major League Baseball

December 23, 1969
Stephen Grant
National Football League

December 23, 1971
Steve Stenstrom
National Football League

December 26, 1964
Jeff King
Major League Baseball

December 27, 1958
Steve Jones
Professional Golfers' Association

December 27, 1964
Steve Wallace
National Football League

December 28, 1972
Adam Vinatieri
National Football League

December 31, 1957
David Ogrin
Professional Golfers' Association

December 31, 1961
Rick Aguilera
Major League Baseball

December 31, 1971
Heath Shuler
National Football League

Part 2

A GUIDE TO SPORTS MINISTRY

Chapter 5

CONTACT INFORMATION

There is something special about having some kind of contact with athletes who are famous. It is especially true when the athlete is someone with whom you as a fan share a special bond. For instance, if you are from the same hometown as an athlete, you feel a special kinship. Or perhaps he or she went to the same college. Or maybe you happened to meet an athlete at a sports camp or at some function. You are forever locked in with this person in some mysterious way.

The bond seems to be even closer, though, when the athlete you have some connection to is a Christian. To share a faith in Christ touches something even more personal than just a sports interest. It is a spiritual connection.

Christian athletes often feel a responsibility to find ways to serve God by being involved in activities that bring them closer to Christian fans. They have to be careful, though, that their time is not dominated by speaking engagements and other things that bring them closer to the public. They have families and other responsibilities.

One of the most frequently asked questions received at *Sports Spectrum* magazine is how to get in touch with professional athletes. The safest answer we can give is to suggest that the interested person get in touch with athletes in care of the team for whom they play. Mail delivered to the players in care of their teams is passed along to the athletes. Although there is no guarantee that the athlete will then respond to a request, the corresponding is often worth the effort.

The most common avenue of contact is through the athlete's agent or through the public relations people for the team for whom he or she plays. Agents' names can sometimes be found by calling the players association of the major sports leagues. Public relations personnel can often be reached through the team phone number. In the interest of assisting fans who want to write to a favorite athlete, the *Christian Fan's Guide* provides the team addresses (and telephone numbers for contacting the public relations department) you would need.

Keep in mind that athletes do get large volumes of mail. There is no guarantee that your mail will receive a reply. To speed the process and to increase the chance that you will get a reply, heed these hints:

1. Be polite.
2. Be brief.
3. Do not try to make the athlete feel guilty or tell the player that he or she is expected to reply because "God told me to write to you" or something like that.
4. Do not ask for more than two items (autographs, photos). One suggestion would be to send an extra of what you want signed (baseball card, for instance) for the athlete to keep.
5. Send a self-addressed, stamped envelope for ease of return. Make the return process as simple as possible, remembering that the athlete may have many similar requests and each eats into his or her free time.
6. Address the note to

   Player
   c/o Team
   Address
   City, State Zip
7. Allow plenty of time for a response. Athletes in season have many demands on their time, and athletes who are not in season often live in a city other than where their home venue is located.

The above notes relate to requests for autographs and other easy-to-answer requests. If you have a more complicated request, such as to ask an athlete to make a speaking engagement, it would be best to do the homework of finding who the athlete's agent is and going that route. Generally, athletes do not handle these arrangements personally.

Keep in mind that if you want to guarantee that you will get a speaker for your event, use the speakers bureaus listed in chapter 6.

BASEBALL

MAJOR LEAGUE BASEBALL

Major League Baseball Players Association
12 East 49th Street, 24th Floor
New York, NY 10017

MLB often can supply some player contact information.

AMERICAN LEAGUE

ANAHEIM ANGELS

Edison International Field
2000 Gene Autry Way
Anaheim, CA 92806
Phone: 714-940-2000

BALTIMORE ORIOLES

333 West Camden Street
Baltimore, MD 21201
Phone: 410-685-9800

BOSTON RED SOX

Fenway Park
4 Yawkey Way
Boston, MA 02215-3496
Phone: 617-267-9440

CHICAGO WHITE SOX

Comiskey Park
333 W. 35th Street
Chicago, IL 60616
Phone: 312-674-1000

CLEVELAND INDIANS

Jacobs Field
2401 Ontario Street
Cleveland, OH 44115
Phone: 216-420-4200

DETROIT TIGERS

Tiger Stadium
2121 Trumbull Avenue
Detroit, MI 48216
Phone: 313-962-4000

KANSAS CITY ROYALS

PO Box 419969
Kansas City, MO 64141-6969
Phone: 816-921-8000

MINNESOTA TWINS

Hubert H. Humphrey Metrodome
34 Kirby Puckett Place
Minneapolis, MN 55415
Phone: 612-375-1366

NEW YORK YANKEES

Yankee Stadium
E. 161st St. and River Avenue
Bronx, NY 10451
Phone: 718-293-4300

OAKLAND ATHLETICS

Oakland-Alameda County Coliseum
7677 Oakport Street, Suite 200
Oakland, CA 94621
Phone: 510-638-4900

SEATTLE MARINERS

PO Box 4100
Seattle, WA 98104
Phone: 206-346-4000

TAMPA BAY DEVIL RAYS

Tropicana Field
One Tropicana Drive
St. Petersburg, FL 33705
Phone: 813-825-3137

TEXAS RANGERS

1000 Ballpark Way
Arlington, TX 76011
Phone: 817-273-5222

TORONTO BLUE JAYS

SkyDome
One Blue Jays Way
Suite 3200
Toronto, Ontario M5V 1J1
Canada
Phone: 416-341-1000

NATIONAL LEAGUE

ARIZONA DIAMONDBACKS

401 East Jefferson
Phoenix, AZ 85003
Phone: 602-514-8500

ATLANTA BRAVES

PO Box 4064
Atlanta, GA 30302
Phone: 404-522-7630

CHICAGO CUBS

1060 West Addison Street
Chicago, IL 60613-4397
Phone: 773-404-2827

CINCINNATI REDS

100 Cinergy Field
Cincinnati, OH 45202
Phone: 513-421-4510

COLORADO ROCKIES

Coors Field
2001 Blake Street
Denver, CO 80205-2000
Phone: 303-292-0200

FLORIDA MARLINS

2267 NW 199th Street
Miami, FL 33056
Phone: 305-626-7400

HOUSTON ASTROS

PO Box 288
Houston, TX 77001-0288
Phone: 713-799-9500

LOS ANGELES DODGERS

1000 Elysian Park Avenue
Los Angeles, CA 90012
Phone: 213-224-1500

MILWAUKEE BREWERS

County Stadium
PO Box 3099
Milwaukee, WI 53201-3099
Phone: 414-933-4114

MONTREAL EXPOS

4549 Pierre-de-Coubertin Avenue
Montreal, Quebec H1V 3N7
Canada
Phone: 514-253-3434

NEW YORK METS

123-01 Roosevelt Avenue
Flushing, NY 11368-1699
Phone: 718-507-6387

PHILADELPHIA PHILLIES

PO Box 7575
Philadelphia, PA 19101
Phone: 215-463-6000

PITTSBURGH PIRATES

600 Stadium Circle
Pittsburgh, PA 15212
Phone: 412-323-5000

ST. LOUIS CARDINALS

250 Stadium Plaza
St. Louis, MO 63102
Phone: 314-421-3060

SAN DIEGO PADRES

PO Box 2000
San Diego, CA 92112-2000
Phone: 619-881-6500

SAN FRANCISCO GIANTS

24 Willie Mays Plaza
San Francisco, CA 94107
Phone: 415-468-3700

MEN'S BASKETBALL

NATIONAL BASKETBALL ASSOCIATION

NBA Players Association
1775 Broadway
Suite 2401
New York, NY 10019

TEAMS

ATLANTA HAWKS

One CNN Center
South Tower, Suite 405
Atlanta, GA 30303
Phone: 404-827-3800

BOSTON CELTICS

151 Merrimac Street, 4th Floor
Boston, MA 02114
Phone: 617-523-6050

CHARLOTTE HORNETS

100 Hive Drive
Charlotte, NC 28217
Phone: 704-357-0252

CHICAGO BULLS

United Center
1901 West Madison Street
Chicago, IL 60612
Phone: 312-455-4000

CLEVELAND CAVALIERS

One Center Court
Cleveland, OH 44115-4001
Phone: 216-420-2000

DALLAS MAVERICKS

Reunion Arena
777 Sports Street
Dallas, TX 75207
Phone: 214-748-1808

DENVER NUGGETS

1635 Clay Street
Denver, CO 80204
Phone: 303-893-6700

DETROIT PISTONS

The Palace of Auburn Hills
Two Championship Drive
Auburn Hills, MI 48326
Phone: 810-377-0100

GOLDEN STATE WARRIORS

1011 Broadway
Oakland, CA 94607
Phone: 510-986-2200

HOUSTON ROCKETS

Two Greenway Plaza
Suite 400
Houston, TX 77046
Phone: 713-627-3865

INDIANA PACERS

125 South Pennsylvania Street

Indianapolis, IN 46204
Phone: 317-917-2500

LOS ANGELES CLIPPERS

1111 South Figueroa Street
Suite 1100
Los Angeles, CA 90015-1306
Phone: 213-742-7500

LOS ANGELES LAKERS

555 Nash Street
El Segundo, CA 90245
Phone: 310-462-6000

MIAMI HEAT

Suntrust International Center
One Southeast 3rd Avenue
Suite 2300
Miami, FL 33131
Phone: 305-577-4328

MILWAUKEE BUCKS

Bradley Center
1001 North Fourth Street
Milwaukee, WI 53203-1312
Phone: 414-227-0500

MINNESOTA TIMBERWOLVES

Target Center
600 First Avenue North
Minneapolis, MN 55403
Phone: 612-673-1600

NEW JERSEY NETS

405 Murray Hill Parkway
East Rutherford, NJ 07073
Phone: 201-935-8888

NEW YORK KNICKERBOCKERS

Madison Square Garden
Two Penn Plaza, 14th Floor
New York, NY 10121-0091
Phone: 212-465-6000

ORLANDO MAGIC

Orlando Arena
2 Magic Place
Orlando, FL 32810
Phone: 407-649-3200

PHILADELPHIA 76ERS

First Union Center
3601 South Broad Street
Philadelphia, PA 19148
Phone: 215-339-7600

PHOENIX SUNS

201 E. Jefferson
Phoenix, AZ 85004
Phone: 602-379-7900

PORTLAND TRAIL BLAZERS

One Center Court
Suite 200
Portland, OR 97227
Phone: 503-234-9291

SACRAMENTO KINGS

One Sports Parkway
Sacramento, CA 95834
Phone: 916-928-0000

SAN ANTONIO SPURS

Alamodome
100 Montana Street
San Antonio, TX 78203-1031
Phone: 210-554-7700

SEATTLE SONICS

190 Queen Anne Avenue North

Suite 200
Seattle, WA 98109-9711
Phone: 206-281-5800

TORONTO RAPTORS

40 Bay Street
Suite 400
Toronto, Ontario M5J 2N8
Canada
Phone: 416-214-2255

UTAH JAZZ

Delta Center
301 West South Temple
Salt Lake City, UT 84101
Phone: 801-325-2500

VANCOUVER GRIZZLIES

General Motors Place
800 Griffiths Way
Vancouver, BC V6B 6G1
Canada
Phone: 604-899-4666

WASHINGTON WIZARDS

MCI Center
601 F Street NW
Washington, DC 20004
Phone: 202-661-5000

WOMEN'S BASKETBALL

WOMEN'S NATIONAL BASKETBALL ASSOCIATION

645 5th Avenue
New York, NY 10022
Phone: 212-688-9622

TEAMS

CHARLOTTE STING

2709 Water Ridge Parkway
Suite 400
Charlotte, NC 28217
Phone: 704-424-9622

CLEVELAND ROCKERS

Gund Arena, 1 Center Court
Cleveland, OH 44115
Phone: 216-263-7625

HOUSTON COMETS

Two Greenway Plaza
Suite 400
Houston, TX 77046
Phone: 713-627-9622

INDIANA FEVER

300 East Market Street
Indianapolis, IN 46204
Phone: 317-263-2100

LOS ANGELES SPARKS

Great Western Forum
3900 W. Manchester Blvd.
Inglewood, CA 90306
Phone: 713-627-9622

MIAMI SOL

Suntrust International Center
One southeast 3rd Avenue
Suite 2300
Miami, FL 33131
Phone: 305-577-4328

NEW YORK LIBERTY

Two Penn Plaza
New York, NY 10121
Phone: 212-564-9622

PHOENIX MERCURY

America West Arena
201 E. Jefferson
Phoenix, AZ 85004
Phone: 602-514-8333

PORTLAND FIRE

One Center Court
Suite 200
Portland, OR 97227
Phone: 503-234-9291

SACRAMENTO MONARCHS

ARCO Arena
One Sports Parkway
Sacramento, CA 95834
Phone: 916-928-0000

UTAH STARZZ

Delta Center
301 West South Temple
Salt Lake City, UT 84101
Phone: 801-355-3865

WASHINGTON MYSTICS

MCI Center
601 F. Street NW
Washington, DC 20004
Phone: 204-661-5000

FOOTBALL

NFL PLAYERS ASSOCIATION

2021 L Street NW
Suite 600
Washington, DC 20036

TEAMS

AMERICAN FOOTBALL CONFERENCE

BALTIMORE RAVENS

11001 Owings Mills Blvd.
Owings Mills, MD 21117
Phone: 410-654-6200

BUFFALO BILLS

One Bills Drive
Orchard Park, NY 14127
Phone: 716-648-1800

CINCINNATI BENGALS

One Bengals Drive
Cincinnati, OH 45204
Phone: 513-621-3550

DENVER BRONCOS

13655 Broncos Parkway
Englewood, CO 80112
Phone: 303-433-9000

INDIANAPOLIS COLTS

PO Box 535000
Indianapolis, IN 46253
Phone: 317-297-2658

JACKSONVILLE JAGUARS

One ALLTEL Stadium Place
Jacksonville, FL 32202
Phone: 904-633-6000

KANSAS CITY CHIEFS

One Arrowhead Drive
Kansas City, MO 64129
Phone: 816-924-9300

MIAMI DOLPHINS

7500 SW 30th Street
Davie, FL 33314
Phone: 954-452-7000

NEW ENGLAND PATRIOTS

Foxboro Stadium
60 Washington Street
Foxboro, MA 02035
Phone: 508-543-8200

NEW YORK JETS

1000 Fulton Avenue
Hempstead, NY 11550
Phone: 516-560-8100

OAKLAND RAIDERS

1220 Harbor Bay Parkway
Alameda, CA 94502
Phone: 510-864-5000

PITTSBURGH STEELERS

300 Stadium Circle
Pittsburgh, PA 15212
Phone: 412-323-0300

SAN DIEGO CHARGERS

Jack Murphy Stadium
Box 609609
San Diego, CA 92160-9069
Phone: 619-874-4500

SEATTLE SEAHAWKS

11220 NE 53rd Street
Kirkland, WA 98033
Phone: 425-827-9777

TENNESSEE TITANS

Baptist Sports Park
460 Great Circle Road
Nashville, TN 37228
Phone: 615-673-1500

NATIONAL FOOTBALL CONFERENCE

ARIZONA CARDINALS

PO Box 888
Phoenix, AZ 85001-0888
Phone: 602-379-0101

ATLANTA FALCONS

One Falcon Place
Suwannee, GA 30024
Phone: 770-945-1111

CAROLINA PANTHERS

800 South Mint Street
Charlotte, NC 28202-1502
Phone: 704-358-7000

CHICAGO BEARS

Halas Hall at Conway Park
1000 Football Drive
Lake Forest, IL 60045
Phone: 847-295-6600

DALLAS COWBOYS

Cowboys Center
One Cowboys Parkway
Irving, TX 75063
Phone: 972-556-9900

DETROIT LIONS

Pontiac Silverdome
1200 Featherstone Road
Pontiac, MI 48342
Phone: 248-335-4131

GREEN BAY PACKERS

1265 Lombardi Avenue
Green Bay, WI 54304
Phone: 920-496-5700

MINNESOTA VIKINGS

9520 Viking Drive
Eden Prairie, MN 55344
Phone: 612-828-6500

NEW ORLEANS SAINTS

5800 Airline Drive
Metairie, LA 70003
Phone: 504-733-0255

NEW YORK GIANTS

Giants Stadium
East Rutherford, NJ 07073
Phone: 201-935-8111

PHILADELPHIA EAGLES

Veterans Stadium
3501 Broad Street
Philadelphia, PA 19148
Phone: 215-463-2500

ST. LOUIS RAMS

Trans World Dome
1 Rams Way
St. Louis, MO 63115
Phone: 314-982-7267

SAN FRANCISCO 49ERS

4949 Centennial Boulevard
Santa Clara, CA 95054-1229
Phone: 408-562-4949

TAMPA BAY BUCCANEERS

1 Buccaneer Place
Tampa, FL 33607
Phone: 813-870-2700

WASHINGTON REDSKINS

Redskin Park
PO Box 17247
Dulles International Airport
Washington, DC 20041
Phone: 703-478-8900

HOCKEY

NATIONAL HOCKEY LEAGUE

ANAHEIM MIGHTY DUCKS

Arrowhead Pond of Anaheim
2695 E. Katella Avenue
PO Box 61077
Anaheim, CA 92803-6177
Phone: 714-940-2900

ATLANTA THRASHERS

One CNN Center
13 South
Atlanta, GA 30303
Phone: 407-827-3394

BOSTON BRUINS

1 Fleet Center, Suite 250
Boston, MA 02114-1303
Phone: 617-624-1950

BUFFALO SABRES

Marine Midland Arena
1 Seymour H. Knox III Plaza
Buffalo, NY 14203-4100
Phone: 716-855-4100

CALGARY FLAMES

Canadian Airlines Saddledome
PO Box 1540 Station M
Calgary, Alberta T2P 3B9
Canada
Phone: 403-777-2177

CAROLINA HURRICANES

Greensboro Coliseum
5000 Aerial Center, Suite 100
Morrisville, NC 27560
Phone: 919-467-PUCK

CHICAGO BLACKHAWKS

United Center
1901 West Madison Street
Chicago, IL 60612
Phone: 312-455-7000

COLORADO AVALANCHE

Pepsi Center
1000 Chopper Place
Denver, CO 80204
Phone: 303-893-6700

DALLAS STARS

211 Cowboys Parkway
Irving, TX 75063
Phone: 972-868-2890

DETROIT RED WINGS

Joe Louis Arena
600 Civic Center Drive
Detroit, MI 48226
Phone: 313-396-7544

EDMONTON OILERS

Edmonton Coliseum
11230 110th Street
Edmonton, Alberta T5B 4M9
Canada
Phone: 403-414-4000

FLORIDA PANTHERS

National Car Rental Center
One Panthers Parkway
Sunrise, FL 33323
Phone: 954-768-1900

LOS ANGELES KINGS

Staples Center
1111 South Figueroa Street
Los Angeles, CA 90015
Phone: 310-426-6000

MONTREAL CANADIENS

Molson Centre
1260 rue de La Gauchetiere Quest
Montreal, Quebec H3B 5E8
Canada
Phone: 514-932-2582

NASHVILLE PREDATORS

Gaylord Entertainment Center
501 Broadway
Nashville, TN 37215
Phone: 615-770-2300

NEW JERSEY DEVILS

Continental Airlines Arena
PO Box 504
East Rutherford, NJ 07073
Phone: 201-935-6050

NEW YORK ISLANDERS

Nassau Veterans Memorial Coliseum
Uniondale, NY 11553
Phone: 516-794-4100

NEW YORK RANGERS
2 Penn Plaza, 14th Floor
New York, NY 10121
Phone: 212-465-6486

OTTAWA SENATORS
Corel Centre
1000 Palladium Drive
Kanata, Ontario K2V 1A5
Canada
Phone: 613-599-0250

PHILADELPHIA FLYERS
First Union Center
3601 South Broad Street
Philadelphia, PA 19148
Phone: 215-465-4500

PHOENIX COYOTES
Cellular One Ice Den
9375 E. Bell Road
Scottsdale, AZ 85260
Phone: 602-473-5600

PITTSBURGH PENGUINS
Civic Arena
66 Mario Lemieux Place
Pittsburgh, PA 15219
Phone: 412-642-1300

ST. LOUIS BLUES
Kiel Center
1401 Clark Avenue
St. Louis, MO 63103
Phone: 314-622-2500

SAN JOSE SHARKS
525 West Santa Clara Street
San Jose, CA 95113
Phone: 408-287-7070

TAMPA BAY LIGHTNING
401 Channelside Drive
Tampa, FL 33602
Phone: 813-229-2658

TORONTO MAPLE LEAFS
Air Canada Centre
40 Bay Street
Toronto, Ontario MSJ 2X2
Canada
Phone: 416-977-1641

VANCOUVER CANUCKS
General Motors Place
800 Griffiths Way
Vancouver, BC V6B 6G1
Canada
Phone: 604-899-4600

WASHINGTON CAPITALS
MCI Center
601 F Street NW
Washington, DC 20004
Phone: 202-628-3200

MISCELLANEOUS

NASCAR
PO Box 2875
Daytona Beach, FL 32120
Phone: 904-253-0611

INDYCAR
755 W. Big Beaver Road
Suite 800
Troy, MI 48084
Phone: 810-362-8800

INDY RACING LEAGUE
4790 West 16th Street

Indianapolis, IN 46222
Phone: 317-484-6526

PROFESSIONAL BOWLERS ASSOCIATION

1720 Merriman Road
Box 5118
Akron, OH 44334
Phone: 330-836-5568

LADIES PROFESSIONAL GOLF ASSOCIATION

100 International Golf Drive
Daytona Beach, FL 32114
Phone: 904-274-6200

PROFESSIONAL GOLFERS ASSOCIATION

112 TPC Boulevard
Ponte Verde, FL 32082
Phone: 904-285-3700

UNITED STATES OLYMPIC COMMITTEE

One Olympic Plaza
Colorado Springs, CO 80909
Phone: 719-632-5551

MAJOR LEAGUE SOCCER

110 East 42nd Street
Suite 1502
New York, NY 10017

ASSOCIATION OF TENNIS PROFESSIONALS (ATP)

200 ATP Tour Boulevard
Ponte Verde Beach, FL 32082
Phone: 904-285-8000

WOMEN'S TENNIS ASSOCIATION (WTA)

1266 East Main Street
Fourth Floor
Stanford, CT 06902
Phone: 203-978-1740

Chapter 6

RESOURCES

One of the outgrowths of sports ministries and the higher profile of Christian athletes during the past couple of decades has been the increased interest in using the tools that Christians in sports make available for outreach. Now people can use speakers' bureaus, magazines, radio programs, videos, and a host of other materials to expand their ministry through sports. Perhaps there is something here you can use to turn your love for sports into a tool for the Lord Jesus Christ.

LITERATURE

BOOKS

ATHLETIC TRAINING

Kenneth H. Cooper, *Faith-based Fitness* (Nelson)
Dr. Cooper is the father of aerobics, and he is a Christian. In this book he combines biblical truth with physical conditioning.

Cross Training Manual (Cross Training Publishing)
A study of key questions Christian athletes face
Cross Training Publishing
PO Box 1541
Grand Island, NE 68802
(Catalog available)
308-384-5762

Elliot Johnson, *Focus on the Finish Line* (Cross Training Publishing)
Helping female athletes overcome tough athletic hurdles

Elliot Johnson, *Growing Stronger: Fundamentals of the Faith* (Cross Training Publishing)
Bible study helps for new Christians, with sports analogies

Wes Neal, *Total Release* (Cross Training Publishing)
A new perspective on winning and losing

BIBLE RESOURCES

Gordon Thiessen, comp., *The Athlete's Topical Bible* (Cross Training Publishing)
A Bible study tool for athletes searching for answers

BIOGRAPHY

Michelle Akers with Judith A. Nelson, *Face to Face With Michelle Akers* (Success Factors Publishing)

Michelle Akers and Tim Nash, *Standing Fast* (JTC Sports)
Olympic gold medalist Michelle Akers talks about overcoming chronic fatigue syndrome to win the gold. Her growing faith is the foundation of her story.
JTC Sports, Inc.
Phone: 919-303-6611

Bob Bardwell with Victor Lee, *Marathons of Life* (Bang Publisher)
Being a paraplegic hasn't stopped Bob Bardwell from running a camp, racing marathons, and raising a family.

Dave Branon, *Competitor's Edge* (Moody)
Profiles of top Christian women athletes

Dave Branon, *First & Goal* (Moody)
Profiles of Christians in pro football

Dave Branon, *Safe at Home 2* (Moody)
Profiles of Christians in major league baseball

Dave Branon, *Slam Dunk* 2 (Moody)
Profiles of Christians in pro basketball

Ron Brown, *I Can* (Cross Training Publishing)
The story of the life of Ron Brown, an assistant coach at Nebraska

Ron Brown, *Unfinished Business* (Cross Training Publishing)
Coach Brown recounts the 1994 Nebraska season.

Brett Butler with Jerry Jenkins, *Field of Hope* (Thomas Nelson)
Butler's biography tells how he overcame obstacles to be a star.

Irving Fryar, *Sunday Is My Day* (Multnomah)
Fryar's story of a great turnaround from troublemaker to follower of Christ.

Chad Hennings, *It Takes Commitment* (Multnomah Publishing)
An Iowa farmboy becomes an Air Force pilot and later a Super Bowl champ.

Jeff Hostetler with Ron Hostetler, *What It Takes* (Multnomah Press)
Hostetler overcomes adversity to star in the NFL.

Art Lindsay, *One Final Pass* (Cross Training Publishing)
A look at the life of Brook Berringer, former Nebraska quarterback

Tom Osborne, *On Solid Ground* (Cross Training Publishing)
Through the 1995 season with Nebraska's coach

Bryce Paup, *What's Important Now* (Multnomah)
One of the NFL's best linebackers talks about what's really important.

Mike Singletary with Russ Pate, *Daddy's Home At Last* (Zondervan)
Hall-of-Fame middle linebacker Mike Singletary talks about making his family the No. 1 priority.

Deion Sanders, *Power, Money, and Sex: How Success Almost Ruined My Life* (Word)
The star football player finds faith and seeks to grow as a Christian.

Charlie Ward with Joe Cooney, *Charlie Ward: Winning By His Grace* (Sports Publishing)
Phone: 800-327-5557
Internet Site: www.SportsPublishing-Inc.com
A photo-packed biography of Charlie Ward

COACHING RESOURCES

Carolyn Allen, *The Coach's Wife* (Cross Training Publishing)
Go through the behind-the-scenes life of a football coach.

Coaches of Destiny (Cross Training Publishing)
Principles of successful living on God's team

Coaching Character (Cross Training Publishing)
This book helps coaches put character in their athletes.

Wes Neal, *The Handbook of Coaching Perfection* (Cross Training Publishing)
Neal offers words of advice for coaches.

FICTION

Jerry Jenkins, *Rookie* (Wolgemuth & Hyatt)
Fictional account of a young athlete

INSPIRATIONAL SPORTS STORIES

All-Star Moment Series (Cross Training Publishing)
Collections of inspirational stories from different sports

Lessons from the Gridiron
Lessons from the Diamond
Lessons from the Hardwood
Lessons from the Fairway
Lessons from the Coaches

Keith Brown, *Intensity With Integrity* (Cross Training Publishing)
Devotional talks given to the Phoenix Suns and Arizona Cardinals

Keith Brown, *Life Above the Rim* (Cross Training Publishing)
Devotional talks given to the Phoenix Suns

Ron Brown, *The Mark Of A Champion* (Cross Training Publishing)
Nebraska's receiver's coach shares the characteristics of God's person.

Peak Performance (Cross Training Publishing)
Biblical principles to help you reach your peak

MEN'S ISSUES

Ken Ruettgers with Dave Branon, *Home Field Advantage* (Multnomah)

Ruettgers addresses the power of role models in a person's life.

Tom Sirotnak with Ken Walker, *Warriors* (Broadman & Holman)

How to be a true warrior for God

Tom Sirotnak with Ken Walker, *Ultimate Warriors* (Broadman & Holman)

More on how to be a true warrior for God

SPECIFIC SPORTS

Robert Bussey, *A Biblical Perspective on the Martial Arts* (Cross Training Publishing)

Bussey helps the reader understand the benefits and dangers of martial arts.

Christian Golf Psychology (Cross Training Publishing)

Helping to apply your Christian faith to your game

The Golfer's Tee Time Devotional (Cross Training Publishing)

Tips on golf and on getting to know God more intimately

The Golfer's Topical Bible (Cross Training Publishing)

Glorify God in your golf game.

Jesus Would Have Been A Scratch Golfer (Cross Training Publishing)

Improve your knowledge of golf while enhancing your relationship with Jesus Christ.

Jim Sheard and Wally Armstrong, *In His Grip* (Nelson)

The authors present a foundation for golf and life.

Jim Sheard and Wally Armstrong, *Playing The Game* (Nelson)

The authors offer inspiring thoughts for golfers

Bob Darden, *The Way Of An Eagle* (Nelson)

Tips and talk from some of the world's best golfers

TRACTS

AMERICAN TRACT SOCIETY

PO Box 462008

Garland, TX 75046-2008

Phone: 1-800-548-7228

E-mail: amtract@aol.com

Tract Samples: gospelcom.net/ats

Auto racing: Davey Allison, "His Last Lap," by Ed Cheek

Baseball: Dave Dravecky, "Comeback"

Mickey Mantle, "His Final Inning"

(Available in NIV, KJV, CD-Rom cybertract)

Basketball: Pete Maravich, "The Unforgettable Pete Maravich," *by* David Robinson

Bow hunting: Charlie Alsheimer, "The Ultimate Hunt"

Cycling: Judy Bowman, "Can We Pedal Our Way To Heaven?"

Football: Reggie White, "Minister of Defense"

"Football and the Post-game Kneel," by Dave Branon

Fishing: Hank Parker, "More Than Winning and Losing"

Golf: Tom Lehman, "Close Is Not Enough"

Olympics: "Go For The Gold," by Phil Rawley

Soccer: John Kregel, "Dealer"

Tennis: Michael Chang, "Michael Chang"

(Available in English, traditional Chinese, simplified Chinese, Japanese)

Track & Field: Olympic athletes, "Go For The Gold"

Track & Field: Madeline Manning Mims, "Running Free"

ATHLETES IN ACTION

PO Box 588
Lebanon, OH 45036

NASCAR: Joe Gibbs, "Success and the Lessons I've Learned"

BASEBALL CHAPEL

Vince Nauss
1315 Main Street
Darby, PA 19023
Baseball: "Let Me Give You Something" (English and Spanish)

DIME PUBLISHERS

PO Box 490
Cupertino, CA 95014
Contact Person: Pedro Dillon

Publisher of sports tracts using sports schedules for football and NASCAR

GOOD NEWS TRACTS

1300 Crescent Street
Wheaton, IL 60187

Golf: Steve Jones, "Winning Isn't Everything"

Tennis: Michael Chang, "The Ultimate Challenge"

Olympics: Dave Johnson, "Our Finest Day"

Baseball: Orel Hershiser, "Success That Counts"

Basketball: Julius Erving, "What Keeps Julius Erving Going?"

General: "What's Your Game Plan?"

SPORTS AMBASSADORS

PO Box 36900
Colorado Springs, CO 80936
"Victory Volleyball"

Pamphlet that provides a clear game plan for the Christian life by using volleyball imagery

MAGAZINES

CHRISTIAN MOTORSPORTS ILLUSTRATED

PO Box 129
Mansfield, PA 16933
Contact Phone: 717-549-2282
Contact Fax: 717-549-3366
Contact Person: Roland Osborne
Internet Site: www.christianmotorsports.com

CMI goes trackside to bring you all kinds of stories about the men and women of motorsports. It covers NASCAR racing, drag racing, motorcyle racing, and everything involved in these and other motor sports.

SHARING THE VICTORY MAGAZINE

8701 Leeds Road
Kansas City, MO 64129
Subscription information: 1-800-289-0909

SPORTS SPECTRUM MAGAZINE

PO Box 3566
Grand Rapids, MI 49501
Subscription information: 1-800-283-8333
Internet Site: www.sport.org
E-mail: ssmag@sport.org

NEWSLETTERS

LA

Life Athletes
400 Plaza Building
210 S. Michigan Street
South Bend, IN 46601
Contact Phone: 219-237-9000
Contact Fax: 219-267-0906
Contact E-mail: info@lifeathletes.org
Internet Site: www.lifeathletes.org
Director: Chris Godfrey

OUT SPOKIN'

International Christian Cycling Club
PO Box 976
Englewood, CO 80151-0976
Contact Phone: 303-781-8672
Contact Person: Marlen Wells

UNLIMITED POTENTIAL, INC.

(UPI) Newsletter
PO Box 1355
Warsaw, IN 46581-1355
Contact Phone: 219-267-7988
Contact Person: Tom Roy

PROFESSIONAL SPORTS CHAPLAINCY PROGRAMS

The chaplains shown below and the chaplaincy program leaders would appreciate your prayers for their teaching, counseling, and evangelizing to professional athletes. Several of these chaplains are available to speak at churches and church youth events. Please note, however, that it's not the responsibility of chaplains and chapel coordinators to arrange speakers for events. Their responsibility entails providing spiritual counsel and guidance. Chaplains cannot jeopardize their relationship with the athletes by becoming their speaker's bureau.

ARIZONA SPORTS

3030 N. Central Avenue
Suite 610
Phoenix, AZ 85012
Contact Person: Keith Brown
Brown is chaplain of the Phoenix Suns.

ALTERNATIVE MINISTRIES

5500 Crestwood Drive
Knoxville, TN 37914
Contact Person: Cris Stevens
Ministry to women professional golfers on the LPGA Tour

ATHLETES EMPOWERED MINISTRIES

3545 Highland Fairways Blvd.
Lakeland, FL 33810-5759
Contact Person: John Venlet
John works with minor league baseball teams but also seeks to disciple other athletes.

BASEBALL CHAPEL

1315 Main Street
Darby, PA 19023
Contact Person: Vince Nauss, executive director

Vince oversees the chaplaincy program in major league and minor league baseball.

BEYOND VICTORY MINISTRIES

16658 NW Dublin
Portland, OR 97229
Contact Person: Al Egg

Egg ministers to the Portland Trail Blazers and other Portland area sports people.

INTERSPORTS ASSOCIATION, INC.

PO Box 143
Wheaton, IL 60189
Contact Person: Henry Soules

Soules is the chaplain of the Chicago Bulls.

PASS MINISTRY

9 Meadowrue Drive
Mt. Laurel, NJ 08054
Contact Person: Bruce McDonald

McDonald is the chaplain for the Philadelphia 76ers, and he ministers to many pro athletes in Philly and elsewhere. Also available for speaking engagements.

PRO BASKETBALL FELLOWSHIP

338 Brisk Avenue
Waterford, CA 95386
Contact Person: Claude Terry
Contact Fax: 209-874-4667

Terry oversees the chaplaincy programs in the NBA.

SEARCH MINISTRIES

5038 Dorsey Hall Drive
Ellicott City, MD 21042
Contact Phone: 410-740-5300
Contact Fax: 410-740-5305
Contact Person: Larry Moody

Larry conducts Bible studies for players on the PGA Tour.

VICTORY MINISTRY

7420 Stone Creek
Anaheim Hills, CA 92808
Contact Person: John Werhas

John is chaplain of the Anaheim Angels.

RADIO, TV, VIDEO

CDR COMMUNICATIONS, INC.

9310-B Old Keene Mill Road
Burke, VA 22015-4204
Contact Phone: 703-569-3400 or 800-729-2237

Five videos made in cooperation with Fellowship of Christian Athletes:

CHALLENGER FILMS, INC.

3361 Cardinal Lake Drive, Suite A
Duluth, MN 30136
Contact Person: Diane Preston-Reilly
Contact Phone: 770-476-3232
Contact Fax: 770-476-2115
Contact E-mail: csus@west.net

Produces sports-related videos that tell the stories of Christian athletes

CHRISTIAN COLLEGE SPORTS NETWORK

PO Box 250
Montreat, NC 28757
Contact Phone: 704-669-9210

Contact Fax: 704-669-6119

Contact Person: Norm Wilhelmi

This radio program tells the stories of what is happening in the world of Christians in sports, including Christian colleges.

GATEWAY FILMS

Vision Video

PO Box 540

Worcester, PA 19490-0540

The Pistol: The Pete Maravich Story

Chariots of Fire: The Eric Liddell Story

Power Play: A fiction account of a pro hockey player whose life is changed

HARK! ENTERTAINMENT

Fredricktown, OH 43019-0237

Contact Phone: 800-824-2637

Contact Fax: 800-427-3511

Sports videos: Give Me The Rock (NBA basketball players testify), Spirit Of The Game (NFL football players testify)

SPORTSWEEK TV

Cornerstone Communications

Host: Tom McGough

Half-hour sports television that explores the game from both the sports angle and the spiritual angle, informing the viewer while also challenging him with the claims of Christ

LINKS CHAMPIONS

40-minute video

U.S. Open champions Betsy King and Scott Simpson talk about what they have learned from the game of golf as they describe the difference Jesus Christ has made in their lives.

Phone: 800-90LINKS

Fax: 703-914-5508

SPEAKERS AND SPEAKERS' BUREAUS

BILL GLASS MINISTRIES

PO Box 9000

Cedar Hill, TX 75104

Contact Phone: 214-291-7895

Contact Fax: 214-293-0173

Note: Founded in 1969, BGM conducts evangelistic crusades as well as prison outreach ministries. Bill Glass is a former player with the Cleveland Browns and Detroit Lions and Pro Bowl starter who brings football stories and sports fervor to his evangelistic crusades, often conducted in local football stadiums.

CHAMPIONS FOR TODAY

551 Exam Court

Lawrenceville, GA 30244

Contact Phone: 770-963-5097

Contact Fax: 770-963-5097

Contact E-mail: BigMike76@aol.com

Speaker: Mike McCoy

Former NFL player Mike McCoy oversees this selection of speakers who are mostly former pro football players. They are usually called on to speak in schools and for youth groups.

Other speakers: Keith Davis, New York Giants; Ken Ellis, Green Bay Packers; José Alvarez, Atlanta Braves; Greg Jensen, Green Bay Packers

CAMERON MILLS MINISTRIES

3319 Ridgecane Road
Lexington, Ky. 40513-1127
Contact Phone: 606-339-3568

DIAMOND YOUTH MINISTRIES

PO Box 501
Wheaton, IL 60189
Contact Phone: 815-899-4011
Contact Person: Chris Paul

"Have baseball cards, will travel" should be Chris Paul's motto. His collection of more than 30,000 sports cards, along with autographs, magazines, books, videos, and other memorabilia is ready to be taken on the road. Chris attempts to use his display, wherever he's called upon to set it up, to introduce fans to Jesus Christ.

JON KREGEL MINISTRIES

PO Box 131480
Tyler, TX 75713
Contact Phone: 903-597-1995
Contact Fax: 903-597-1995
Speaker: Jon Kregel

Former pro soccer player Jon Kregel tells of his brush with the law and with danger as he teaches his listeners about the right kind of life.

Resources: Tracts, videos, printed materials

LIFELINE MINISTRIES

8730 Town & Country Boulevard
Ellicott City, MD 21043
Contact Phone: 410-203-9248
Speaker: Pat Kelly

Former major leaguer Pat Kelly is an evangelist at heart, and he can make the gospel extremely clear in his exciting presentations.

MILES AHEAD MINISTRIES

9888 Carroll Center Road #235
San Diego, CA 92126
Contact Phone: 619-271-0700
Contact Fax: 619-566-0804
Contact Person: Elaine Franklin
Speaker: Miles McPherson

Former NFL player for the San Diego Chargers Miles McPherson uses his ability to speak in public and numerous resources to spread the gospel and challenge young people to apply practical Bible principles.

Resources: Audio cassettes, discipleship materials, training programs, video

PLAN TO WIN

5 Sonora Court
Madison, WI 53719
Contact Phone: 608-231-0728
Contact Fax: 608-231-0708
Contact E-mail: jensenfca@aol.com
Speaker: Greg Jensen

Former NFL player Greg Jensen travels the country to speak out against the devastation of alcohol and drug abuse, while giving hope in Jesus Christ.

SPORTS WORLD

104 Main Street
PO Box 558
New Tazewell, TN 37825
Contact Phone: 800-832-6546
Contact Person: Sam Sample

SW offers former professional basketball and football players for speaking engagements in schools and churches.

US SPORTS

PO Box 13291
Charlotte, NC 28270
Contact Phone: 704-536-2446
Contact Person: Robert Walker

Robert Walker has put together an impressive array of speakers: David Thompson, NBA; Bobby Jones, NBA; Bobby Richardson, baseball; Sam Rutigliano, football, John Lotz, assistant AD at North Carolina; Gary Lavelle, former major leaguer; Tully Blanchard, one-time pro wrestler; Darrell Green, NFL; Todd Fuller, NBA; Phil Ford, former NBA star.

WORLD IMPACT

2001 S. Vermont Avenue
Los Angeles, CA 91007
Contact Person: Keith Phillips
Contact Phone: 213-735-1137
Contact Fax: 213-735-2576
Web Site: www.worldimpact.org

Rosey Grier, former NFL player

YES! MINISTRIES

1033 Newton Road
Santa Barbara, CA 93103
Contact Phone: 805-962-7579
Contact Fax: 805-962-7579
Contact E-mail:
70373.701@compuserve.com
Speaker: Jay Carty

Former NBA player Jay Carty seeks to reach the unreached by relating to a changing contemporary society with an engaging speaking style.

Resources: Audio interviews, video interviews, printed materials, videos

SPORTS APPAREL

ChristianiTee
12806 Oakmont Street
Overland Park, KS 66213
Contact Phone: 913-685-3226
Contact Fax: 913-685-0902
Toll-free: 800-388-2848
Web Site: www.christianitee.com

Types of sports-related clothes: nine unique Christian golf logos that go on T-shirts, golf shirts, and golf caps. Also, golf towels

FELLOWSHIP OF CHRISTIAN ATHLETES

8701 Leeds Road
Kansas City, MO 64129
Contact Phone: 800-289-0909
Brochure available

Types of sports-related clothes: T-shirts, shorts, caps, jackets

Other merchandise: golf balls, golf towels, tees, sport bags

KERUSSO

238 Spur 62
PO Box 32
Berryville, AR 72616
Contact Phone: 800-424-0943
Contact Fax: 870-423-3568
Endorsers: Andre Wadsworth, Arizona Cardinals

Types of sports-related clothes: T-shirts, caps, tank tops, ties

SOLID LIGHT

PO Box 26060
Columbus, OH 43226
Contact Phone: 614-846-9606
Contact Fax: 614-846-8740
Toll-free: 800-726-9606

Types of sports-related clothes: T-shirts, caps

VERSES WEAR

PO Box 102
Tallahassee, FL 32302
Contact Phone: 850-224-7760 extension 13
Contact Fax: 850-224-7760

Endorsers: Danny Wuerffel, Peter Boulware

Types of sports-related clothes: T-shirts

TRAINING RESOURCES

CHAMPIONS OF EXCELLENCE

PO Box 627
200 Woodson Bend Rd.
Branson, MO 65611
Contact Phone: 417-334-7037
Contact Fax: 417-334-7037
Contact E-mail:
Wesnealcoe@aol.com
Contact Person: Wes Neal

Neal, who has done extensive studying and writing about athletes, has made available a wide range of audio interviews, printed materials, and sports tips materials that help the athlete and the coach understand sports and their ramifications.

GATOR GOLF ENTERPRISES

PO Box 941911
Maitland, FL 32794
Contact Phone: 407-699-2803
Contact Fax: 407-644-9093
Contact Person: Wally Armstrong

Gator Golf offers golf training videos and several other golf-related materials.

SPORTSNET

1160 Old Johnson Ferry Road
Atlanta, GA 30319
Contact Phone: 404-303-7215
Contact Fax: 404-303-9398
Contact E-mail:
dansportsnet@csi.com

SportsNet is developing a number of printed resources that can help sports fans grow in faith by studying role models. Many of these resources are based on profiles found in Sports Spectrum *magazine and* Path To Victory *New Testaments.*

Resources: newsletter, TimeOut curriculum

UPWARD BASKETBALL

127 Ninth Avenue North
Nashville, TN 37234
Contact Phone: 800-585-4721

Upward Basketball is a ready-made basketball league. Order the curriculum, and you'll be equipped to run a first-class outreach basketball circuit.

WIN THE PRIZE

Concordia Publishing House
3558 South Jefferson Avenue
St. Louis, MO 63118-3968
Contact Phone: 800-774-0274

Win The Prize is a resource for coaches who want to incorporate Christian principles into their coaching plan.

The kit includes materials for distribution as well as practical help for coaches as they apply biblical principles.

WINNING RUN FOUNDATION
255 B Settlers Road
Longview, TX 75605
Contact Phone: 903-663-6256
Contact Fax: 903-663-9382
Contact E-mail: nurniw@aol.com
Director: Elliot Johnson

Winning Run produces a number of sports-related materials that promote evangelism and spiritual growth.

Resources: printed materials, tracts, videos

Languages: English, French, German, Japanese, Polish, Portuguese, Russian, Spanish

WEB SITES

MICHELLE AKERS www.michelleakers.com
MARK BRUNELL www.mark-brunell.com
MICHAEL CHANG www.mchang.com
THEGOAL.COM www.thegoal.com
DAVID ROBINSON www.theadmiral.com
SPORTS SPECTRUM www.sport.org
CHARLIE WARD www.1stewards.com
GILL BYRD www.heartofachampion.com
A. C. GREEN www.acgreen.com
DARRELL GREEN www.dgylf.com

Chapter 7

SPORTS MINISTRIES

As the influence of sports has proliferated during the past thirty years, so has the influence of people who have learned that sports can be used in a multitude of ways to bring people to faith in Christ and to help them grow spiritually. Some of the early pioneers of sports ministry work, such as Fellowship of Christian Athletes, are still going strong, but their work is now aided by hundreds of other groups who are reaching out through what was at one time called muscular Christianity. These resources are available for any Christian who wants to get involved in reaching people through sports.

ALASKA MOUNTAIN ADVENTURES

PO Box 80444
Fairbanks, AK 99708
Contact Phone: 907-457-2907
Contact Person: Tim Brill
Web Site:
www2.polarnet.com/~Tim
Scope: Alaska

Adventure-based fellowship for young people who want to show God's love and experience the power of the gospel in what AMA calls "God's great outdoor church"

ATHLETES IN ACTION

PO Box 588
Lebanon, OH 45036
Contact Phone: 513-459-9597
Contact Fax: 513-459-9697
Web Site: www.aiasports.org/aia

AIA exists to reach the United States and resource the world for Jesus Christ through the influence of sports.

CAROLINA SPORTS OUTREACH

9432 Sardis Glen Drive
Matthews, NC 28105
Contact Phone: 704-451-2698
Contact Fax: 704-844-2785
Contact E-mail: dyarbob@aol.com
Contact Person: Bob Dyar
Scope: The Carolinas

The purpose of CSO is to use sports to reach the Carolinas with the gospel.

CSO is mostly involved in motor sports ministries, especially NASCAR.

CHARLOTTE EAGLES SOCCER CLUB

2101 Sardis Road North, Suite 201
Charlotte, NC 28227
Contact Phone: 704-841-8644

Contact Fax: 704-841-8652
Contact E-mail:
Info@CharlotteEagles.com
Web Site: www.charlotteeagles.com
Scope: United States and sending teams overseas

The Charlotte Eagles sets out to do what no other pro sports team tries. Its reason for existence is to spread the gospel. It does this through its team, which plays in the United System of Independent Soccer League (USISL). Other ministries include youth soccer teams, international tours, summer camps, and other local programs.

CHRISTIAN ATHLETIC ASSOCIATION

2302 Zanker Road
San Jose, CA 95150
Contact Phone: 601-453-3266
Contact E-mail: jondet@usa.net
Scope: Local

CAA uses sports to spread the gospel through clinics, leagues, camps, and leadership development programs. Each year, CAA touches more than 1,000 young lives who are interested in baseball, basketball, field hockey, golf, soccer, softball, volleyball, and wrestling.

CHRISTIAN BOWHUNTERS OF AMERICA

3460 W. 13th Street
Cadillac, MI 49601
Contact Phone: 616-775-7744
Director: David L. Roose
Scope: North America

More than 2,000 members in all fifty states and Canada participate in this outreach that brings together hunters who are interested in being accountable to God and honoring the Creator.

CHRISTIAN GOLFER'S ASSOCIATION

Contact E-mail: tomwin@infoave.net
757 Bultman Drive, Suite B
Sumter, SC 29150
Contact Phone: 803-773-2171
Contact Fax: 803-773-7757
Contact Person: Tom Winstead

Mission: To help spread the word of Jesus Christ by using golf as the platform and vehicle for witnessing and evangelism

CHRISTIAN MOTORSPORTS INTERNATIONAL

Team RFC
433 West Allen Avenue, Suite 105
San Dimas, CA 91773-4704
Contact Phone 909-599-9833
Contact Fax: 909-592-0836
Director: Ken Owen

Team RFC sponsors a two-pronged ministry: Racing For Christ works in motor racing and Rodders For Christ works in street rods and custom machines. These two ministries make up the world's largest racing organization, Christian Motorsports International. Team RFC conducts race chapel services and many other activities that help racers know Jesus Christ.

Resources: Tracts

CHRISTIAN RODDERS ASSOCIATION

6157 Callaway Place
Alta Loma, CA 91737

Contact Phone: 909-466-9311
Contact Fax: 909-948-1566
Contact Persons: Dale or Jeannie Daly
Scope: United States

CRA attempts to hold chapel services at street rodding events across the country.

CHRISTIAN RUNNERS ASSOCIATION

1025 Grand Road
Meadow Vista, CA 95722
Contact Person: Nick Vogt
Web Site: www.c3online.net/ctm

Christian runners learn how to respect Jesus Christ through their sport.

CHURCH RECREATION PROGRAM

127 Ninth Avenue North
Nashville, TN 37234-0158
Contact Phone: 615-251-3848
Contact Fax: 615-251-2066
Contact E-mail: jgarner@BSSB.com
Director: John Garner
Scope: North America

CRP is a resource for churches who want to use sports as a ministry tool. With a long history of serving churches, CRP is able to suggest successful strategies for reaching people with the gospel. Resources include a newsletter, sports ministry development tools, and training programs.

CHURCH SPORTS INTERNATIONAL

6023 Calle de Felice
San Jose, CA 95124
Contact Phone: 408-978-3764
Contact Fax: 408-269-2033
Contact E-mail: chsports@aol.com
Web Site: www.churchsports.org
Director: Rodger Oswald
Scope: Worldwide

A church sports expert, Oswald seeks to help churches or mission agencies use sports as a church planting or church growth tool. Resouces include audio cassettes, training programs, and videos.

COACH'S CORNER SPORTS MINISTRIES

2358 Clearwater Drive
Marietta, GA 30067
Contact Phone: 770-971-7390
Contact Fax: 770-509-8820
Contact E-mail: jwe484@aol.com
Director: Bobby Lankford
Scope: Southeast United States

This ten-plus-year-old ministry seeks to minister to coaches and athletes on high school campuses. Resources include discipleship materials and training programs.

COACHES OF INFLUENCE (COIN)

c/o Sports Outreach Los Angeles
1605 Elizabeth
Pasadena, CA 91104
Contact Phone: 626-398-2370
Contact Fax: 626-398-2471
Contact E-mail: SOLA12@aol.com
Contact Person: Steve Quatro
Scope: Southern California

Using the local church as its base, COIN seeks to encourage and strengthen coaches in their spiritual, family, and professional lives through camps, discipleship groups, and a newsletter.

COLLEGE GOLF FELLOWSHIP

2005 Peninsula Drive
Flower Mound, TX 75028-5478
Contact Person: Rik Massengale

Former pro Rik Massengale seeks to help young golfers in their faith.

CROSSFIRE MINISTRIES

31 College Place B #223
Ashville, NC 28801
Contact Persons: Randy Shepherd and Jamie Johnson
Contact Phone: 704-255-9111
Scope: National, international

Crossfire attempts to preach the gospel through athletics. Their activities include ministry trips to places such as Romania and Guatemala; basketball camps, outreaches, and All-Star games; softball ministries; pulpit supply; Bible conferences; and Holy Land tours.

DARRELL GREEN LEARNING CENTERS

1713 Benning Road NE
Suite 45
Washington, DC 20002

Founded by Darrell Green of the Washington Redskins Darrell has set up a variety of programs to help inner-city kids in Washington, D.C.

DAVE DRAVECKY'S OUTREACH OF HOPE

13840 Gleneagle Drive
Colorado Springs, CO 80921
Contact Phone: 719-481-3528
Contact Fax: 719-481-4689
Contact Person: Carey Hubert
Scope: National

Outreach of Hope offers hope and encouragement through Jesus Christ to people suffering from cancer or amputation. OH has a newsletter and other printed materials available to those in need.

DIAMOND CLUB

PO Box 91
Theodore, AL 36590
Contact Phone: 334-653-5621
Director: Bernie Carbo
Scope: Regional

Former major leaguer Bernie Carbo uses baseball training to spread the gospel as he speaks at baseball camps and clinics.

THE DOOR

219 N. Chester Street
Baltimore, MD 21231

An inner-city Baltimore ministry begun by former Colt Joe Ehrmann.

FAST TRACK MINISTRIES

18921 Hawthorne Drive
Independence, MO 64057
Contact Phone: 816-795-0883
Contact Person: Mike Weddle

Fast Track attempts to bring inspiration to motor racing through chapel programs at local tracks, Bible studies for drivers, and a bimonthly newsletter.

FELLOWSHIP OF CHRISTIAN ATHLETES

8701 Leeds Road
Kansas City, MO 64129
Contact Phone: 816-921-0909
Contact Fax: 816-921-8755
Web Site: www.fca.org

Scope: Worldwide

Mission statement: To present to athletes and coaches, and all whom they influence, the challenge and adventure of receiving Jesus Christ as Savior and Lord, serving Him in their relationships and in the fellowship of the church

FELLOWSHIP OF CHRISTIAN COWBOYS

PO Box 3010
Colorado Springs, CO 80934-3010
Contact Phone: 719-630-7636
Contact Fax: 719-630-7611
Scope: National

FCC seeks to reach out to and encourage cowboys through the gospel. It sponsors chapel programs at rodeos and provides discipleship for the men and women of rodeo.

Resources: Line Rider newsletter, testimony tracts of top cowboys

FEMALE DRAG RACERS FOR CHRIST

197 County Road 230
Niota, TN 37826
Contact Phone: 423-337-0469
Contact Person: Sandy Malone
Scope: National

FDRFC is open to drivers, tech crew members, pit crew members, wives, daughters, sisters, anyone involved in drag racing. The goal is to encourage people in the sport to walk closer to Jesus Christ and to learn from the lessons taught on the track. The organization has a newsletter.

FOCAS

RR 2 Box 506-1
Salina, KS 74365
Contact Person: George Braswell
Scope: National

This ministry reaches out to fishermen with the gospel.

FOUR WINDS CHRISTIAN ATHLETICS

PO Box 189
Danbury, WI 54830
Contact Phone: 715-244-3503
Director: Steve McConkey
E-mail: fourwind@centurytel.net
Web Site: 4wca.org
Scope: Worldwide

Outreach for track and field athletes throughout the world

FRANK STARK RACEWAY MINISTRIES, INC.

PO Box 56
Strafford, MO 65757
Contact Phone: 417-736-3073
Contact Fax: 417-736-9091
Contact E-mail: raceway@dialus.com
Contact Person: Frank Stark
Scope: National

An organization whose purpose is to take the gospel of Jesus Christ to race fans and teams on the ARCA and NASCAR circuits.

HOME PLATE

280 East Lincoln Street
Birmingham, MI 48009-3673
Contact Phone: 810-646-2000
Contact Fax: 810-646-2213
Contact Person: Jeff Totten
Scope: Detroit area

Each year this event is held in conjunction with a Detroit Tiger home game. Participants are treated to testimonies by such men as Travis Fryman, Ernie Harwell, and Frank Tanana.

HOOPS OF HOPE BASKETBALL MINISTRY

5510 Jennifer Lane
Colorado Springs, CO 80917
Contact Phone: 719-573-5647
Contact Fax: 719-573-5952
Contact E-mail: brent@hoops.org
Web Site: www.hoops.org
Director: Brent Fuqua
Scope: Worldwide

Hoops of Hope presents the gospel in the U.S. and abroad through camps, clinics, assemblies, and exhibitions. It seeks athletes to participate through its traveling basketball programs.

INDIANA SPORTS OUTREACH

6900 South Gray Road
Indianapolis, IN 46237
Contact Phone: 317-783-5461
Contact Fax: 317-783-5469
Contact E-mail: Indsports@aol.com
Contact Person: David W. Cox
Scope: National

The goal of ISO is to help equip local churches to make a difference in their communities through sports events.

INFINITY SPORTS

PO Box 3006 T.S.
Reston, VA 71272
Contact E-mail:
bsutech@popalex1.linknet.net
Contact Person: David-Andrew Fox
Scope: Worldwide

By using people around the world as resources, Infinity is able to gain access for sports teams in sometimes restricted areas, especially in the so-called 10/40 window (those countries located between latitudes 10 and 40). The group sponsors clinics, missions trips, sports leagues, and training programs.

INTERNATIONAL BIBLE SOCIETY

1820 Jet Stream Drive
Colorado Springs, CO 80921
Contact Phone: 719-488-9200
Contact E-mail: ibs@gospelcom.net
Web Site: www.gospelcom.net/ibs/
Contact Person: Dwight Anderson
Scope: Worldwide

The mission of IBS is to aid evangelism and discipleship by providing God's Word. IBS has produced several sports Bibles that feature the testimonies of Christian athletes.

Resources: Path To Victory *New Testaments*

INTERNATIONAL CHRISTIAN CYCLING CLUB

PO Box 976
Englewood, CO 80151
Contact Phone: 303-781-8672
Contact Fax: 303-781-8745
Contact E-mail: ICCCWells@aol.com
Web Site: www.jps.net/iccc/
Contact Person: Marlen Wells
Scope: Worldwide

A two-fold approach: Working with pro bikers to win them to Christ, and developing a network of recreational bikers nationwide

Club personalities: Brenda Brashears, Kim Morrow, Marilyn Wells, Nadia Kibardina, Peg Hill

INTERNATIONAL SPORTS FEDERATION

8227 Mt. Eden Road
Shelbyville, KY 40065
Contact Phone: 502-738-5592
E-mail: keredadnil@aol.com
Contact Person: Derek Coleman
Scope: Worldwide

ISF works with the Foreign Mission Board of the Southern Baptist Convention to send sports missions teams overseas.

JIM RYUN MINISTRIES

16718 Thirteenth Street
Lawrence, KS 66044
Contact Phone: 913-749-3325
Contact Fax: 913-749-3325
Contact Person: Heather Ryun
Scope: Kansas

Track and field camps run by the former Olympian, Jim Ryun.

J.U.M.P.

1051 15th Avenue S
St. Cloud, MN 56301
Contact Phone: 320-253-6097
Contact Fax: 320-253-6097
Contact Person: Rick Rassier
Scope: National

JUMP is an acronym for Jumping Up with Mighty Power. Using volleyball and his ability to take on entire teams by himself, Rick Rassier reaches young people with the gospel.

LET'S GO FISHING INC.

PO Box 434
Moraga, CA 95446
Contact Phone: 510-376-8277
Contact Person: Jim Grassi
Scope: National

This multifaceted outreach endeavors to strengthen families and encourage spiritual growth. By teaching recreational skills, LGF seeks to promote confidence and cooperation while making memories.

Newsletter: The Lure

LIFE ATHLETES

400 Plaza Building
210 S. Michigan Street
South Bend, IN 46601
Contact Phone: 219-237-9000
Contact Fax: 219-267-0906
Contact E-mail: info@lifeathletes.org
Web Site: www.lifeathletes.org
Director: Chris Godfrey
Scope: National

This organization celebrates life in all stages, from newborn to the aged. Many professional athletes are a part of this organization.

MIKE BARBER PRISON MINISTRY

951 Echo Lane, Suite 324
Houston, TX 77024
Contact Phone: 713-461-4144

A former NFL player, Mike Barber has created a unique, successful ministry of reaching out to prisoners with the gospel of Jesus Christ.

MINISTRY OF BASKETBALL IN JESUS

7410 11th Avenue
Brooklyn, NY 11228
Contact Phone: 718-745-7587
Contact E-mail: petert@brass.com
Contact Person: Peter Terranova
Scope: New York City

This New York City basketball

league attempts to use hoops to attract non-Christians and introduce the gospel to them.

MISSIONARY ATHLETES INTERNATIONAL

PO Box 25010
Colorado Springs, CO 80936
Contact Phone: 719-528-1636
Contact Fax: 719-528-1638
Contact Person: Mark Schrock

"Committed to communicating the revelation of Jesus Christ to all cultures through the environment of soccer." MAI carries out this commitment through camps, clinics, missions trips, and sports leagues.

MOTOR RACING OUTREACH

Smith Tower Suite 405
Highway 29 N
Harrisburg, NC 28075
Contact Phone: 704-455-3828
Contact Fax: 704-455-5806
Contact E-mail: mrocms@aol.com
Director: Max Helton
Scope: National

MRO is an evangelistic and discipleship ministry that reaches out to the men and women of motor racing, including NASCAR, the Craftsman Truck Series, and the Busch Series.

MOTORSPORTS MINISTRIES

2460 West Third Street, Suite 260
Santa Rosa, CA 95401
Contact Phone: 707-523-4780
Contact Fax: 707-523-0935
Contact: Hunter Floyd
Internet Site:
www.MotorsportsMinistries.org
Directors: Richard and Beth Anderson
Scope: National

This organization assists the spiritual growth of racers on a number of racing circuits, including CART, SCCA, USA Midgets, and several others.

Resource: newsletter, The Pit Board

NATIONAL ASSOCIATION OF CHURCH RECREATORS AND SPORTS MINISTERS (NACRSM)

11705 Mountain View Road
Knoxville, TN 37922
Contact Phone: 423-690-2047
Contact Fax: 423-693-6611
Contact E-mail:
butchsport@compuserve.com
Director: Butch Garman
Scope: National

This organization is designed to help churches that are interested in using sports as an outreach ministry. NACRSM seeks to facilitate a network of church recreation and sports professionals.

NBC CAMPS THUNDER TEAM

N 21808 Panorama Road
Colbert, WA 99005
Contact Phone: 509-466-4690
Contact Fax: 509-467-6289
Scope: National

A Division I college basketball exhibition basketball team that uses former college players to compete against major college competition

NEW LIFE MINISTRIES

PO Box 1984
Tracy, CA 95378
Contact Phone: 209-839-9569

Contact Fax: 209-835-6618
Contact E-mail: RevNev@aol.com
Scope: Local

A local sports ministry that coordinates all adults sports sites for the city, this ministry is a prototype for other cities. More than 2,000 people hear the gospel regularly through this ministry.

Sports: baseball, basketball, football, racquetball, volleyball

NEWS RELEASE BASKETBALL

7157 Townsend Drive
Highlands Ranch, CO 80126
Contact Phone: 303-470-0763
Contact Fax: 303-470-0720
Contact E-mail:
sorensen@pogo.ast.lmco.com
Director: Steve Sorensen
Scope: International

News Release sends high-quality basketball teams overseas for evangelism. The teams conduct clinics and camps in addition to playing games against local teams.

ONE ON ONE INTERNATIONAL

PO Box 503
8692 B Skillman Street
Dallas, TX 75243
Contact Phone: 214-349-9753
Contact Fax: 214-349-9753
Director: Mark Murdock
Scope: International

One On One uses NBA and NCAA players to man teams of traveling basketball teams that conduct camps and clinics in other countries.

OPERATION SPORT HELP

PO Box 6484
Bend, OR 97708-6484
Contact Phone: 541-388-8210
Contact Fax: 541-388-0065
Contact E-mail:
Sporthelp@empnet.com
Contact Person: Ron Roley
Scope: International

The goal of Operation Sport Help is to gather new and used cycling equipment and distribute it overseas where it is needed most, including former Soviet bloc countries, Asia, and Latin America. In addition, OSH distributes thousands of Bibles at cycling venues.

PRO ATHLETES OUTREACH

PO Box 1044
Issaquah, WA 98027
Contact Phone: 425-392-6300
Contact Fax: 425-392-7640
Contact E-mail: paooffice@aol.com
Web Site: www.pao.org
Directors: Norm and Bobbie Evans
Scope: North America

PAO offers a unique ministry to professional athletes and their spouses by sponsoring programs to help disciple and train them to grow in their Christian life. Norm Evans, a former member of the Miami Dolphins, also takes speaking assignments. PAO does not set up speaking arrangements for athletes.

PROFESSIONAL SKIERS FELLOWSHIP

401 Ute Lane
Gunnison, CO 81230
Contact Person: Rick Barton

PSF gives encouragement to Christian skiers.

RACERS FOR JESUS

PO Box 1208
Gilbert, AZ 85299-1208
Contact Phone: 602-507-5323
Contact Fax: 602-507-5393
Contact E-mail: TeamRF@aol.com
Contact Person: Ken Owen

An arm of Christian Motorsports International

RACING FOR JESUS

100 Cascade Lane
Columbia, SC 29045
Contact Phone: 803-788-9628
Contact E-mail: raftcross@aol.com
Web Site: www.racingforjesus.org/
Contact Person: Dennis Dyches
Scope: South Carolina

Concentrated in the state of South Carolina, RFJ seeks to have a working ministry going at every local auto sports racing track in the state. RFJ endeavors to minister to both fans and drivers.

THE RIGHT CLUB MINISTRIES

29015 Willow Creek Lane
Highland, CA 92346
Contact Phone: 909-862-4115
Contact Fax: 909-425-1083
Contact E-mail:
70423.74@compuserve.com
Contact Person: Ron Harvey
Scope: North America

Right Club conducts Bible studies and chapels for golfers in the PGA and on the Senior PGA Tour.

RUN & SHOOT BASKETBALL LEAGUE

13808 W. Maple Road, Suite 114
Omaha, NE 68164
Contact Phone: 402-496-0979
Contact Fax: 402-496-1140
Contact E-mail: BAllen7@aol.com
Web Site:
www.eagleheightschurch.com
Scope: Local

Using basketball as the main tool, R & S Basketball seeks to reach kids and their families with the gospel through basketball leagues and clinics.

RUN TO WIN

17905 Bothell-Everett Highway, Suite 103
Mill Creek, WA 98012
Contact Phone: 425-487-1946
Contact Fax: 425-487-0552
Contact Person: Mike Rohrbach
Scope: Regional

The outreach of this Seattle-based organization can be seen as a model for other groups who want to reach out through sports. RTW conducts chapels and discipleship ministries among local college and pro teams while running sports camps and other activities.

Resources: Newsletter, discipleship materials, book of chapel talks

SAINTS PRISON MINISTRIES

PO Box 681
235 W. Main Street
Moorestown, NJ 08057-0681
Contact Phone: 609-866-4428
Contact Fax: 609-235-8077
Contact E-mail: JSK1963@IX.net
Director: Dale M. Glading
Scope: Northeastern United States

This unique ministry works in

dozens of prisons in at least nine states by using sports teams who compete against prisoners. Thousands have turned to Christ through this outreach, and the Saints have more than 1,000 prisoners enrolled in Bible correspondence courses.

Sports teams: basketball and softball

SCORE INTERNATIONAL

PO Box 5385
Ft. Oglethorpe, GA 30742
Contact Phone: 706-937-6778
Contact Fax: 706-937-6779
Director: Ron Bishop
Scope: International

Both men and women athletes can participate in this opportunity to use their athletic ability on sports teams that travel overseas to spread the gospel of Jesus.

Sports: basketball, volleyball, softball, baseball, cheerleading

SKYDIVING

Jacksonville Skydiving Center, Inc.
9838 Old Baymeadows Road, Suite 290
Jacksonville, FL 32256
Contact Phone: 904-641-2886
Contact E-mail: jaxsky@bellsouth.net
Scope: Local

The goal of this group is to use skydiving as a way to provide a setting in which to strengthen family unity with Christian values.

SOCCER OUTREACH INTERNATIONAL

530 Dog Track Road
Longwood, FL 32750
Contact Fax: 407-830-9840
Director: Michelle Akers, 1996 Olympic gold medalist, soccer
Scope: International

Michelle Akers, one of the best women soccer players alive, uses her platform to reach out with the gospel through a number of tools, including her own remarkable story of overcoming.

Resources: books, video, speaking

SOLID ROCK: CLIMBERS FOR CHRIST

630 Autumn Crest Circle, Suite C
Colorado Springs, CO 80919
Contact Phone: 719-593-8954
Contact Fax: 719-593-0829
Director: Gary Scott
Scope: National

Solid Rock provides a support network for men and women who like to participate in mountain climbing. The group seeks to introduce climbers to Christ and encourage fellow Christian climbers. Activities include a newsletter, Bible studies, and climbers' conferences.

SPORTS AMBASSADORS

PO Box 36900
Colorado Springs, CO 80936-6900
Contact Phone: 719-592-9292
Contact Fax: 719-592-0693
Web Site: www.oci.org/sa/
Director: Robin Cook
Scope: International

One of the oldest sports ministry organizations in the United States, Sports Ambassadors sends sports teams on missions trips around the world. SA's Venures for Victory teams have played more than 5,000 games overseas.

SPORTS AND CULTURAL EXCHANGE

PO Box 554
320 Walnut Street
Pekin, IL 61555-0554
Contact Phone: 309-347-3309
Contact Fax: 309-347-3309
Contact E-mail: davidej@dpc.net
Contact Person: Dave Johnson
Scope: International

Traveling sports teams are used by SCE to take the gospel to people around the world. The ministry looks for athletes who are willing to use their skills in baseball, basketball, soccer, softball, tennis, and volleyball to spread the Good News.

SPORTS OUTREACH AMERICA

PO Box 3566
Grand Rapids, MI 49501
Contact Phone: 616-974-2663
Contact Fax: 616-957-5741
E-mail: sola12@aol.com
Contact Person: Tom Felten

SOA is a consortium of sports ministries around the United States that are attempting to use sports as a tool for reaching people with the gospel.

SPORTS OUTREACH LOS ANGELES

324 N. Magnolia Avenue
Monrovia, CA 91016
Contact Person: Steve Quatro

SOLA reaches out through sports in the southern California area.

SPORTSNET

1160 Old Johnson Ferry Road
Atlanta, GA 30319
Contact Phone: 404-303-7215
Contact Fax: 404-303-9398
Contact E-mail:
dansportsnet@csi.com
Web Site: www.sportsnet-yets.org/
Scope: Atlanta area

Leagues and camp programs have been developed by SportsNet to teach positive values and life skills in the following sports: baseball, basketball, golf, soccer, softball, tennis.

Resources: clinics, sports ministry development, training programs

SPURRIN' WITH JESUS

PO Box 1405
Weatherford, TX 76086
Contact Person: Scott Mendes
Scope: National

Presenting the life-changing truth of the gospel to audiences who are interested in rodeo

TEAM FAITH RACING MINISTRY

813 Cantton Hollow Road
Knoxville, TN 37922
Contact Phone: 423-671-3066
Contact E-mail: Teamfaith@aol.com
Web Site:
http://members.aol.com/teamfaith/index.htm
Contact Person: Brian O'Rourke
Scope: National

A competitor on the International Jet Sports Boating Association National Tour Personal Watercraft Racing Series, Brian O'Rourke uses his interest in this fast-growing sport to introduce his competitors to Christ.

Resource: Team Faith Racing video

TEAM FISH—ADVENTURE RACING FOR CHRIST

550 Hidden Valley Raod
Wilmington, NC 28409
Contact Phone: 910-799-8701
Contact E-mail:
rogerw@vision911.com
Contact Person: Roger Wyatt
Scope: Local

Using nontraditional sports such as climbing, equestrian events, mountain biking, and various water sports, Team Fish seeks to show non-churched people that life in Christ is something they need to investigate.

TEAM JESUS MOTORSPORTS EVANGELISM

Little Country Church
PO Box 494640
Redding, CA 96049
Contact Phone: 916-275-5265
Contact Fax: 916-222-2631
Contact Persons: Kim and Paul Grasty
Scope: National

Team Jesus uses contemporary Christian music in chapel services at racing events to share the gospel with racing fans.

ULTIMATE GOAL MINISTRIES

PO Box 110334
Nashville, TN 37222
Contact Phone: 615-331-4339
Contact Fax: 815-331-3862
Contact E-mail: UGMin@aol.com
Contact Person: John Stayscal
Scope: International

Through soccer teams made up of teenage soccer players, Ultimate Goal takes the gospel to several countries.

UNCHARTED WATERS

2501 W. Colorado, #204
Colorado Springs, CO 80904
Contact Fax: 719-447-0347
Contact Person: Tim Conrad
E-mail: Uwaters@aol.com

Uncharted Waters is an equipping ministry that enhances the vision of the church by providing sports resources for the effective communication of the gospel. They come alongside the local church and help them develop sports programs for themselves.

UNLIMITED POTENTIAL, INC.

PO Box 1355
Warsaw, IN 46581-1355
Contact Phone: 219-267-7988
Contact Fax: 219-267-6190
Contact E-mail:
73322.2521@compuserve.com
Web Site: www.upi.org
Director: Tom Roy
Scope: International

One of the key purposes of UPI is to disciple major league baseball players, urging them to use their platform to witness of their faith. During the off-season, UPI takes some of the players overseas to conduct camps and clinics.

VANGUARDS

PO Box 2170
Orange, CA 92859
Contact Phone: 714-634-7456
Contact Person: David Irby
Scope: California, Oregon, and International

Besides sponsoring soccer teams in semipro leagues in Oregon and California, the Vanguards take traveling teams overseas for evangelism and encouragement.

WHEEL POWER CHRISTIAN CYCLING

PO Box 4791
Lynchburg, VA 24502
Contact Phone: 804-385-7213
Contact Fax: 804-385-7214
Director: Judy Bowman
Scope: National

Wheel Power is an acronym for Witnessing, Helping, Evangelizing, Encouraging, and Loving as we Pedal Our Way to Eternal Rewards. Wheel Power sponsors cross-country cycling tours that are used as witnessing outreaches.

WORLD SPORTS

PO Box 2607
Bonita Springs, FL 34133
Contact Phone: 941-498-9000
Contact Fax: 941-498-9099
Contact E-mail: waxer@ibm.net
Director: Eddie Waxer
Scope: International

The heart of this ministry is international sports outreach. World Ministry seeks to work with nationals to establish sports ministries where none exists.

YOUTH SOCCER INTERNATIONAL

2617 Dahlia Drive
Ft. Worth, TX 76123
Contact Phone: 817-263-9574
Contact Fax: 817-263-9574
Contact E-mail:
103435.3017@compuserve.com
Contact Person: Robert Burns
Scope: National

Through professional training in soccer, YSI seeks to communicate the gospel of Jesus Christ.

Chapter 8

CHRISTIAN SPORTS ABROAD

Just as sports ministries are growing and multiplying in the United States, so are they gaining strength in countries outside the U.S. One indication of the wide-ranging interest of sports abroad was the activity that surrounded the 1998 World Cup of Soccer, which was held in France.

The following report about the outreach of the gospel during the World Cup is just a sampling of the ways the Good News is being presented in dozens of countries around the world. It shows that the U.S. is not alone in using sports to win people to Jesus Christ. Special videos and booklets were prepared for this outreach, as these reports testify.

WORLD CUP OUTREACH: 1998

BANGLADESH: More than 80,000 Bengali tracts were handed out. The tract, *World Champion,* was distributed through a network of 400 churches.

BRAZIL: The greatest testimony came when soccer star Taffarel was able to declare his faith after helping Brazil win the semifinal game. Also, 50,000 New Testaments were distributed, and 7,250 *Will Brazil Do It Again?* videos were used.

BULGARIA: Twelve thousand copies of *To Be The Best* booklets were dispersed.

COSTA RICA: Executives were reached through 500 copies of the sports edition of the video *Jesus*.

EGYPT: More than 800 churches had World Cup outreaches.

IRAQ: Four hundred *To Be The Best* booklets were distributed in Baghdad.

KENYA: Watume Football Fellowship used *To Be The Best* booklets; University Fellowship used the video *Will Brazil Do It Again?* Ministries such as Scripture Union, International Bible Society, and Youth for Christ also worked on World Cup outreaches.

KOREA: A sports edition of the *Jesus* video was used.

LEBANON: Thirty churches used *To Be The Best* and *Will Brazil Do It Again?* A program called *More Than Gold* was shown on television. A 20,000-seat stadium was equipped with large screens for the finals. Booklets were given to attendees.

LITHUANIA: The sports edition of the *Jesus* video was used.

MALAYSIA: About twenty-five churches showed *Will Brazil Do It Again?*

MIDDLE EAST: Six thousand Arabic versions of the *Jesus* video were distributed.

MOLDOVA: Five thousand copies of *To Be The Best* were used.

MOROCCO: Tens of thousands of copies of *The Wonder Book* were distributed. This booklet, prepared by Child Evangelism Fellowship, had a testimony by Brazilian footballer Jorghino as well as a strong gospel presentation.

MOZAMBIQUE: Five thousand copies were distributed of a booklet called *Goal*.

MYANMAR: (formerly Burma): National television twice broadcast a video with testimonies of Brazilian soccer stars.

NETHERLANDS: Dutch television showed five programs that detailed the testimonies of Brazilian star Taffarel and others. Ten thousand copies of a Dutch Sports New Testament were distributed.

ROMANIA: Almost 50,000 copies of *To Be The Best* were distributed.

SOUTH AFRICA: More than 100,000 copies of *Goal* were produced.

ZIMBABWE: More than 10,000 copies of *Goal* were given out. Also, the videos *Will Brazil Do It Again?* and the *Jesus* video were shown.

In summary, more than 110 countries had ministries that used soccer as an outreach tool to tell sports fans about Jesus Christ.

SOCCER RESOURCES

The following resources were developed and distributed worldwide in conjunction with World Cup 1998 in France. For more information about these resources and for continuing information on future soccer outreaches, use the contact information at the end of the listing.

Sports New Testament (Brazil)

Children's Soccer Comic Book (United Kingdom)

Football (soccer) Dramatic Video (Middle East)

Jesus Video, Special Soccer Edition (22 languages)

Goal (World Cup-related booklet)

More Than A Game (Video)

Sports Music Video (Middle East)

World Cup Booklet (Thailand)

To Be The Best (World Cup Booklet, 10 languages)

Who Won The World Cup? (Book, 5 languages)

Will Brazil Do It Again? (Video, 10 languages)

Wonder Book (children, North Africa)

Contact: Michael Wozniak, *Sports Spectrum,* Box 3566, Grand Rapids, MI 49501. E-mail at mwozniack@rbc.org

INTERNATIONAL MINISTRIES

The following outreach ministries use sports as a tool for letting people know about the saving power of Jesus Christ.

ACTS

Association of Christian Triathletes
Contact Person: Andrew Stanfield
[AUTHOR: Please add address and contact phone]

An arm of Athletes In Action Australia, ACTS uses tracts and testimonies to reach the unreached.

AMBASSADORS IN SPORT

Claremont House
St. George's Road
Bolton BL1 2BY
England
Contact Phone: 01204-36306
Contact E-mail:
ais.uk@btinternet.com
Contact Person: John Boggs

AIS is the European arm of Missionary Athletes International.

Resource: newsletter: The Goal Post

Athletes In Action International
421 East Woodman Road
Colorado Springs, CO 80919
Contact Phone: 513-933-2421
Contact Fax: 513-933-2422

ATHLETES MINISTRIES INTERNATIONAL

PO Box 241076
Memphis, TN 38124
Contact Person: Dennis Cantrell

ATLETAS DE CRISTO

Brazilian address:
Caixa Postal (Box) 55011
São Paulo, SP CEP 04799-970
U.S. address:
Gabor Becht
3869 NW 166th Drive
Beaverton, OR 97006
Contact E-mail: gabor@ctletus.org
or atletas@ibm.net
Contact Phone: 11-246-6538
Contact Fax: 11-524-9444
Director: Alex Ribiero
Country: Brazil

A Brazilian sports outreach that uses sports to proclaim the gospel and to train leaders to know Christ better

Resources include books, videos, brochures, and merchandise.

CHRISTIAN SPORTS INTERNATIONAL

6023 Calle De Felice
San Jose, CA 95124
Contact Fax: 408-269-2033
Contact Person: Rodger Oswald

CSI seeks to help churches and other groups use sports both to begin and grow churches

CHRISTIANS IN SPORT

PO Box 93
Oxford OX2 7YP
Great Britain
Phone: 01865-311211
Fax: 01865-311334
E-mail:
stuart@christiansinsport.org.uk
Contact Person: Stuart Weir
Internet Site:
www.christiansinsport.org.uk
Country: Great Britain

Christians In Sport is a wide-ranging ministry that seeks to reach out through many different sports. Working with churches and with athletes both professional and amateur, CIS reaches thousands with the gospel.

CHRISTIANS IN RUGBY

14 Dehlsen Avenue
West Pennant Hills
NSW 2125
AUSTRALIA
Contact Phone: 61-2-9873-5145
Contact E-mail:
peterfurst@hotmail.com
Director: Peter Furst
Country: Australia

Started in 1996 by footballer Peter Furst, Christians in Rugby seeks to encourage Christian rugby players and to spread the gospel.

CHRISTIAN SPORTS OUTREACH INTERNATIONAL

PO Box 2823
Vero Beach, FL 32961-2823
Contact Phone: 800-451-3643
Contact Fax: 561-778-6781
Contact E-mail: coihq@sprynet.com
Director: Jack Isleib
Scope: Worldwide

CSOI sponsors athletic missions trips to a variety of countries. Sports included in these teams are baseball, basketball, cheerleading, football, golf, gymnastics, martial arts, soccer, street hockey, tennis, volleyball, and wrestling.

GOOD SPORTS

The Navigators
PO Box 6000
Colorado Springs, CO 80934
Contact E-mail:
tslobodian@interhop.net
Countries: Slovakia and Hungary

Good Sports has learned that one universal language is baseball. By teaching the sport to kids in Slovakia and Hungary, Good Sports personnel have had the opportunity to share the gospel with them.

INTERNATIONAL SPORTS COALTION

160 Harbor Drive
Key Biscayne, FL 33149
Contact Phone: 305-361-2058
Contact Person: Eddie Waxer

The organization develops sports ministries internationally, helping ministries around the world use sports as a way to spread the gospel.

KRISTEN IDRETTSKONTAKT (KRIK)

PB 3822 UllevAl Hageby
Sognsvn 75F, UllevAl Stadion
Norway
Contact Phone: 00-47-22-23-51
Contact Fax: 00-47-22-23-60
Contact E-mail: krik@krik.no
Contact Person: Anne Lene Tangen
Country: Norway

Headed by Kjell Markset, sports minister, KRIK is a youth organization in Norway that combines sports and faith.

SPORTS OUTREACH NEW ZEALAND

PO Box 2298
Wellington, New Zealand
Contact E-mail: mobsol@ihug.co.nz
Contact Person: Robert Blok
Country: New Zealand

In its formative stages, SONZ is striving to promote sports and other ministry related activities.

SPORTS SERVICES INTERNATIONAL

Box 576
Shatin, NT
Hong Kong
Contact Phone: 852-2524-6057
Contact Fax: 852-2810-5198
Contact E-mail: ssi@hk.super.net
Contact Person: Merja Ruokonen
Country: China (Hong Kong)

Hong Kong-based SSI seeks to train sports people to use athletics in evangelism and discipleship. Also, the ministry runs basketball and volleyball camps.

WITHIN THE WALLS

PO Box 721
Forest, VA 24551
Contact Phone: 804-582-2381

This prison ministry is run from the United States, but the work takes place in England. Bill Bell, soccer coach at Liberty University, along with his wife Mary, go inside the prisons of England to tell the people there about faith in Jesus Christ. Bell is a former player for the Scottish national team.

Chapter 9

CHRISTIAN COLLEGE ATHLETICS

1. DIRECTORY

NATIONAL CHRISTIAN COLLEGE ATHLETIC ASSOCIATION

According to data released by the National Christian College Athletic Association (NCCAA) in 1999, the association had 115 member schools that were divided into two divisions: Division I (Christian liberal arts colleges) and Division II (Bible colleges). These schools field a variety of sports, and they all participate in NCCAA competitions leading to national championships in various sports. The competitive sports offerings are listed below, including whether there are men (M) or women's (W) teams. Baseball is offered to men only; softball is offered to women only.

This information may be helpful for someone hoping to attend a Christian college and play sports, or perhaps it will direct a reader who simply might be looking for Christian sports information.

National championships won by member schools are shown as well, using the following *national champs key:* WVB, women's volleyball; WBB, women's basketball; WS, women's softball; WTF, womens' track and field; WCC, womens' cross-country; WSO, womens' soccer; MBB, men's basketball; MB, men's baseball; MW, men's wrestling; MTF, men's track and field; MCC, men's cross-country; MS, men's soccer; MT, men's tennis.

DIVISION 1

ASBURY COLLEGE EAGLES

Enrollment: 1,176
Affiliation: Interdenominational
Sports: Baseball, basketball (M & W), cross-country (M & W), soccer (M), softball, swimming (M & W), tennis (M & W), volleyball (W)
Athletic Director: David Baillie
1 Macklem Drive
Wilmore, KY 40390-1198
Phone: 606-858-3511 x2163
Fax: 606-858-3511 x 2473

BARTLESVILLE WESLEYAN COLLEGE EAGLES

Enrollment: 476
Affiliation: Wesleyan
Sports: Basketball (M & W), soccer (M & W), volleyball (W)
Athletic Director: Jere Johnson
2201 Silver Lake Road
Bartlesville, OK 74006
Phone: 918-335-6259
Fax: 918-335-6244

BETHEL COLLEGE PILOTS

Enrollment: 1,600
Affiliation: Missionary Church
Sports: Baseball, basketball (M & W), cross-country (M & W), golf (M), soccer (M & W), softball, tennis (M & W), track & field (M & W), volleyball (W)
Athletic Director: Mike Lightfoot
1001 W. McKinley Avenue
Mishawaka, IN 46545
Phone: 219-257-3343
Fax: 219-257-3385
E-mail: webmaster@bethel-IN.edu
National champs: WVB, 1993, 1994; WSB, 1995; MBB, 1992, 1993; MB, 1986, 1990

BRYAN COLLEGE LIONS

Enrollment: 445
Affiliation: Nondenominational
Sports: Basketball (M & W), soccer (M & W), tennis (M & W), volleyball (W)
Athletic Director: Dr. Sanford Zensen
Box 7000, Mercer Drive
Dayton, TN 37321
Phone: 423-775-7255
Fax: 423-775-7330
E-mail: zensensa@bryannet.bryan.edu
National champs: MCC, 1975; MS, 1975–77

CASCADE COLLEGE THUNDERBIRDS

Enrollment: 251
Affiliation: Church of Christ
Sports: Basketball (M), cross-country (M & W), soccer (M), track and field (M & W), volleyball (W)
Athletic Director: Eric Littleton
9101 E. Burnside
Portland, OR 97216
Phone: 503-257-1207
Fax: 503-257-1222
E-mail: bpink@cascade.edu

CEDARVILLE COLLEGE YELLOW JACKETS

Enrollment: 2,484
Affiliation: Baptist
Sports: Baseball, basketball (M & W), cross-country (M & W), golf (M), soccer (M & W), softball, tennis (M & W), track & field (M & W),

volleyball (W)
Athletic Director: Pete Reese
PO Box 601
Cedarville, OH 45314
Phone: 937-766-7755
Fax: 937-766-5556
E-mail: reesep@cedarville.edu
National champs: WTF, 1985, 1986, 1994–98; WCC, 1985, 1991, 1996; MTF, 1975, 1976, 1983, 1984; MCC, 1978, 1979, 1985

CENTRAL CHRISTIAN COLLEGE TIGERS

Enrollment: 114
Affiliation: Free Methodist
Sports: Baseball, basketball (M & W), cross-country (M & W), golf (M & W), soccer (M & W), softball, volleyball (W)
Athletic Director: Gary Turner
PO Box 1403
McPherson, KS 67460
Phone: 316-241-0723
Fax: 316-241-4318
E-mail: garyt@centralcollege.edu

EAST TEXAS BAPTIST UNIVERSITY TIGERS

Enrollment: 1,141
Affiliation: Baptist
Sports: Baseball, basketball (M & W), golf (M & W), soccer (M & W), softball, volleyball (W)
Athletic Director: Kent Reeves
1209 North Grove Street
Marshall, TX 75670
Phone: 903-935-7963 x271
Fax: 903-935-0162
E-mail: klreeves@etbu.edu

CHRISTIAN HERITAGE COLLEGE HAWKS

Enrollment: 354
Affiliation: Independent
Sports: Basketball (M & W), soccer (M), volleyball (W)
Athletic Director: Paul Berry
2100 Greenfield Drive
El Cajon, CA 92109
Phone: 619-441-2280
Fax: 619-590-1734
E-mail: info@cbcag.edu
National champs: WVB, 1996, 1999; MBB, 1990, 1997, 1998

CONCORDIA COLLEGE CARDINALS

Enrollment: 568
Affiliation: Lutheran
Sports: Baseball, basketball (M & W), cross-country (M & W), soccer (M & W), softball, track & field (M & W), volleyball (W)
Athletic Director: Robert Kasten
4090 Geddes Road
Ann Arbor, MI 48105
Phone: 734-995-7342
Fax: 734-995-4883
National champions: Women's volleyball, 1986; Women's softball, 1998

EMMANUEL COLLEGE LIONS

Enrollment: 657
Affiliation: Pentecostal
Sports: Baseball, basketball (M & W), softball, tennis (M & W)
Athletic Director: Mike Bona
PO Box 129
Franklin Springs, GA 30639
Phone: 706-245-3139

Fax: 706-245-4424
E-mail: mbona@emmanuel-college.edu

FAULKNER UNIVERSITY EAGLES

Enrollment: 666
Affiliation: Church of Christ
Sports: Baseball, basketball (M), cross-country (M & W) softball, volleyball (W)
Athletic Director: Jim Sanderson
5345 Atlanta Highway
Montgomery, AL 36109
Phone: 334-386-7148
Fax: 334-386-7277
E-mail: jsanderson@faulkner.edu

GENEVA COLLEGE GOLDEN TORNADOES

Enrollment: 1,488
Affiliation: Reformed Presbyterian Church
Sports: Baseball, basketball (M & W), cross-country (M & W), football, soccer (M & W), softball, tennis (M & W), track & field (M & W)
Athletic Director: Geno DeMarco
3200 College Avenue
Beaver Falls, PA 15010
Phone: 724-847-6650
Fax: 724-847-5001
National champs: MS, 1994

GRACE COLLEGE LANCERS

Enrollment: 598
Affiliation: Grace Brethren
Sports:Baseball, basketball (M & W), soccer (M & W), softball, tennis (M & W), track & field (M & W), volleyball (W)
Athletic Director: Roger Haun
200 Seminary Drive
Winona Lake, IN 46590
Phone: 219-372-5217
Fax: 219-372-5137
E-mail: hustedjl@grace.edu
National champs: WVB, 1995

GREENVILLE COLLEGE PANTHERS

Enrollment: 823
Affiliation: Free Methodist
Sports: baseball, basketball (M & W), cross-country (M & W), football, golf (M), soccer (M & W), softball, tennis (M & W), track & field (M & W), volleyball (W)
Athletic Director: Sharon Alger
315 E. College Avenue
Greenville, IL 62246-1145
Phone: 618-664-2800 x 4371
Fax: 618-664-2800 x 4377
E-mail: panther@greenville.edu

HANNIBAL-LAGRANGE COLLEGE TROJANS

Enrollment: 727
Affiliation: Southern Baptist
Sports: Baseball, basketball (M & W), golf (M), softball, volleyball (W)
Athletic Director: Ben Pitney
2800 Palmyra Road
Hannibal, MO 63401-1999
Phone: 573-221-3675 x300
Fax: 573-221-9424
E-mail: bpitney@hlg.edu

INDIANA WESLEYAN UNIVERSITY WILDCATS

Enrollment: 3,798
Affiliation: Wesleyan
Sports: Baseball, basketball (M & W), cross-country (M & W), golf (M), soccer (M & W), softball, tennis

(M & W), track & field (M & W), volleyball (W)
Athletic Director: Dr. Mike Fratzke
4201 S. Washington Street
Marion, IN 46953
Phone: 765-677-2318
Fax: 765-677-2328
E-mail: lneill@indwe.edu
National Championships: WVB, 1985; WSO, 1997; MTF, 1994; MBB, 1995

JOHNSON BIBLE COLLEGE PREACHERS/EVANGELS

Enrollment: 364
Affiliation: Christian
Sports: Baseball, basketball (M & W), soccer (M & W), softball, tennis (M), volleyball (W)
Athletic Director: Douglas Karnes
7900 Johnson Drive
Knoxville, TN 37998
Phone: 423-251-2210
Fax: 423-251-2333
E-mail: dkarnes@jbc.edu

JUDSON COLLEGE LADY EAGLES

Enrollment: 331
Affiliation: Baptist
Sports: Basketball (W), softball, volleyball (W)
Athletic Director: Michele Templin
PO Box 120
Marion, AL 36756
Phone: 334-683-5249
Fax: 334-683-5158

JUDSON COLLEGE EAGLES

Enrollment: 827
Affiliation: Baptist
Sports: Baseball, basketball (M & W), cross-country (M & W), soccer (M & W), softball, tennis (M & W), volleyball (W)
Athletic Director: Steve Burke
1151 N. State Street
Elgin, IL 60123
Phone: 847-695-2500 x3800
Fax: 847-695-9252
National champs: MS, 1991, 1992, 1995, 1997

LEE UNIVERSITY FLAMES

Enrollment: 2,584
Affiliation: Church of God
Sports: Baseball, basketball (M & W), cross-country (M & W), golf (M), soccer (M & W), softball, tennis (M & W), track & field (M & W), volleyball (W)
Athletic Director: Larry Carpenter
1120 N. Ocoee Street
Cleveland, TN 37311
Phone: 423-614-8440
Fax: 423-614-8443
E-mail: athletics@leeuniversity.edu
National champs: WBB, 1985, 1999; MBB, 1968, 1973, 1994; MT, 1997

LETOURNEAU UNIVERSITY YELLOW JACKETS

Enrollment: 837
Affiliation: Nondenominational
Sports: Baseball, basketball (M & W), cross-country (M), soccer (M), volleyball (W)
Athletic Director: Dr. Bill Elder
PO Box 7001
Longview, TX 75607
Phone: 903-233-3370
Fax: 903-233-3822
E-mail: brewerm@lctu.edu
National champs: WBB, 1997, 1998

LIBERTY UNIVERSITY FLAMES

Affiliation: Baptist
Sports: Baseball, basketball (M & W), cross country, football, golf (M & W), softball, track & field (M &W), volleyball
Athletic Director: Kim Graham
1971 University Boulevard
Lynchburg, VA 24502
Phone: 800-543-5317
Fax: 800-628-7977
E-mail: admissions@liberty.edu
Internet Site: www.liberty.edu
NCCAA National champs (Liberty now competes in the NCAA): WTF, 1979, 1981; MBB, 1980; MW, 1977–81; MTF, 1979

MALONE COLLEGE PIONEERS

Enrollment: 1,717
Affiliation: Evangelical Friends
Sports: Baseball, basketball (M & W), cross-country (M & W), football, golf (M), soccer (M & W), softball, tennis (M & W), track & field (M & W), volleyball (W)
Athletic Director: Hal Smith
515 25th Street NW
Canton, OH 44709
Phone: 330-471-8300
Fax: 330-471-8298
National champs: WTF, 1987–89; WCC, 1986, 1987, 1989, 1990, 1992, 1993, 1997; MBB, 1996; MTF, 1973, 1989, 1991; MCC, 1986–92, 1994, 1995, 1997; MG, 1999

THE MASTER'S COLLEGE MUSTANGS

Enrollment: 910
Affiliation: Nondenominational
21726 Placerita Canyon Road
Santa Clarita, CA 91321
Phone: 661-259-3540 x 222
Athletic Director: Bill Oats
Sports: Baseball, basketball (M & W), cross-country (M & W), golf (M), soccer (M & W), volleyball (W)
National champs: MS, 1987, 1989, 1993

MIDAMERICAN NAZARENE UNIVERSITY PIONEERS

Enrollment: 1,155
Affiliation: Nazarene
Sports: Baseball, basketball (M & W), cross-country (M & W), football, softball, track & field (M & W), volleyball (W)
Athletic Director: Ron Hill
2030 E. College Way
Olathe, KS 66062
Phone: 913-791-3278
Fax: 913-791-3456
E-mail: rhill@mnu.edu
National champs: MTF, 1983

MID-CONTINENT COLLEGE COUGARS

Enrollment: 135
Affiliation: Baptist
Sports: Baseball, softball
Athletic Director: Hannibal Najjar
99 Powell Road East
Mayfield, KY 42066
Phone: 502-247-8521
Fax: 502-247-3115
E-mail: mcc@midcontinent.edu

MOUNT VERNON NAZARENE COLLEGE CRUSADERS

Enrollment: 1,631
Affiliation: Nazarene
Sports: Baseball, basketball (M & W), golf (M), soccer (M), softball,

volleyball (W)
Athletic Director: Scott Flemming
800 Martinsburg Road
Martinsburg, OH 43050
Phone: 740-397-9000 x 3100
Fax: 614-392-5079
E-mail: sflemming@mvnc.edu
National champs: WBB, 1994; MB, 1989, 1995–97, 1999

NORTHWEST CHRISTIAN COLLEGE CRUSADERS

Enrollment: 446
Affiliation: Disciples of Christ
Sports: Baseball, basketball (M)
Athletic Director: Dave Lipp
828 E. 11th Street
Eugene, OR 97401
Phone: 541-343-1641
Fax: 541-343-9159

NORTHWEST COLLEGE EAGLES

Enrollment: 824
Affiliation: Assemblies of God
Sports: Basketball (M & W), cross-country (M), soccer (M), track & field (M), volleyball (W)
Athletic Director: Wayne Mendezona
5220 108th Avenue NE
Kirkland, WA 98033
Phone: 425-889-4207
Fax: 425-889-5323
E-mail: stephanie.baller@ncag.edu
National champs: WBB, 1988, 1990, 1991, 1993, 1994; MBB, 1993

NORTHWESTERN COLLEGE EAGLES

Enrollment: 1,524
Affiliation: Nondenominational
Sports: Baseball, basketball (M & W), cross-country (M & W), football, golf (M), soccer (M & W), softball, tennis (M), track & field (M & W), volleyball (W)
Athletic Director: Joseph L. Smith
3003 Snelling Avenue N
St. Paul, MN 55113
Phone: 612-631-5219
Fax: 612-628-3350
National champs: (Division I): MW, 1992; MTF, 1977, 1978; (Division II): WBB, 1984, 1985; MBB, 1980

NYACK COLLEGE PURPLE PRIDE

Enrollment: 829
Affiliation: Christian and Missionary Alliance
Sports: Baseball, basketball (M & W), cross-country (M & W), soccer (M & W), softball, volleyball (W)
Athletic Director: Keith Davie
1 South Boulevard
Nyack, NY 10960
Phone: 914-358-1710
Fax: 914-353-2147
E-mail: daviek@Nyack.edu

OAKLAND CITY UNIVERSITY MIGHTY OAKS

Enrollment: 329
Affiliation: General Baptist
Sports: Baseball, basketball (M & W), cross-country (M & W), golf (M & W), softball, volleyball (W)
Athletic Director: Mike Sandirar
Johnson Center
Oakland City, IN 47660
Phone: 812-749-1264
Fax: 812-749-1291

OLIVET NAZARENE UNIVERSITY TIGERS

Enrollment: 1,727
Affiliation: Nazarene
Sports: Baseball, basketball (M & W), cross-country (M & W), football, golf (M), soccer (M & W), softball, tennis (M & W), track & field (M & W), volleyball (W)
Athletic Director: Larry Watson
Athletics Department
240 E. Marsile Street
Kankakee, IL 60914
Phone: 815-939-5372
Fax: 815-939-7933
E-mail:tbakewel@olivet.edu
National champs: WSB, 1996, 1997; WCC, 1994, 1995; MBB, 1975; MW, 1987–90, 1993; MT, 1998

HOPE INTERNATIONAL UNIVERSITY ROYALS

Enrollment: 702
Affiliation: Christian Church/Church of Christ
Sports: Baseball, basketball (M & W), golf (M & W), soccer (M & W), softball, volleyball (M & W)
Athletic Director: Dr. Glenn Snyder
2500 E. Nutwood Avenue
Fullerton, CA 92831
Phone: 714-879-3901
Fax: 714-526-0231

PENSACOLA CHRISTIAN COLLEGE EAGLES

Enrollment: 3,818
Affiliation: Nondenominational
Sports: Baseball, basketball (M), volleyball (W), wrestling
Athletic Director: Jim Wagenschutz
PO Box 18000
Pensacola, FL 32503
Phone: 904-478-8496 x 2783
Fax: 904-479-6571
National champs: MW, 1994–96, 1998

ROBERTS WESLEYAN COLLEGE RAIDERS

Enrollment: 1,215
Affiliation: Free Methodist
Sports: Basketball (M & W), cross-country (M & W), soccer (M & W), softball, track & field (M & W), volleyball (W)
Athletic Director: Michael Faro
2301 Westside Drive
Rochester, NY 14624
Phone: 716-594-6130
Fax: 716-594-6580
E-mail: farom@roberts.edu
National champs: MCC, 1993

SOUTHERN WESLEYAN UNIVERSITY

Enrollment: 1,247
Affiliation: Wesleyan
Sports: Baseball, basketball (M & W), cross-country (M & W), golf (M), soccer (M & W), softball, volleyball (W)
Athletic Director: Dr. Keith Connor
1 Wesleyan Drive
Central, SC 29630
Phone: 864-639-2453
Fax: 864-639-4526

SPRING ARBOR COLLEGE COUGARS

Enrollment: 1,906
Affiliation: Free Methodist
Sports: Baseball, basketball (M &

W), cross-country (M & W), golf (M), soccer (M & W), softball, tennis (M & W), track & field (M & W), volleyball (W)
Athletic Director: Hank Burbridge
106 E. Main Street
Spring Arbor, MI 49283
Phone: 517-750-1200
Fax: 517-750-2745
E-mail: melissa@admin.arbor.edu
National champions: WVB, 1992; WBB, 1983, 1987; WTF, 1982; WCC, 1981, 1982; MB, 1992, 1993, 1998

TAYLOR UNIVERSITY TROJANS

Enrollment: 1,904
Affiliation: Nondenominational
Sports: Baseball, basketball (M & W), cross-country (M & W), football, golf (M), soccer (M & W), softball, tennis (M & W), track & field (M & W), volleyball (W)
Athletic Director: David B. Bireline
500 W. Reade Avenue
Upland, IN 46989-1001
Phone: 765-998-5311
Fax: 765-998-4920
E-mail: jfmarsee@tayloru.edu
National champs: WVB, 1989–91; WTF, 1984; MTF, 1985–87, 1995–99; MCC, 1996

TAYLOR UNIVERSITY-FORT WAYNE FALCONS

Enrollment: 328
Affiliation: Nondenominational
Sports: Basketball (M & W), soccer (M), volleyball (W)
Athletic Director: Bud Hamilton
1025 W. Rudisill Boulevard
Ft. Wayne, IN 46807
Phone: 219-456-211
Fax: 219-456-2119
E-mail: bdhamilton@tayloru.edu

TENNESSEE TEMPLE UNIVERSITY CRUSADERS

Enrollment: 525
Affiliation: Baptist
Sports: Baseball, basketball (M & W), soccer (M), volleyball (W)
Athletic Director: Kevin Templeton
1815 Union Avenue
Chattanooga, TN 37404
Phone: 423-493-4220
Fax: 423-493-4219
E-mail: COACHRJ@juno.com
National champs: MBB, 1979, 1981–83, 1988, 1989

TRINITY CHRISTIAN COLLEGE TROLLS

Enrollment: 593
Affiliation: Interdenominational
Sports: Baseball, basketball (M & W), soccer (M & W), softball, volleyball (W)
Athletic Director: David L. Ribbens
6601 W. College Drive
Palos Heights, IL 60463
Phone: 708-239-4779
Fax: 708-396-7460

TRINITY INTERNATIONAL UNIVERSITY WARRIORS

Enrollment: 325
Affiliation: Evangelical Free
Sports: Baseball, soccer (M), volleyball (W)
Athletic Director: Jud Damon
500 NE 1st Avenue
Miami, FL 33101

Phone: 305-577-4600 x 133
Fax: 305-577-4612
E-mail: jdamon@trin.edu

TRINITY INTERNATINAL UNIVERSITY TROJANS

Enrollment: 775
Affiliation: Evangelical Free
Sports: Baseball, basketball (M & W), cross-country (M & W), football, soccer (M & W), tennis (M & W), volleyball (M & W)
Athletic Director: William Washington
2065 Half Day Road
Deerfield, IL 60015
Phone: 847-945-7095
Fax: 847-317-8056

UNION UNIVERSITY BULLDOGS

Enrollment: 1,650
Affiliation: Baptist
Sports: Baseball, basketball (M & W), golf (M), softball, tennis (M & W), volleyball (W)
Athletic Director: Dr. David Blackstock
1050 Union University Drive
Jackson, TN 38305
Phone: 901-661-5130
Fax: 901-661-5182

WESTERN BAPTIST COLLEGE WARRIORS

Enrollment: 617
Affiliation: Baptist
Sports: Baseball, basketball (M & W), soccer (M & W), volleyball (W)
Athletic Director: Tim Hills
5000 Deer Park Drive SE
Salem, OR 97301
Phone: 503-375-7021
Fax: 503-315-2947
E-mail: athletics@wbc.edu
National champs: WVB, 1997; WBB, 1977 (Div. II), 1995, 1996; MS, 1996

YORK COLLEGE PANTHERS

Enrollment: 426
Affiliation: Church of Christ
Sports: Baseball, basketball (M & W), cross-country (M & W), soccer (M & W), softball, tennis (M & W), track & field (M & W), volleyball (W)
Athletic Director: Gerald Nixon
912 Kiplinger Avenue
York, NE 68467
Phone: 402-363-5622
Fax: 402-363-5623

ASSOCIATE MEMBERS

CORNERSTONE COLLEGE

Enrollment: 1,100
Affiliation: Baptist
Sports: Basketball (M & W), cross-country (M & W), soccer (M & W), softball, tennis (M & W), track & field (M & W), volleyball (W)
Athletic Director: Robert Fortosis
1001 East Beltline NE
Grand Rapids, MI 49505
Phone: 616-949-5300

HOUGHTON COLLEGE HIGHLANDERS

Enrollment: 1,243
Affiliation: Wesleyan
Sports: Baseball, basketball (M & W), cross-country (M & W), soccer (M & W), track & field (M & W), volleyball (W), field hockey

Athletic Director: Skip Lord
PO Box 128
Houghton, NY 14744
Phone: 716-567-9360
Fax: 716-567-9365
National champs: MS, 1979, 1980, 1986

HUNTINGTON COLLEGE FORESTERS

Enrollment: 697
Affiliation: United Brethren in Christ
Sports: Baseball, basketball (M & W), cross-country (M & W), golf (M), soccer (M & W), softball, tennis (M & W), track & field (M & W), volleyball (W)
Athletic Director: Lori Culler
2303 College Avenue
Huntington, IN 46750
Phone: 219-356-4090
Fax: 219-359-4212
E-mail: Lculler@huntington.edu
National champions: WVB, 1988; WBB, 1984, 1991, 1992; WTF, 1990–93

DIVISION II

APPALACHIAN BIBLE COLLEGE WARRIORS

Enrollment: 244
Affiliation: Independent
Sports: Basketball (M & W), soccer (M), volleyball (W)
Athletic Director: Tim Barton
PO Box AB
Bradley, WV 25818
Phone: 304-877-6427

ARLINGTON BAPTIST COLLEGE PATRIOTS

Enrollment: 189
Affiliation: Baptist
Sports: Basketball (M), volleyball (W)
Athletic Director: Durward Cash
3001 W. Division
Arlington, TX 76012
Phone: 817-274-0785

ATLANTA CHRISTIAN COLLEGE CHARGERS

Enrollment: 300
Affiliation: Christian Church
Sports: Baseball, basketball (M & W), golf (M), soccer (M), tennis (M & W), volleyball (W)
Athletic Director: Joe Griffin
2605 Ben Hill Road
East Point, GA 30344
Phone: 404-669-2052
National champs: MBB, 1991 (Division II-A)

BAPTIST BIBLE COLLEGE PATRIOTS (MISSOURI)

Enrollment: 829
Affiliation: Baptist
Sports: Basketball (M & W), golf (M), volleyball (W)
Athletic Director: Hilly Bect
628 E. Kearney
Springfield, MO 65803
Phone: 417-268-6038

BAPTIST BIBLE COLLEGE DEFENDERS (PENNSYLVANIA)

Enrollment: 488
Affiliation: Baptist
Sports: Basketball (M & W), cross-country (M & W), soccer (M & W),

track & field (M & W), volleyball (W), wrestling
Athletic Director: Jim Huckaby
538 Venard Road
Clarks Summit, PA 18411
Phone: 570-585-9323
National champs: WBB, 1983; MBB, 1978, 1979, 1981–84, 1992; MS 1990–92; 1995

BAPTIST BIBLE COLLEGE EAST CRUSADERS

Enrollment: 101
Affiliation: Baptist
Sports: soccer (M); volleyball (W)
Athletic Director: Gary Coleman
950 Metropolitan Avenue
Boston, MA 02136
Phone: 617-364-3510

BARCLAY COLLEGE BEARS

Enrollment: 92
Affiliation: Nondenominational
Sports: Basketball (M & W), soccer (M & W), volleyball (W)
Athletic Director: Amy Fleener
PO Box 288
Haviland, KS 67059
Phone: 316-862-5876

CALIFORNIA CHRISTIAN COLLEGE RUNNIN' ROYALS

Enrollment: NA
Affiliation: Freewill Baptist
Sports: Baseball, basketball (M), volleyball (W)
Athletic Director: Wes Bigelow
4881 E. University
Fresno, CA 93703
Phone: 559-251-4215

CALVARY BIBLE COLLEGE WARRIORS

Enrollment: 400
Affiliation: Nondenominational
Sports: Basketball (M & W), cross-country (M), golf (M), volleyball (W)
Athletic Director: Jeanette Regier
15800 Calvary Road
Kansas City, MO 64147
Phone: 816-332-5152 x 1210

CARVER BIBLE COLLEGE COUGARS

Enrollment: 200
Affiliation: Independent
Sports: Basketball (M)
Athletic Director: Martin Cartin
437 Nelson Street SW
Atlanta, GA 30313
Phone: 404-527-4520

CENTRAL BIBLE COLLEGE SPARTANS

Enrollment: 986
Affiliation: Assemblies of God
Sports: Basketball (M), volleyball (W)
Athletic Director: Kirk Hanson
3000 N. Grant Avenue
Springfield, MO 65803
Phone: 417-833-2551 x 1105
National champs: MBB, 1994

CINCINNATI BIBLE COLLEGE GOLDEN EAGLES

Enrollment: 537
Affiliation: Church of Christ
Sports: Basketball (M & W), golf (M), soccer (M), volleyball (W)
Athletic Director: John Garrett
2700 Glenway Avenue
Cincinnati, OH 45204

Phone: 513-244-8442
E-mail: john.garrett@cincybible.edu
National champs: MBB, 1985–87

CIRCLEVILLE BIBLE COLLEGE CRUSADERS (DIVISION IIA)

Enrollment: 185
Affiliation: CCCU
Sports: Baseball, basketball (M & W), soccer (M), volleyball (W)
Athletic Director: Rev. Larry Olson
PO Box 458
Circleville, OH 43113
Phone: 614-477-7702

CLEARWATER CHRISTIAN COLLEGE COUGARS

Enrollment: 511
Affiliation: Nondenominational
Sports: Baseball, basketball (M & W), soccer (M), softball, volleyball (W)
Athletic Director: Del Wubbena
3400 Gulf-to-Bay Boulevard
Clearwater, FL 33759-4595
Phone: 813-726-1153
National champs: WVB, 1995–97; MB, 1997

COLORADO CHRISTIAN UNIVERSITY COUGARS

Affiliation: Independent
SportsL Basketball (M & W), cross-country (M & W), soccer (M & W), tennis (M & W), volleyball
180 South Garrison
Lakewood, CO 80226
Phone: 303-238-5386
Fax: 303-233-2735
Internet Site: www.ccu.edu

COLUMBIA BIBLE COLLEGE

Enrollment: 349
Affiliation: Mennonite
Sports: Basketball (M), hockey, soccer (M & W), volleyball (M & W)
Athletic Director: Tim Demant
2990 Clearbrook Road
V2T 2Z8
Abbottsford BC, Canada
Phone: 604-853-3567 x 311

CROWN COLLEGE CRUSADERS

Enrollment: 529
Affiliation: Christian and Missionary Alliance
Sports: Baseball, basketball (M & W), cross-country (M & W), football, golf (M & W), soccer (M), volleyball (W)
Athletic Director: Don Rekoske
6425 County Road 30
St. Bonifacius, MN 55375
Phone: 612-446-4179

CROWN COLLEGE ROYAL CRUSADERS

Enrollment: 339
Affiliation: Baptist
Sports: Basketball (M), soccer (M), volleyball (W)
Athletic Director: Dwayne Hickman
PO Box 159
Powell, TN 37849
Phone: 423-938-8186

DALLAS CHRISTIAN COLLEGE CRUSADERS

Enrollment: 190
Affiliation: Christian Church
Sports: Basketball (M & W), soccer (M), volleyball (W)

Athletic Director: Mark Worley
2700 Christian Parkway
Dallas, TX 75234-7299
Phone: 972-241-3371

EMMAUS BIBLE COLLEGE EAGLES

Enrollment: 255
Affiliation: Nondenominational
Sport: Basketball (M & W)
Athletic Director: Marilee Mertz
2570 Asbury Road
Dubuque, IA 52001
Phone: 319-588-8000 x 164

FAITH BAPTIST BIBLE COLLEGE EAGLES (DIVISION IIA)

Enrollment: 244
Affiliation: Baptist
Sports: Basketball (M & W), soccer (M), volleyball (W)
Athletic Director: Dave Walter
1900 NW Fourth Street
Ankeny, IA 50021
Phone: 515-964-0601 x 24

FLORIDA CHRISTIAN COLLEGE SUNS (DIVISION IIA)

Enrollment: 156
Affiliation: Christian
Sports: Basketball (M & W), volleyball (W)
Athletic Director: Dale Buchanon
1011 Bill Beck Boulevard
Kissimmee, FL 34744
Phone: 407-847-8966 x 265

FREE WILL BAPTIST BIBLE COLLEGE FLAMES

Enrollment: 322
Affiliation: Free Will Baptist
Sport: Basketball (M & W)
Athletic Director: Byron Deel
3606 West End Avenue
Nashville, TN 37205
Phone: 615-844-5276

GEORGE FOX UNIVERSITY BRUINS

Sports: Baseball, basketball, cross-country, soccer, softball, tennis, track & field, volleyball
414 North Meridian Street
Newberg, OR 97132-2697
Phone: 800-765-4369
Internet Site: www.georgefox.edu

GRACE BIBLE COLLEGE TIGERS

Enrollment: 143
Affiliation: Grace Gospel Fellowship
Sports: Basketball (M & W), soccer (M & W), softball, tennis (M), volleyball (W)
Athletic Director: John Spooner
PO Box 910
Wyoming, MI 49509
Phone: 616-538-1770
National champs: MBB, 1994, 1995 (Division II-A)

GRACE UNIVERSITY ROYALS

Enrollment: 343
Affiliation: Nondenominational
Sports: Basketball (M & W), soccer (M), volleyball (W)
Athletic Director: Jim Classen
1311 S. 9th Street
Omaha, NE 68108
Phone: 402-449-2906

GREAT LAKES CHRISTIAN COLLEGE CRUSADERS

Enrollment: 139
Affiliation: Nondenominational
Sports: Baseball, basketball (M), soccer (M)
Athletic Director: Ron Klepal
6211 W. Willow Highway
Lansing, MI 48917
Phone: 517-321-0242 x 230

HILLSDALE FREE WILL BAPTIST COLLEGE SAINTS

Enrollment: 105
Affiliation: Free Will Baptist
Sports: Baseball, basketball (M & W), volleyball (W)
Athletic Director: Kelly Archer
PO Box 7208
Moore, OK 73160
Phone: 405-912-9033
National Champs: MB, 1999

KENTUCKY CHRISTIAN COLLEGE KNIGHTS

Enrollment: 517
Affiliation: Christian Church/Church of Christ
Sports: Basketball (M & W), soccer (M), softball, volleyball (W)
Athletic Director: Bruce W. Dixon
100 Academic Parkway
Grayson, KY 41143-2205
Phone: 606-474-3215
National champs: WBB, 1989, 1995–98; MBB, 1988, 1989, 1991, 1995–97

LANCASTER BIBLE COLLEGE CHARGERS

Enrollment: 537
Affiliation: Nondenominational
Sports: Baseball, basketball (M & W), soccer (M), softball, volleyball (W)
Athletic Director: Vickie Byler
901 Eden Road
Lancaster, PA 17601
Phone: 717-560-8267

LIFE BIBLE COLLEGE WARRIORS

Enrollment: 368
Affiliation: Foursquare Gospel
Sports: Basketball (M), volleyball (W)
Athletic Director: Rick Meyer
1100 Covina Boulevard
San Dimas, CA 91773
Phone: 909-599-5433 x 500

LINCOLN CHRISTIAN COLLEGE PREACHERS

Enrollment: 505
Affiliation: Christian Church/Church of God
Sports: Baseball, basketball (M & W), soccer (M & W), volleyball (W)
Athletic Director: Randy Kirk
100 Campus View Drive
Lincoln, IL 62656
Phone: 217-732-3168 x 2358

MANHATTAN CHRISTIAN COLLEGE CRUSADERS

Enrollment: 296
Affiliation: Independent Christian Church
Sports: Basketball (M), soccer (M), volleyball (W)
Athletic Director: Shawn Condra
1415 Anderson Avenue
Manhattan, KS 66502
Phone: 785-539-3571
National champs: MB, 1996 (Division II-A)

MARANATHA BAPTIST BIBLE COLLEGE CRUSADERS

Enrollment: 640
Affiliation: Independent Baptist
Sports: Baseball, basketball (M), cross-country (W), football, soccer (M), softball, volleyball (W), wrestling
Athletic Director: Greg Weniger
745 W. Main Street
Watertown, WI 53094
Phone: 920-206-2376
National champs (Division I): MW, 1986, 1991; (Divison II): WVB, 1987, 1989–92, 1994; MBB, 1990; WBB, 1999

MARYLAND BIBLE COLLEGE EAGLES

Enrollment: NA
Affiliation: Nondenominational
Sports: Baseball, basketball (M)
Athletic Director: Rev. Steve Stevens
6023 Moravia Park Place
Baltimore, MD 21206
Phone: 410-485-0700 x 235

MID-AMERICA BIBLE COLLEGE EVANGELS

Enrollment: 468
Affiliation: Church of God
Sports: Baseball, basketball (M & W), soccer (M), softball, volleyball (W)
Athletic Director: Willey Holley
3500 SW 119th Street
Oklahoma City, OK 73170
Phone: 405-692-3141
National champs: MBB, 1998; MB, 1998

MOODY BIBLE INSTITUTE ARCHERS

Enrollment: 1,483
Affiliation: Nondenominational
Sports: Basketball (M & W), soccer (M), softball, volleyball (W)
Athletic Director: Sheldon Bassett
320 N. LaSalle Blvd.
Chicago, IL 60610
Phone: 312-329-4039
National champs: WBB, 1987; MS, 1994

MULTNOMAH BIBLE COLLEGE AMBASSADORS

Enrollment: 508
Affiliation: Nondenominational
Sports: Baseball, basketball (M & W), volleyball (W)
Athletic Director: Chris Reese
8435 NE Gilsan Street
Portland, OR 97220
Phone: 503-251-5395

NEBRASKA CHRISTIAN COLLEGE PARSONS

Enrollment: 136
Affiliation: Independent Christian
Sports: Baseball, basketball (M & W), soccer (M), volleyball (W)
Athletic Director: Todd Gordon
1800 Syracuse Avenue
Norfolk, NE 68701
Phone: 402-379-5020

NORTH CENTRAL UNIVERSITY FLAMES

Enrollment: 913
Affiliation: Assemblies of God
Sports: Basketball (M & W), soccer (M), volleyball (W)
Athletic Director: Greg Hayton

910 Elliot Avenue SE
Minneapolis, MN 55404
Phone: 612-343-4755

NORTHLAND BAPTIST BIBLE COLLEGE PIONEERS

Enrollment: 579
Affiliation: Independent Baptist
Sports: Baseball, basketball (M & W), cross-country (M & W), soccer (M), volleyball (W)
Athletic Director: Jim Phillips
W10085 Pike Plains Road
Dunbar, WI
Phone: 715-324-6900 x 6900
National champs: MS, 1993, 1997

OKLAHOMA BAPTIST COLLEGE PROPHETS

Enrollment: 135
Affiliation: Independent Baptist
Sports: Basketball (M), track & field (M)
Athletic Director: Dr. Mark Elliott
5517 NW 23rd
Oklahoma City, OK 73127
Phone: 405-943-3334

OZARK CHRISTIAN COLLEGE AMBASSADORS

Enrollment: 615
Affiliation: Independent Christian
Sports: Basketball (M & W), soccer (M), volleyball (W)
Athletic Director: Charlie Williams
1111 N. Main
Joplin, MO 64801
Phone: 417-624-2518

PHILADELPHIA COLLEGE OF BIBLE CRIMSON EAGLES

Enrollment: 650
Affiliation: Independent
Sports: Baseball, basketball (M & W), soccer (M), softball, volleyball (M & W)
Athletic Director: Mike Shaker
200 Manor Avenue
Langhorne, PA 19047
Phone: 215-702-4268
National champs: MS, 1984–89, 1996

PIEDMONT BAPTIST COLLEGE CONQUERORS

Enrollment: 222
Affiliation: Baptist
Sports: Baseball, basketball (M), volleyball (W)
Athletic Director: Nathan Rasey
716 Franklin Street
Winston-Salem, NC 27101
Phone: 336-725-8344

PUGET SOUND CHRISTIAN COLLEGE ANCHORS

Enrollment: 166
Affiliation: Nondenominational
Sports: Basketball (M & W), volleyball
Athletic Director: Troy McNichols
410 4th Avenue N
Edmonds, WA 98020
Phone: 425-775-8686 x 239

PILLSBURY BAPTIST BIBLE COLLEGE COMETS

Enrollment: 125
Affiliation: Baptist
Sports: Baseball, basketball (M & W), golf (M), soccer (M), softball, volleyball (W)
Athletic Director: Gary Garrson
315 S. Grove Street

Owatonna, MN 55060
Phone: 507-451-2710

PRACTICAL BIBLE COLLEGE SWORDSMEN

Enrollment: 204
Affiliation: Nondenominational
Sports: Baseball, basketball (M & W), soccer (M)
Athletic Director: Thomas O'Conor
440 Riverside Drive
Johnson City, NY 13790
Phone: 607-729-1581

PROVIDENCE COLLEGE FREEMEN

Enrollment: 296
Affiliation: Independent
Sports: Basketball (M & W), hockey, soccer (M), volleyball (M & W)
Athletic Director: Darel Lepp
Otterburne, Manitoba
R0G 1G0, Canada
Phone: 204-433-7488

SAINT LOUIS CHRISTIAN COLLEGE

Enrollment: 144
Affiliation: Christian Church
Sports: Baseball, basketball (M & W), volleyball (W)
Athletic Director: Danny Wolford
1360 Grandview Drive
Florissant, MO 63033
Phone: 314-837-6777

SIMPSON COLLEGE VANGUARDS

Enrollment: 589
Affiliation: Christian and Missionary Alliance
Sports: Baseball, basketball (M & W), soccer (M & W), softball, volleyball (M & W)
Athletic Director: Vern Howard
2211 College View Drive
Redding, CA 96003
Phone: 530-224-5600 x 217

SOUTHEASTERN COLLEGE CRUSADERS

Enrollment: 1,079
Affiliation: Assemblies of God
Sports: Baseball, basketball (M & W), soccer (M), volleyball (W)
Athletic Director: Scott Laing
1000 Longfellow Boulevard
Lakeland, FL 33801
Phone: 941-667-5138

SOUTHWESTERN ASSEMBLIES OF GOD UNIVERSITY LIONS

Enrollment: 1,225
Affiliation: Assemblies of God
Sports: Basketball (M & W), volleyball (W)
Athletic Director: Rev. Steve Garippa
1200 Sycamore
Waxahachie, TX 75165
Phone: 972-937-4010

SOUTHWESTERN COLLEGE EAGLES

Enrollment: 204
Affiliation: Conservative Baptist
Sports: Basketball (M), volleyball (W)
Athletic Director: Stephen H. Morley
2625 E. Cactus Road
Phoenix, AZ 85032
Phone: 602-992-6101

SOUTHWESTERN COLLEGE OF CHRISTIAN MINISTRIES EAGLES

Enrollment: 181
Affiliation: Pentecostal/Holiness

Sport: Basketball (M)
Athletic Director: Mark Arthur
PO Box 340
Bethany, OK 73008
Phone: 405-789-7661 x 3436
National champs: MB, 1998 (Division II-A)

TOCCOA FALLS COLLEGE EAGLES

Enrollment: 830
Affiliation: Interdenominational
Sports: Baseball, basketball (M & W), golf (M), soccer (M & W), volleyball (W)
Athletic Director: Lance Martin
PO Box 818
Toccoa Falls, GA 30598
Phone: 706-886-6831 x 5377
National champs: WBB, 1986, 1992

TRINITY BAPTIST COLLEGE EAGLES

Enrollment: 300
Affiliation: Baptist
Sports: Basketball (M), volleyball (W)
Athletic Director: Pat Milligan
426 S. McDuff Avenue
Jacksonville, FL 32254
Phone: 904-596-2454

TRINITY BIBLE COLLEGE LIONS

Enrollment: 301
Affiliation: Assemblies of God
Sports: Basketball (M & W), cross-country (M & W), football, track & field (M & W), volleyball (W)
Athletic Director: Jesse Godding
50 S. 6th Avenue
Ellendale, ND 58436
Phone: 701-349-5440

VALLEY FORGE CHRISTIAN COLLEGE PATRIOTS

Enrollment: 470
Affiliation: Assemblies of God
Sports: Baseball, basketball (M & W), cross-country (M & W), soccer (M & W), softball, volleyball (W)
Athletic Director: Dan Boothman
1401 Charlestown Road
Phoenixville, PA 19460
Phone: 610-917-1467

WARNER PACIFIC COLLEGE KNIGHTS

Enrollment: NA
Affiliation: Church of God
Sports: Basketball (M & W), soccer (M), volleyball (W)
Athletic Director: Bart Valentine
2219 SE 68th Avenue
Portland, OR 97215
Phone: 503-517-1000
Fax: 503-517-1350
E-mail:
bvalentine@warnerpacific.edu

WASHINGTON BIBLE COLLEGE COUGARS

Enrollment: 222
Affiliation: Nondenominational
Sports: Baseball, basketball (M & W), soccer (M), volleyball (W)
Athletic Director: Rev. Brian Smith
6511 Princess Garden Parkway
Lanham, MD 20706
Phone: 301-552-1400 x 283

WESLEY COLLEGE WARRIORS

Enrollment: 81
Affiliation: Congregational Methodist

Sport: Basketball (M)
Athletic Director: William Devore Jr.
PO Box 170
Florence, MS 39073
Phone: 601-845-2265

2. NCCAA: ARCHIVES

Professional Athletes from NCCAA Schools

Sid Bream	Baseball	Liberty University
Randy Tomlin	Baseball	Liberty University
Lee Geutterman	Baseball	Liberty University
Christian Okoye	Football	Azusa Pacific University
Dave Johnson	Decathlon	Azusa Pacific University
Todd Worrell	Baseball	Biola University
Tim Worrell	Baseball	Biola University
Tim Belcher	Baseball	Olivet Nazarene University

NCCAA Hall of Fame

Year Inducted	Award Winner
1991	E. C. Haskell
1991	Jim Huckaby
1991	Norm Wilhelmi
1992	Dr. Don Callan
1992	Dr. Ralph Swearngin
1993	Hank Burbridge
1993	Elvin King
1994	Jim Kessler
1994	Dick Patterson
1995	Ron Bishop
1995	Kristi Brodin
1995	Dr. Mike Fratzke
1996	Tom Fink
1996	Dr. Ken Rhoden
1997	Dr. John Bratcher
1997	Willie Holley
1997	Larry Maddox
1998	Dr. Barry May
1998	Harold Williams

3. Other Christian Colleges

The following institutions are not in the NCCAA. They do, however, provide a variety of sports for students to participate in on the varsity level, often against other division III schools.

ANDERSON UNIVERSITY RAVENS

Affiliation: Church of Christ
Sports: 16 NCAA Division III sports for men and women
Athletic Director: Barrett Bales
1100 East Fifth Street
Anderson, IN 46102-3495
Phone: 800-94RAVEN
E-mail: info@anderson.edu
Internet Site: www.anderson.edu
NCCAA champs: WCC, 1983, 1984; MB, 1991; MTF, 1988, 1990, 1992, 1993; MCC, 1980–84; MT, 1996

BIOLA UNIVERSITY

Affiliation: Nondenominational
13800 Biola Avenue
La Mirada, CA 90639-0001
Sports: 11 NAIA sports for men and women
Phone: 310-903-6000
Fax: 310-903-4748
Internet Site: www.biola.edu
NCCAA champs: MBB, 1976, 1978, 1984; MW, 1985

CALVIN COLLEGE KNIGHTS

Affiliation: Christian Reformed Church
Sports: NCAA Division III; 17 teams (8 M, 9 W)
3201 Burton SE
Grand Rapids, MI 49546
Phone: 800-688-0122
E-mail: admissions@calvin.edu
Internet Site: www.calvin.edu

CARSON-NEWMAN COLLEGE EAGLES

Sports: 12 NCAA Division II sports
1646 Russell Avenue
Jefferson City, TN 37760
Phone: 800-678-9061
Internet Site: www.cn.edu
NCCAA national champs: MW, 1982–84; MTF, 1980

CENTRAL COLLEGE FLYING DUTCHMEN

Affiliation: Reformed Church in America
Sports: 17 NCAA Division III sports
812 University
Pella, IA 50219
Phone: 877-GO-CENTRAL
E-mail: admissions@central.edu
Internet Site: www.central.edu

EASTERN COLLEGE EAGLES

Affiliation: Independent
Sports: 9 NCAA Division III sports
1300 Eagle Road
St. Davids, PA 19087
Phone: 610-341-1736
E-mail: ugadm@eastern.edu
Internet Site: www.eastern.edu

GORDON COLLEGE FIGHTING SCOTS

Affiliation: Nondenominational
Sports: 14 NCAA Division III sports
255 Grapevine Road
Wenham, MA 01984-1899
Phone: 800-343-1379
Internet Site: www.gordonc.edu

GRAND CANYON UNIVERSITY ANTELOPES

Affiliation: Southern Baptist
9 NCAA Division II sports
3300 West Camelback Road
PO Box 11097
Phoenix, AZ 85061
Phone: 602-249-3300
Fax: 602-589-2895

HOUSTON BAPTIST UNIVERSITY HUSKIES

Affiliation: Baptist
7502 Fondren Road
Houston, TX 77074
Phone: 281-649-3211
Internet Site: www.hbu.edu

JOHN BROWN UNIVERSITY GOLDEN EAGLES

Affiliation: Interdenominational
Sports: 8 NAIA sports
2000 West University
Siloam Springs, AR 72761
Phone: 800-634-6969
Fax: 402-341-9587
E-mail: jbinfo@acc.jbu.edu
Internet Site: www.jbu.edu
NCCAA national champs: MBB, 1991; MS, 1983, 1984

MESSIAH COLLEGE FALCONS

Enrollment: 2,400
Sports: Baseball, basketball (M & W), cross-country (M & W), golf (M), lacrosse (M & W), soccer (M & W), track (M & W), field hockey, volleyball, wrestling
Grantham, PA 17027
Phone: 800-233-4220
E-mail: admiss@messiah.edu
Internet Site: www.messiah.edu
National champs: WTF, 1983; MW, 1975, 1976; MTF, 1982; MS, 1978, 1981

POINT LOMA NAZARENE UNIVERSITY CRUSADERS

Affiliation: Church of the Nazarene
Sports: 13 NAIA sports
3900 Lomaland Drive
San Diego, CA 92106
Phone: 619-221-2000
Fax: 619-221-2579
Internet Site: www.ptloma.edu
NCCAA national champs: MBB, 1985–87

STERLING COLLEGE WARRIORS

Affiliation: Presbyterian USA
Sports: 15 NAIA sports
PO Box 98
Sterling, KS 67579
Phone: 800-346-1017
Internet Site: www.sterling.edu

VANGUARD UNIVERSITY OF SOUTHERN CALIFORNIA LIONS

Enrollment: 1,200
Sports: 9 NAIA sports
55 Fair Drive
Costa Mesa, CA 92626

Phone: 714-556-3610
E-mail: admissions@sccu.edu
Internet Site: sccu.edu

WARNER SOUTHERN COLLEGE EAGLES

Affiliation: Church of God
Sports: NAIA in basketball (M & W), baseball, cross-country (M & W), volleyball
5301 US 27 South
Lake Wales, FL 33853
Phone: 800-949-7248
E-mail: admissions@warner.edu
Internet Site: www.warner.edu

WESTMONT COLLEGE

Affiliation: Nondenominational
Sports: 10 NAIA sports
955 La Paz Road
Santa Barbara, CA 93108
Phone: 805-565-6000
Fax: 805-565-6234
Internet Site: www.westmont.edu

WHEATON COLLEGE CRUSADERS

Enrollment: 2,283
Affiliation: Nondenominational
Sports: 18 NCAA Division II sports
Athletic Director: Dr. Tony Ladd
501 E. College Avenue
Wheaton, IL 60187
Phone: 603-752-5125
Fax: 603-752-7007
E-mail: Tony.Ladd@wheaton.edu

Chapter 10

SPORTS CAMPS

This listing of camps includes those run by colleges, those run by Christian coaches at secular colleges, and those run by other organizations.

A. C. GREEN BASKETBALL CAMP

P. O. Box 1709
Phoenix, AZ 85001
Contact Phone: 800-327-9371

JANE ALBRIGHT-DIETERLE

University of Wisconsin
Womens' Basketball Camp
University of Wisconsin
Madison, Wisconsin
Contact Phone: 608-263-5506

ATHLETES IN ACTION SPORTS CAMPS

General information
PO Box 588
Lebanon, OH 45036
Contact E-mail: aiacom@aol.com
Internet Site: www.aiasports.org/aia

Girls basketball
Contact: Stephanie Zonars
Contact Phone: 513-933-2421
Contact E-mail: szonars@aol.com

Boys basketball
Contact: Craig Sladek
Contact Phone: 513-933-2421
Contact E-mail: aiahoops@aol.com

Swimming
Contact: Craig Harriman
Contact Phone: 719-593-8200
Contact E-mail: chorsaia@aol.com

Track & field
Contact: Tim Ellis
Contact Phone: 513-771-4292
Contact E-mail:
aiatrck4hm@aolc.com

Wrestling
Contact: Steve Burack
Contact Phone: 719-593-8200
Contact E-mail:
102552.456@compuserve.com

BAPTIST BIBLE COLLEGE SPORTS CAMPS

Baptist Bible College
538 Venard Road
Clarks Summit, PA 18411
Camp Dates: Late June, July, August
Number of Camp Weeks: Four
- Girls basketball: one week
- Boys basketball: two weeks
- Boys/girls soccer: one week

Place: Campus, Clarks Summit, Pennsylvania
Contact Phone: 717-585-9323
Contact E-mail: athletics@bbc.edu
Camp notes: Morning instruction; afternoon competition

BOB BARDWELL CAMPS

Route 1
Stewartville, MN 55976
Contact Phone: 507-533-4315
Wheelchair sports and recreation camps

CAMP OZARK

HC64, Box 190
Mt. Ida, AR 71957
Camp Dates: All summer
Sports: baseball, football, lacrosse, soccer, tennis, weight training, basketball, golf, softball, track, wrestling, Tae Kwon Do, volleyball
Contact Phone: 870-867-4131
Contact Fax: 870-867-4344
Contact E-mail:
campozark@campozark.com
Web Site: www.campozark.com

CAMPBELLSVILLE UNIVERSITY SPORTS CAMPS

Campbellsville University
1 University Drive
Campbellsville, KY 42718
Camp Dates: June, July, August
Number of Camp Weeks: Five
- Basketball (guards): boys age 3–12 (day camp)
- Baseball: day camp
- Girls Basketball: day camp and a team camp
- Football: two day pass-o-rama
- Cheerleading: two weeks

Place: Campus, Campbellsville, Kentucky
Contact Phone: 502-789-5018

CHARLOTTE EAGLES

2101 Sardis Road, Suite 201
Charlotte, NC 28227
Contact Phone: 704-841-8644
Contact Fax: 704-841-8652
Contact E-mail:
Info@CharlotteEagles.com
Note: Soccer camp sponsored by the Christian semipro team, Charlotte Eagles

CHRISTIAN ATHLETIC ASSOCIATION

PO Box 5151
San Jose, CA 95150
Contact Phone: 408-227-0160
Contact Fax: 408-227-9286
Contact E-mail: jondet@usa.net
Contact Person: Jonathan Detweiler
For more than twenty years CAA has used competitive sports to introduce athletes to the gospel of Jesus Christ.
Activities: Clinics and camps
Sports: baseball, basketball, golf, soccer, street hockey

CINCINNATI BIBLE COLLEGE SPORTS CAMPS

Cincinnati Bible College
2700 Glenway Avenue
Cincinnati, OH 45204
Camp Dates: June, July
Number of Camp Weeks: Three
- Boys: grades 4–8
- Girls: grades 6–12
- Boys: grades 9–12

Place: Campus, Cincinnati
Contact Phone: 513-244-8442
Contact Fax: 513-244-6028
Contact E-mail:

john.garrett@cincybible.edu

Camp notes: Overnight camps, camper receives basketball and T-shirt. Small group devotions and plenary sessions for devotions.

CITYVISION SPORTS CAMPS

PO Box 251
Rifton, NY 12471
Contact Phone: 914-658-8579
Contact E-mail:
itchar@mindspring.com

Hoop Heaven is the flagship camp of CityVision's sports camps. This camp gives inner-city, unchurched kids a chance to get out of the city, play basketball in a camp setting, learn from Christian instructors, and hear the gospel.

CROSSPOINT

127 Ninth Avenue North
Nashville, TN 37234
Camp dates: Throughout the summer
Place: Crosspoint camps are held in about two dozen locations in the following states: Kentucky, Alabama, Georgia, South Carolina, Tennessee, Missouri, Florida, Maryland, Texas, and Mississippi
Sports offered: basketball, baseball, softball, soccer, team handball, cheerleading, gymnastics, volleyball, flag football, tennis, track & field.
Contact Phone: 615-251-3834
Contact Fax: 615-251-5699
Contact E-mail: dhartze@bssb.com

Camp notes: Crosspoint offers an incredible array of opportunities in a wide variety of sports. Besides individual coaching at most camps, Crosspoint also has team camps available.

FELLOWSHIP OF CHRISTIAN ATHLETES CAMPS

8701 Leeds Road
Kansas City, MO 64124
Sports: Athletic training, basketball, baseball, cheerleading, cycling, field hockey, golf, football, karate, lacrosse, power lifting, roller hockey, soccer, softball, surfing, swimming, tennis, track & field, volleyball, wrestling; located throughout the United States
Contact Phone:1-800-289-0909
FCA Extreme Sports Camp
Sports: Rock climbing, whitewater rafting, kayaking, rappelling
Location: West Virginia
Contact Phone: 1-888-FCA-TEEN

HOCKEY MINISTRIES INTERNATIONAL

Hockey Camps
2915 St. Charles Blvd.
Suite 101, Kirkland
Montreal, Quebec
Canada H9H 3B5
Contact Phone: 514-694-6440

Camps for young hockey players between the ages of 10 and 17 are held at numerous camps across North America and Canada. Campers receive instruction from NHL players past and present

HOUGHTON COLLEGE SPORTS CAMPS

Houghton College
1 Willard Avenue

Houghton, NY 14744
Number of Camp Weeks: Six
Girls basketball: one
Boys basketball: one
Girls volleyball: one
Boys/girls soccer: two
Cross-country: one
Field hockey: one
Place: Campus, Houghton, New York
Contact Phone: 716-567-9645
Contact Fax: 716-567-9365
Contact E-mail:
hlord@houghton.edu

JIM MOLINARI'S

Bradley University Basketball Camps
Peoria, Illinois
Contact Phone: 309-677-2668
Ask for Peggy.

KIDS ACROSS AMERICA KAMPS

Kanakuk Kamps
1429 Lakeshore Drive
Branson, Mo 65616
Contact Phone: 417-335-8400
Contact Person: Jim Subers
Camp notes: KAAK uses thirty different sports and activities to interest campers and introduce Christ to them.

MALONE COLLEGE SPORTS CAMPS

Malone College
515 25th Street NW
Canton, OH 44709
Camp Dates: Summer
Number of Camp Weeks: Three
Golf: ages 13–18
Track: ages 12–18
Cross-country: ages 12–18
Place: Campus, Canton, Ohio
Contact Phone: 330-471-8300
Camp notes: Open to day campers; camps run by Malone head coaches

MAI CAMPS

PO Box 945
LaHabra, CA 90631-0945
Contact Fax: 719-528-1638
E-mail:
10316.115@compuserve.com

MOUNT VERNON NAZARENE COLLEGE SPORTS CAMPS

Mount Vernon Nazarene College
800 Martinsburg Road
Martinsburg, OH 43050
Camp Dates: Summer
Sports:Soccer, basketball
Place: Campus, Martinsburg, Ohio
Contact Phone: 740-397-6862
x 3112

NBC CAMPS

N. 21808 Panorama Road
Colbert, WA 99005
Camp Sports: Basketball, soccer, volleyball
Contact Phone: 509-466-4690
Contact Fax: 509-467-6298
Contact E-mail:
nbccamps@soar.com
Contact Person: Jennifer Ferch
Camp Notes: One of the largest sports camps in the U.S., Northwest Basketball Camp services more than 7,000 camps each summer.

NYACK COLLEGE SPORTS CAMPS

Nyack College
1 South Boulevard
Nyack, NY 10960
Camp dates: July, August
Number of Camp Weeks: Six
Basketball: boys day camp (ages 6–17), boys overnight, twice (ages 9–17), girls day camp, (ages 6–17), girls overnight (ages 9–17)
Soccer: Boys/Girls
Place: Campus, Nyack, New York
Contact Phone: 914-358-1710 x 181

ONE-ON-ONE INTERNATIONAL

Basketball Camps
PO Box 503
8692 Skillman Street
Dallas, TX 75243
Contact Phone: 214-349-9753

QUICK HANDLE BASKETBALL CAMPS

Northwest College
5220 108th Avenue NE
Kirkland, WA 98033
Camp Director: Wayne Mendezona
Camp Dates: Late June and July
Number of Camp Weeks: Three
Place: Campus, Kirkland, Washington
Contact Phone: 1-800-928-9004
Camp notes: Emphasis on offensive moves; based on instruction book Quick Handle

ROBERTS WESLEYAN COLLEGE CAMPS

Roberts Wesleyan College
2301 Westside Drive
Rochester, NY 14624
Sports:
- basketball (ages 6–17)
- swimming (ages 6–17)
- tennis (ages 6–17)
- volleyball (ages 6–17)
- soccer (ages 6–17)

Place: Campus, Roberts Wesleyan, Rochester, New York
Contact Phone: 716-594-6514
Camps Director: Greg Gidman

JIM RYUN RUNNING CAMP

16718 Thirteenth Street
Lawrence, KS 66044
Sport: Long-distance running
Contact Phone: 913-749-3325
Contact Person: Heather Ryun
Camp notes: This camp mixes training in both running and the spiritual life.

RWJ GOOD NEWS SPORTS OUTREACH

4809 Mayfair Street
Fort Worth, TX 76116
Contact Phone: 817-763-9631
Contact E-mail: jjsalandr@aol.com
Director: Joseph A. La Salandra
Run With Jesus! Outreach runs sports activities, camps, and clinics that are designed to introduce participants to Jesus Christ.
Sports: Baseball, basketball, soccer, tennis

SUMMER'S BEST TWO WEEKS

111 Lake Gloria Road
Boswell, PA 15531-9274
Contact Phone: 814-629-8744

Contact Fax: 814-629-9744
Contact Person: James S. Welch
SBTW offers an almost endless array of sports opportunities for young people to grow and learn.
Sports: archery, basketball, cycling, field hockey, football, gymnastics, hockey, kayaking, canoeing, rafting, mountain biking, rowing, sailing, scuba diving, skiing, soccer, softball, swimming, diving, track and field, volleyball, wrestling

T BAR M SPORTS CAMP

PO Box 310600
New Braunfels, TX 78131-0600
Contact Phone: 214-692-4254
Contact Fax: 214-692-4255
Contact E-mail: sturpin@gte.com
T Bar M seeks to help young people grow in wisdom, stature, and in favor with God and men through sports and adventure.
Sports: baseball, basketball, cheerleading, football, golf, gymnastics, soccer, swimming, diving, tennis, volleyball

TRIPLE THREAT BASKETBALL CAMP

Contact Phone: 516-689-1682
Contact E-mail:
jfea@ccmail.sunysb.edu
Contact Person: John Fea
Scope: Northeast United States
A basketball camp with a Christian emphasis, Triple Threat combines strong basketball teaching with inspirational messages.

WALKING ON WATER (WOW) SURF CAMPS

3900 Lomaland Drive
Flex 45D
San Diego, CA 92106
Contact Phone: 619-849-7719
Director: Bryan Jennings
Location: Point Loma Nazarene College
Number of Camp Weeks: Two
Camp notes: Bryan Jennings, a pro surfer, conducts the camps.

WESTERN BAPTIST COLLEGE CAMPS

Western Baptist College
5000 Deer Park Drive SE
Salem, OR 97301
Camp Dates: August
Number of Camp Weeks: Two
Boys age 8–17 (day camp)
Girls age 8–17 (day camp)
Place: Campus, Salem, Oregon
Contact Phone: 503-375-7021
Camp notes: Boys camp goes all day, with lunch; girls is morning, with no lunch.

WINNING RUN FOUNDATION

255 B Settlers Road
Longview, TX 75605
Contact Phone: 903-663-6256
Contact Fax: 903-663-9382
Contact E-mail: nurniw@aol.com
Director: Elliot Johnson
Longtime baseball coach Johnson conducts a number of camps and clinics that encourage the development of baseball skills.

Moody Press, a ministry of Moody Bible Institute,
is designed for education, evangelization, and edification.
If we may assist you in knowing more about Christ
and the Christian life, please write us without obligation:
Moody Press, c/o MLM, Chicago, Illinois 60610.